# Bringing the Social Sciences Alive

# RELATED TITLES OF INTEREST

**New Kids on the Net: Internet Activities in Secondary Mathematics**
Sheryl Burgstahler and Christine Murakami
ISBN: 0-205-28593-7

**New Kids on the Net: Internet Activities in Secondary Science**
Sheryl Burgstahler and Kurt Sahl
ISBN: 0-205-28594-5

**An Educator's Guide to Block Scheduling: Decision Making,
 Curriculum Design, and Lesson Planning Strategies**
Mary M. Bevevino, Dawn M. Snodgrass, Kenneth M. Adams,
and Joan A. Dengel
ISBN: 0-205-27847-7

**Quantum Teaching: Orchestrating Student Success**
Bobbi DePorter, Mark Reardon, and Sarah Singer-Nourie
ISBN: 0-205-28664-X

**Affirming Middle Grades Education**
Carl W. Walley and W. Gregory Gerrick
ISBN: 0-205-17128-1

For more information or to purchase a book, please call 1-800-278-3525

# Bringing the Social Sciences Alive

## 10 Simulations for History, Economics, Government, and Geography

Frederick M. Hess
*University of Virginia*

Foreword by Vito Perrone

Allyn and Bacon

Boston    London    Toronto    Sydney    Tokyo    Singapore

*Series editor:* Frances Helland
*Series editorial assistant:* Bridget Keane
*Manufacturing buyer:* Suzanne Lareau

Copyright © 1999 by Allyn & Bacon
A Viacom Company
Needham Heights, MA 02494

Internet: www.abacon.com

Library of Congress Cataloging-in-Publication Data

Hess, Frederick M.
        Bringing the social sciences alive : 10 simulations for history,
    economics, government, and geography / Frederick M. Hess;
    foreword by Vito Perrone.
                p.        cm.
        Includes bibliographical references and index
        ISBN 0-205-28170-2
        1. Social sciences—Study and teaching—Simulation methods.
    I. Title.
    H62.H476  1999
    300'.71--dc21                                          98-31394
                                                              CIP


Printed in the United States of America
10 9 8 7 6 5 4 3 2 1     03 02 01 00 99

*For my brother Sanford,*
*the historian*

# CONTENTS

*Foreword*   *xi*

*Preface*   *xiii*

Chapter 1   Introduction   1
What Simulations Can Add to Your Classroom   3
Some Practical Thoughts on Designing and Using Simulations   5
Layout of the Book   8
References   10

Chapter 2   Constructing a New American Government   11
Teacher's Note   11
Background on the Constitutional Convention   12
Using This Simulation   15
How the Simulation Works   16
Comments From Experience   18
Possible Modifications   19
Assessment   19
Appendix—Materials   21

Chapter 3   The Mighty Dorito Cartel   32
Teacher's Note   32
Background on the Free Rider Syndrome, Oliogopolies,
   and OPEC   33
Using This Simulation   38
How the Simulation Works   39
Comments from Experience   41
Possible Modifications   41
Assessment   42
Appendix—Materials   44

Chapter 4   Letting the Bulls Run   49
Teacher's Note   49
Background on the Equity Markets   50
Using This Simulation   55
How the Simulation Works   55
Comments from Experience   58
Possible Modifications   59
Assessment   59
Appendix—Materials   61

Chapter 5   Forging a Lasting Middle East Peace   64
Teacher's Note   64
Background on Middle East Conflict   65

Using This Simulation     68
How the Simulation Works     69
Comments from Experience     71
Possible Modifications     73
Assessment     73
Appendix—Materials     75

Chapter 6     Choosing a President     88

Teacher's Note     88
Background on Political Party Conventions     89
Using This Simulation     91
How the Simulation Works     93
Comments from Experience     98
Possible Modifications     98
Assessment     99
Appendix—Materials     100

Chapter 7     A Whirlwind American Tour     129

Teacher's Note     129
Background on Low-Budget Travel     130
Using This Simulation     130
How the Simulation Works     131
Comments from Experience     133
Possible Modifications     135
Assessment     136
Appendix—Materials     137

Chapter 8     Passing a Crime Bill     140

Teacher's Note     140
Background on the Legislative Process     140
Using This Simulation     142
How the Simulation Works     143
Comments from Experience     147
Possible Modifications     147
Assessment     147
Appendix—Materials     149

Chapter 9     Living on a Paycheck     165

Teacher's Note     165
Background on Budgeting     166
Using This Simulation     167
How the Simulation Works     167
Comments from Experience     169
Possible Modifications     170
Assessment     171
Appendix—Materials     172

Chapter 10     The Delicate Balance of Power     175

Teacher's Note     175
Background on Europe Before World War I     176
Using This Simulation     179
How the Simulation Works     180
Comments from Experience     184

Possible Modifications     185
Assessment     186
Appendix—Materials     187

Chapter 11    Making the United Nations Work     196
Teacher's Note     196
Background on the United Nations     197
Using This Simulation     198
How the Simulation Works     199
Comments from Experience     200
Possible Modifications     202
Assessment     203
Appendix—Materials     204

Chapter 12    Final Thoughts     208
Assessing Simulations     208
Assessment Materials     210

Index     215

# FOREWORD

In our teacher education program, I often invoke John Dewey's thoughts about the need for teachers to be *students of teaching*, persons who are articulate about their practice. I suggest that the path to this articulateness is through reflection and writing. Frederick (Rick) Hess has taken this message to heart. *Bringing the Social Sciences Alive* is an excellent example of the kind of writing I wish more teachers would engage in and share.

As part of a research project around a *pedagogy of understanding*, I had the occasion to ask students at all levels about times in school when their education was particularly engaging intellectually, when they sensed that their learning was larger and their understandings deeper than usual. What comes up most often are longer-term projects, complex ideas, room for interpretation, multiple resources, space for collaboration, opportunities to share their learning, among other ideas. The simulations described in this text relate well to that outlook. They are the kinds of activities that bring life to a classroom as they begin with genuine questions and focus on complex issues. They call for student investment and interpretation. There aren't any predetermined answers.

More important, the simulations call on students to assume many different roles and to engage in a variety of performance-oriented activities. They are asked to see the world as others might see it and actually *do* something. They role-play, read and interpret primary historical documents and various social and economic data, write in a number of different genres, participate in debates, and engage in research.

Hess notes, "The most obvious benefit [of simulations] is that sometimes students get so taken with one experience that they begin to look at the entire subject through a new lens." That is my experience with simulations. They help create a questioning disposition, a willingness to hear many different points of view. Moreover, it is my experience with all teaching approaches that stress depth over coverage (which is the case with the kinds of simulations described in this text) that students seem to continue with many aspects of the subject matter on their own. They come, in the process, to understand the subject matter, to internalize it, to make it their own. In contrast, most coverage models just end, with little continued study and considerable forgetting. Engagement tends to be very low.

This book provides a good rationale for simulations and their use, and clearly outlines a process for constructing simulations. While I don't usually support "how-to" guides, this book carries out the task of sharing a process in a conversational, collaborative style. As a reader, I am respected. The text makes it especially clear that any simulation that I or other teachers construct will likely work better in our classrooms than the simulations constructed by others, including those here. I think this is generally the case. Teachers do, after all, have to make the lessons they teach their own. Nonetheless, I like the simulations in this text and believe I could make use of many aspects of all of them. They are imaginative and stimulating.

Rick also makes it clear that the materials a teacher uses matter greatly—this is not textbook territory. He also speaks of the importance of careful preparation and ongoing assessment. In the best of teaching and learning circumstances, students are the workers but teacher preparation for each of the days remains critical—not just in making sure that the requisite materials are present but in taking the time to consider possible questions students might pose; rehearsing possible responses to keep the inquiry moving productively, and, in the end, having more resources and other examples that can be called on.

Further, it is difficult to move to ever higher levels of learning without ongoing assessment. This is particularly the case as the activities grow in their complexity. Built into the simulations are a variety of scaffolding directions to ensure that students can take the next steps. This is important because students need to know how to proceed if they are to do their best work.

I am pleased that Rick has written such a useful and stimulating book. I believe that teachers will find it enormously helpful as they work at the creation of more intense, more stimulating classrooms.

Vito Perrone
*Director of Teacher Education Programs*
*Harvard Graduate School of Education*
*Cambridge, Massachusetts*

# *PREFACE*

This book represents the more or less successful culmination of a great deal of trial and error. From my first efforts as a student teacher, I have found simulated exercises to be an engaging and effective way to teach substantive material. In this book, I have brought together ten exercises that have emerged from these efforts at lesson design. The lessons assembled here have been tried, refined, and tried again, both by myself and by some of the colleagues with whom I have worked. What has emerged is a mix of the theoretical and the practical, a combination of ambitious lessons tempered by the realities of the working classroom.

After spending the better part of the last decade teaching high school, supervising student teachers, teaching sections of government to students at the university level, and teaching courses at the university level, I feel comfortable with the widespread applicability of these lessons. I hope and expect that colleagues in a variety of situations will find this book to be a helpful and interesting complement to their own instructional repertoire.

I have found these simulations to be valuable tools for teaching content, enriching understanding, teaching "soft skills" that I value, and building classroom interest and camaraderie. In the belief that every teacher can always make use of another idea or another lesson, I present these exercises, along with some thoughts on how teachers might approach the design and use of simulation.

In constructing these lessons and in assembling this book, I have received assistance and input from a number of people. I would like to offer special thanks to those colleagues at Belmont High School, Scotlandville Magnet High School, South Boston High School, Boston English High School, Harvard University, and the University of Virginia, who have offered input and insights over the years. More times than I can remember, casual conversations with colleagues at these schools have helped me to become a better teacher.

I would particularly like to thank John Ameer, Vicki Jacobs, and Vito Perrone, who offered guidance and advice from my earliest days in the profession. I offer special thanks to Loren Baron, whose insight and comments have been a great help at numerous stages of this book. I would like to offer a special thanks to my own social science teachers over the years, at both the high school and university levels, particularly Mo Fiorina, Mary Hoch, Michael Macy, Shep Melnick, Paul E. Peterson, Barney Schwalberg, Paula Spencer, and Peter Woll. For support of a different kind, I'd like to thank Todd Anderman, David Leal, Mandy Magallanes, Scott Orenstein, David Romano, Dave Walsh, and Eric Yanco.

I'd like to thank Phyllis Palmore and Stephanie Timmons for their assistance in preparing this work. I am also indebted to my editor, Frances Helland, and her assistant Bridget Keane, for their assistance.

My appreciation goes to the following reviewers for their comments on the manuscript: Jo Ellen Read, Leawood Middle School, Leawood, KS; Loren Baron, Richard Montgomery High School, Rockville, MD; Noel Hammatt, Louisiana State University; Karen Grace, Oakland Unified School District, Oakland, CA; and John Ameer, Simmons College, Boston.

# Bringing the Social Sciences Alive

# CHAPTER 1
## Introduction

Teaching is hard work. It is made even more difficult because there is little incentive for teachers to share their ideas and because teachers have only minimal amounts of time to seek out ideas from their colleagues. The isolation of teachers in their classrooms means that they are rarely able to observe the lessons or teaching of their colleagues first-hand. The result is that most teachers I know are hungry for more exposure to substantive, interesting ideas they can actually use. This book presents a set of such lessons and offers an introduction to *simulations*—a type of teaching exercise many teachers find to be effective and rewarding. In simulations, students learn by being thrust into reality-based scenarios. These scenarios illustrate the requisite material and force students to apply their knowledge and skills in order be successful. This book's exercises are intended as a practical source of ideas for new teachers and as an easy-to-use supplement for time-starved veteran teachers who are interested in experimenting with some new types of lessons.

As a high school teacher and then as a university professor, I have taught a variety of courses in social studies, political science, and education policy. In various classrooms, I have observed that the same students can be either fascinated or repelled by the social sciences. The difference often seems to come down to whether students find the material to be relevant and stimulating. The difficulty of the material does not seem to matter nearly as much as does its vividness. I have found simulations to be one consistently effective tool for sparking students' interest. By giving students the opportunity to exercise judgment, simulations can bring material to life—without sacrificing content learning. These exercises can also offer teachers an excellent opportunity for interdisciplinary instruction.

I initially created and refined these exercises as a high school social studies teacher. I have found them to be an excellent way to integrate substantive content with interpersonal and ancillary skills, while making my classroom more enjoyable and more cohesive.

The simulations here include seven group-based and individual classroom games, lessons that are conventionally thought of as simulations. There are also three project-oriented exercises that force students to "simulate" real-world dynamics, but are less typically thought of as simulations. Teachers are sometimes put off by simulations that require weeks of class time, lack intellectual content, or foster student interaction by encouraging wandering talkfests. These exercises were designed to require only a few days of class time and to foster student interaction around substantive academic material.

These lessons attempt to bridge the frequent trade-off between content-driven computer simulations devoid of interpersonal contact and interpersonally oriented exercises that are weak on content. The exercises here require no technology. Research components of the exercises are often aided by computer access, but the simulations themselves require no hardware or software. This is particularly relevant for those teachers who do not have the classroom technology, the resources, or the training necessary to use computer-driven simulations in their classes. More important, to my mind, these exercises integrate student interaction and substantive content in a manner that electronic simulations cannot replicate. Increasingly, the allure of technology has led to simulations designed almost exclusively for multimedia and software applications. Although there is nothing wrong with this per se, computer-driven simulations do shortchange the interpersonal skills that simulations can develop so effectively. The result has been a dearth of simulations that allow teachers to foster camaraderie and student interaction within their classes.

I believe that just about all experienced social sciences teachers are capable of designing useful simulations. If you have designed or used simulations in the past, some of the ones in this book will probably have a familiar feel. If you are a veteran teacher who has used simulations extensively, there is probably little in here that you could not assemble yourself given sufficient time. On the other hand, if you are not a veteran, lack experience with simulations, and/or lack the time to design and refine them, I hope you will find this book a valuable source of lessons and ideas.

Well-crafted simulations provide an excellent opportunity to integrate intellectual substance, practical skills, and constructive student interaction. Nonetheless, simulations are used only infrequently. Why? I believe there are several reasons. First, the difficult and time-consuming process of creating simulations often deters teachers from designing them. Second, most teacher education programs do not pay much attention to this issue, and most teachers have not been taught how to construct simulations. This is even more true for university and college faculty who generally receive almost no pedagogical training during the course of their studies. Third, most packaged simulations are relatively expensive and often are not readily available. Finally, those simulations that are available generally emphasize student interaction at the expense of content knowledge.

I started to design these exercises as a student teacher when I was unable to find any existing simulations that paid adequate attention to theory and substantive knowledge. Looking for a practical guide that would offer some sensible advice on creating simulations, I found very little that was useful and devoid of jargon. Consequently, I relied primarily on trial and error. With time and practice, as I grew more comfortable with simulation design and management, my rough early attempts improved. Teaching colleagues in various educational settings have also used these simulations and have reported the lessons to be productive and enlivening. These colleagues have generously suggested many refinements that I have incorporated into the exercises. There is nothing sacrosanct about any of these simulations; I simply offer them as tested, effective ideas. I don't think a teacher can ever be offered too many good ideas.

This book is intended for a variety of users. First, beginning teachers and student teachers preparing for the profession may find these pieces to be helpful time-savers and useful models for ideas of their own. Second, it is intended for teachers who want to use simulations but have neither the time nor experience to create their own. Third, teachers may simply want to use these field-tested and substantive lesson plans to help enliven a course while lightening their burden. Fourth, teachers who are asked to teach a new course may find exercises that can help to enliven their new preparation without requiring them to invest extensive time and energy. This book is intended for teachers who teach high school or junior high school social studies, as well as undergraduate political science and history professors.

Devising useful and interesting alternative lessons can be difficult and time-consuming. Teachers squeezed by multiple demands simply may not have time to design as many interesting lessons as they would like. Additionally, it often takes several iterations to refine a new activity or lesson. The lack of time for preparation and the need to refine lessons particularly weigh on overburdened novice teachers. In that spirit, I especially hope that teachers beginning their careers will find these lessons useful. After working with numerous student teachers as a supervisor during a five-year association with the Harvard Graduate School of Education, I became convinced that making these kinds of lessons widely available in an easy-to-use format would be especially helpful to newer teachers.

Each of the exercises in this book has been used multiple times and then subsequently modified to eliminate the most obvious kinks. These lessons were generally designed for classes of 25 to 30 students, but most of them will work effectively for classes ranging in size from 15 to 40 students. Most of the simulations require roughly one to three days of classtime to actually play, though several of these also involve some student preparation before the exercise begins. Also included here are three multi-week projects for students to work on primarily at home.

Various simulations in this collection emphasize factual knowledge, mathematical applications, cooperative learning, negotiation and persuasive argument, and creative writing. The lessons in the following ten chapters cover the broad spectrum of social studies so that almost any social studies teacher will be able to find at least one attractive lesson. Further, I hope that these simulations will provide useful models that will encourage others to dabble in simulation design.

Each chapter notes modifications teachers may want to make, depending on class size and the level of the students. The necessary content background for each lesson is presented in each chapter, the rules are laid out for the teacher, the necessary materials are prepared and ready for photocopying, and the recommended assessment tools are discussed. The result is that a teacher should be able to use any of these simulations based on two or three hours of effort. Once the teacher has decided if and how an exercise fits into the curriculum, the rest is fairly straightforward. After that decision is made, the teacher simply needs to read the chapter, photocopy the appropriate materials, decide how to use the background information provided, and then introduce the exercise to the class at the appropriate juncture.

This book is not just intended to serve as a set of prepackaged lesson plans. It is intended to be a platform from which teachers can explore simulations in ways that they find productive and comfortable. Each exercise comes with some suggested modifications that can be used to make it more appropriate for more advanced or for less advanced students. Teachers can use these modifications as starting points for reshaping the exercises. This introductory chapter and Chapter 12 include some down-to-earth discussions about how to think about designing and assessing simulations. This is intended to help teachers expand and refine their pedagogical repertoire.

## WHAT SIMULATIONS CAN ADD TO YOUR CLASSROOM

The greatest strength of simulation-based exercises is that they can help to bring a classroom to life and to integrate it into the daily world. When students start to get enthused about material, they start to care about it. For me, it was always a thrill to be on cafeteria duty and to overhear a table of football-crazy tenth-grade boys arguing about how to verify Dorito production limits or about the reliability of the enforcement mechanism they designed (see The Mighty Dorito Cartel, Chapter 3). I can think of few other approaches that bring students charging into the classroom, anxious to check the paper's stock listings to see how their holdings fared (see Letting the Bulls Run, Chapter 4), or that cause students to skip their normal before-school chat sessions to wrangle about constitutional provisions (see Constructing a New American Government, Chapter 2).

The competitive nature of many simulations lends an urgency to collaboration that is lacking in more traditional group projects. This urgency increases the value of each student's participation because the compact time frame and competitive dynamics make the unique contribution of each student significant. For instance, at any given point during A Delicate Balance of Power (see Chapter 10), students in a group may need to send out multiple negotiators, to receive multiple ambassadors, to coordinate these sets of negotiations, and to track resources and information on the condition of other countries. Once the simulation is up and running, no group tolerates a member who just wants to chew gum and read *Cosmo* or *Sports Illustrated* in a corner. Additionally, because I have frequently seen good friends double-cross each other in the course of the exercise when a more attractive offer came along (very much like Italy in 1915), students learn to move beyond their traditional classroom cliques in the conduct of diplomacy.

These simulations are not only enjoyable, they also produce highly beneficial spin-off effects in the classroom. The most obvious benefit is that students sometimes get so taken with one exercise that they begin to look at the entire subject through a new lens.

Students who always thought politics was uncool, economics was irrelevant, or history was boring can sometimes come at the material in a whole new way. Even if the transformation isn't total or permanent, just getting that student interested in one unit or for a period of time is valuable.

These changes in the behavior of individual students can also feed very positive changes in class atmosphere. If a class becomes so interesting that it begins to be a topic of conversation on the school bus or in the lunchroom, it becomes much easier to get students to commit to the class and to participate. In effect, an exciting class can invert the classroom social hierarchy so that participation and interest become cool (or at least cease to be signs of social retardation). Increased interest helps to make the class a friendlier and more welcoming environment, which leads to more comfortable interaction and discussion. As students start to see each other as valuable resources, teammates, savvy politicians, economists, negotiators and/or analysts, I have found it becomes substantially easier to get them to abide by bromides about tolerance, collegiality, and consideration.

Depending on the design and structure of the exercise, some simulations are particularly effective at breaking students out of their traditional friendship groups and cliques. Not only is this good for the students, but this aspect of the exercises particularly tends to foster positive classroom interaction over the course of the year. Sustained interaction between students who rarely speak can lead to increased friendliness, understanding, and even friendship. These incremental gains can be seen when teammates from two different social circles show up before school to plan some strategic stroke or when students are suddenly swapping phone numbers with the bookish and insular student who turns out to be a whiz at locating travel information on the Internet.

Simulations can also allow students to explore personas and roles that they do not explore in the daily course of classroom or personal life. In the course of simulations, I have routinely seen students step out of their classroom roles and interact across clique lines. One common example is that reserved female students become more assertive as they have a chance to fulfill leadership roles in these various exercises. The variety of leadership roles and other responsibilities creates opportunities for quiet students to display previously obscured talents. I remember a colleague telling me about one student, an academically gifted but very shy girl, who turned out to be a fabulous negotiator. Apparently, by the end of the second day, she was wheeling about the classroom while simultaneously conducting three negotiations. These kinds of opportunities can help students to emerge from traditional gender or classroom roles, and can allow students to explore different personalities and behavior.

These exercises are particularly useful because they force students to use a broad array of skills that, too often, are underutilized in social studies classes. Different exercises force students to use skills such as written and oral persuasion, note-taking, mathematical calculation, research skills, and negotiation. Forced to apply these skills, students have an opportunity to see their practical value. For instance, rather than merely writing a persuasive essay, students need to frame cogent and persuasive arguments that appeal to the self-interest of fellow players. The analytic skills required include "big-think" strategic and tactical concerns, but also demand that students pay careful attention to classroom activity, take careful notes, apply basic mathematical and deductive skills, and use good interpersonal skills.

Whatever our individual goals as teachers, our ability to fulfill our larger objectives almost always benefits from livelier and more creative curricula (Ornstein & Hunkins, 1993). As a staunch advocate of rigorous substantive content, however, I have sometimes found myself looking at activities promising to enliven my classroom and wondering, "Where's the beef?" Well-designed simulations can provide that beef and help to teach content and energize the classroom, even as they cultivate a range of analytic and interpersonal skills (Raffini, 1996). The exercises in this book were designed and tested with these multiple purposes in mind.

Simulations are a particularly attractive tool in the social studies classroom. Like all teachers, the social studies teacher confronts multiple expectations (Lazerson et al., 1985;

Sizer, 1992). Like our colleagues in other subject areas, we are expected to teach students important historical and social scientific concepts and facts. However, due to the "soft" nature of our material and the opportunities for discussion and interaction intrinsic in the social sciences, we are also expected to structure lessons that will cultivate interpersonal and analytic skills (Dobkin et al., 1985).

Well-crafted simulations are attractive precisely because they address both content-based and interaction-based goals. First, they call on a variety of skills and intelligences. Well-honed social studies lessons seek to cultivate analytic, interpersonal, and management skills; to practice team coordination and data collection; and to absorb and organize factual material. Simulations can do precisely these kinds of things, and can do them within a rigorous substantive framework.

Second, simulations and group activities can help to foster classroom relationships and to energize new patterns of classroom interaction. This kind of interaction can help to overcome resistance implicit in traditional teacher-centered lessons, particularly for teachers who are working with students from diverse backgrounds (Alpert, 1991). It is not that there is anything magical about simulations, but that using a diverse range of approaches and lessons increases the chance of forging a connection with students who are not learning.

Third, the variety of skills summoned forth in a well-designed exercise permits the teacher to simultaneously accommodate the developmental needs of a variety of learners (Slavin, 1994). By creating a variety of roles, and encouraging student-on-student interaction, the teacher is freed to interact with individual students much more easily than when interacting with the class as a whole.

## SOME PRACTICAL THOUGHTS ON DESIGNING AND USING SIMULATIONS

### Designing Simulations

***Creating a Simulation***   First things first. I strongly recommend that you do not sit down and attempt to design a simulation for a unit you are teaching next week, not unless you want to invite serious frustration. Getting the materials just right, in order to minimize student confusion, always seems to take as long as the rest of the simulation process combined. Simulations that are rushed into the classroom without clear student materials and without having been given an extra once-over often produce a great deal of confusion.

Give yourself a total of at least 15 hours of work time if you want to build, from scratch, a simulation in which each student will play a different role. Give yourself at least 10 hours to build one that will feature five or eight classroom groups. You might be able to get by with five or six hours of preparation for a more project-driven exercise in which students do not have particular roles (see Living on a Paycheck, Chapter 9, or A Whirlwind American Tour, Chapter 7); however, don't plug the exercise into your lesson planning until after it is designed. One of the infuriating things about designing simulations is that constructing the materials and dotting the "i's" and crossing the "t's" often seems to take more time than all of the heavy lifting that goes into brainstorming, researching, designing, and organizing the exercises.

***Pick a Focus***   I find creating an intellectually substantive and content-driven simulation to be easiest if the teacher starts in one of two ways. The most effective way is to begin with a general social science concept, one that will be illustrated through the use of specific content. For instance, in creating The Mighty Dorito Cartel (Chapter 3), I began with the intention of illuminating the "free rider syndrome" and the theoretical problems of securing multi-party cooperation. These are fundamental social science notions, which I then decided to embed in problems that plagued the OPEC oil cartel during the 1980s.

More important than choosing a specific factual occurrence (e.g., the Civil Rights Movement, the Yalta Conference, or the 1987 stock market crash) is that the teacher select an illuminating social science concept that will be brought to life through the simulation. I find it is easiest to keep a simulation alive and fresh if the exercise is written around systemic incentives that shape student activity. What do I mean by "systemic incentives"? Rather than simply giving the students a role and asking them to remain faithful to that role, I structure the role of each player or team so that they are likely to fare best by behaving in ways that increase the simulation's authenticity. Whether the larger aim is to pass a piece of legislation, forge a Constitution, win a nomination, or conquer a continent, the incentives for each player and/or team are designed so that effective play will help to illustrate the tensions that the simulation was designed to teach. Once I have chosen the concept to illuminate, and figured out how to build it into an interesting exercise, I have generally found numerous locations in the curriculum where the content is appropriate for integrating the exercise.

A second approach to simulation design is to select an important area of practical knowledge in which students have little understanding, such as the stock market, traveling, or budgeting, and design the exercise so that students will be steeped in the requisite material. I find this second approach to be less intellectually rewarding for the students, but it often does a better job of instilling practical skills. The first approach lends itself to classroom games and exercises, while the "practical knowledge" approach is more conducive to simulation-based projects.

Once the theme of the lesson is in place, there are two major ways to approach the incorporation of interpersonal and other complementary skills. If there are certain student skills you wish to emphasize, it is not very difficult to develop and shape an exercise that incorporates those. Such skills might be math reasoning, negotiating, creative writing, research, debate, or public speaking. An alternative approach is to play with the content until an exercise begins to take shape, and then to simply incorporate those ancillary skills suggested by the lesson design. The simulations in this book help to develop a wide range of skills, including oral communication, written communication, note-taking, strategic thinking, negotiation, applied mathematics, and budgeting.

I find clear and carefully structured exercises to be particularly helpful for the less talented students. One criticism that is sometimes leveled at structured approaches is that the structure in these exercises impedes the ability of students to be creative. I have definitively found that not to be the case. I have found students to be more comfortable and interested in the exercise when they have a clear sense of the parameters and the objectives. Over time, I have sought to increase the structure of these exercises in order to permit students to focus their energy on devising creative strategies within those structures. I have found that meandering exercises, rather than inspiring student creativity, all too often lose the targeted students.

***The "Right" Dynamic***   I'm quite sure that there is no *best* way to invigorate a simulation. You will notice that this book includes both competitive and noncompetitive exercises, exercises that require group cooperation, and ones that students can pursue alone. On the other hand, there is a particular dynamic that I feel more comfortable with. As you will note, I have a preference for negotiation-based exercises in which students have incentives to cooperate, while various obstacles make cooperation difficult. I find that the quasicompetitive nature of this dynamic keeps students engaged, rewards constructive student interaction, and teaches large theoretical lessons which I think are central to the social sciences. However, rather than advocating this particular focus, I suggest that you try to get a sense of the dynamic with which you are most comfortable.

***Authenticity versus Manageability***   Teachers need to decide how concerned they are about specificity and precise historical authenticity. More complicated and more precise exercises promise to teach students more specific content and to create more sophisticated interaction. On the other hand, increased precision and complexity require that the exercises become more complicated and more confusing. Each teacher needs to strike an appropriate balance, given a particular course, a particular group of students, and that teacher's particular goals for the exercise. I will note that several of the exercises in this book, even though they feature stylized data and stripped-down versions of authentic interaction, still require careful instruction to avoid student confusion and frustration. Too much concern with getting historical data precisely right can greatly increase complexity, while adding little intellectual substance.

## Using Simulations

***Before Introducing the Simulation***    I like to prepare the substantive groundwork for the exercise a day or two before introducing simulation. The exercises contained in this book generally require that the students be taught a certain amount of prior content in order for the context and nature of the exercise to make sense. Each chapter begins with a Background section, which contains content sufficient to handle this introduction for those teachers unfamiliar with the topic at hand. Failure to prepare the students with some prior background may lead to unproductive confusion regarding vocabulary, basic concepts, and just what the exercise is intended to illustrate.

You will notice that, in most cases, there are not extensive prepared materials for distribution to the students. This is by design. While some simulations come with packets of information for the teacher to give each participant, I have always thought that requiring students to collect some background information on their own is a desirable way to integrate the development of research skills into the larger lesson. It is certainly possible for the teacher to write up brief fact sheets on the countries students represent in Forging a Lasting Middle East Peace (Chapter 10) or Constructing a New American Government (Chapter 2), for instance, but I would advise against doing so for most intermediate and advanced students. One bonus of having students do their own research is that students who take the trouble to do more thorough research tend to enjoy real advantages during the course of the exercise.

***Logistics and Planning***    Simulations can be structured in whatever fashion is deemed most productive. In this book, most of the simulations run for two or three 40-minute periods, while others are activities that students do at home over the course of several weeks. There are two key factors to keep in mind when thinking about using simulations. The first is to make sure that you have planned out how to integrate the time and the content into the larger curriculum so that you don't wind up feeling pressured to rush through the simulation. To get the full benefit from a simulation requires that students sink their teeth into it, take it seriously, and be assessed on the activity. Hurried half-measures inhibit this.

Second, consider in advance how the time and work demands of a simulation will affect your workload and that of your students. Some simulations require relatively little effort (at least on the students' part), while others require a great deal. It is useful to mesh these demands with your ongoing units and assignments, as well as with the rhythms of the school year.

***Classroom Management During a Simulation***    Be deliberate in handling the pace of in-class exercises. Don't try to move too quickly, particularly in complex simulations, or you will wind up confusing yourself and frustrating the class. Instead, settle on a sustainable and smooth pace. Once students get into the flow of a simulation, they are able to fill most slack time with figuring, plotting, strategizing, and negotiating.

Particularly for simulations that are more complex, such as those involving numerical calculations, I strongly recommend having a student assist with the calculations. However, I hate to ask the student assistant to sit out the exercise, and the teacher can safely rely on a participating student (at least in a group exercise) if the student is regarded as competent and fair.

***Assessment***    The issue of assessment is crucial. Too often, simulations are regarded as a break from the substance of the course. Simulations become a fun sidelight, but are largely irrelevant to the class. The key to making simulation-based exercises educationally valuable is to integrate them fully into the larger course. One key way to do this is by having students treat the substance, the lessons, and the skills of the exercise with the seriousness they would accord to regular material. I try to achieve this effect by building assessments into each exercise. This prompts students to pay attention, gives me a way to check learning and involvement, and encourages all students to participate in a meaningful fashion.

Multiple assessments also permit the teacher to evaluate the intellectual substance taught, the skills developed, and the students' ability to apply the dynamics illustrated by the exercise. The one proviso is that the teacher be careful to design assessments that are manageable, complementary, and not too time-consuming. A number of suggestions are included in the Assessment section of each chapter. The approaches I tend to prefer include student essays, quizzes, projects, research briefs and teacher observation.

***Modifications for Students of Various Levels***    A given simulation will not prove equally effective with students at varying levels of intellectual, cognitive, and emotional development. Exercises that work well with older students may prove too burdensome or confusing for younger students, while other exercises may excite younger students but fail to sustain interest among older students. Exercises that require cooperation and student negotiation tend to work better with more mature students, while those that require a good deal of research or recordkeeping fare particularly well with students who have had an opportunity to develop those skills.

Because the capacities of students and classroom cultures vary within any given grade level, teachers need to use their own professional judgment and experience to determine appropriate adjustments. Teachers will find that this task becomes easier as they become accustomed to the rhythms and demands of simulations. Flexibility is a particularly attractive element of simulations. It increases your ability to fit simulations into the requirements of your classroom and to shape the exercises in a way that makes them the most valuable for your students.

The exercises here were designed for high school students and were refined to work well with the student population I taught. Consequently, teachers at other levels may want to modify the lessons in some ways. To facilitate fine-tuning, each chapter includes a short discussion of possible modifications that can make an exercise more appropriate for more advanced students or for junior high school students.

***The Role of Bonuses***    Personally, I always like to assign rewards (bonus points or such) for performance. For some exercises, this means rewarding a victor, but more commonly it means integrating points into a game so that all students are chasing bonus points as part of their roles. I have found that bonus points heighten the seriousness with which students tackle the simulation and help students to remain clear on their primary objectives. The teacher can achieve similar effects by incorporating observations of student activity into the exercise assessment, but I find the bonus points approach helps to lend a competitive excitement which serves to enhance the game.

In truth, though, I am somewhat ambivalent on bonuses. I compromise by integrating both my assessment of the activity and the bonus-point dimension into most exercises, while explicitly and implicitly making the point that the bonus points are not the focus of the exercise. Using a multiplicity of assessment tools and making the purpose and nature of the exercise clear to students help to keep the significance of rewards in perspective. It is easy for me to use bonus points in this manner because my students accumulate a large amount of points over the course of a quarter and have frequent opportunities to earn bonuses. For other teachers, with other styles, in other classrooms, I would recommend taking the approach that feels most comfortable for you.

## LAYOUT OF THE BOOK

To make this book as useful and accessible as possible for practitioners, I have organized it around 10 self-contained, original simulations and exercises. If you refer to Table 1.1, you will see that all of the simulations have been listed according to the courses and the

**TABLE 1.1.  Which Exercises Can Be Used with Various Courses**

| Chapter | *World Geography* | *World History* | *European History* | *American History* | *Contemporary Issues* | *American Government/ Political Science/Civics* | *Free Enterprise/ Economics* |
|---|---|---|---|---|---|---|---|
| **2** Constructing a New American Government | | | | 1780s | | Constitution | |
| **3** The Mighty Dorito Cartel | Middle East | 20$^{th}$ century | | 1970s | Natural Resources | | Cartels |
| **4** Letting the Bulls Run | | | | 1920s | Investing | | Investing |
| **5** Forging a Lasting Middle East Peace | Middle East | 20$^{th}$ century | | 1970–80s | | | |
| **6** Choosing a President | | | | Political Machines, President-ial Politics | American Politics | Presidency | |
| **7** A Whirlwind American Tour | United States | | | Urban Geography | Travel and Budgeting | | Money Management |
| **8** Passing a Crime Bill | | | | Congress's Role | National Policy | Congress | |
| **9** Living on a Paycheck | | | | | Budget Skills | | Budgeting and Living Skills |
| **10** The Delicate Balance of Power | Europe | Europe | Pre–World War I | Pre–World War I | | International Relations | |
| **11** Making the United Nations Work | Global | Global | Post–Cold War | Post–World War II | World Issues | | |

suggested units for which they may be applicable. Teachers may also find it helpful to examine Table 1.2, which shows which skills are emphasized in each of the exercises.

Each simulation is introduced by an extended note to the teacher which discusses the purpose and the nature of the exercise. The note also suggests the kinds of courses in which the simulation may be useful and says a bit about my thinking during the creation of the exercise. Included are relevant background materials on the target topic, guidelines on when and with whom each exercise is intended to work, careful step-by-step instructions on how each simulation operates, and suggested modifications for more and less advanced students. Each chapter also includes a boxed check-off list of the materials to prepare for each lesson and an abbreviated list of step-by-step instructions suitable for reference during each exercise. Each simulation includes all necessary supplementary materials, presented in ready-to-photocopy form. Finally, each chapter also includes a discussion of recommended assessments for that exercise and a discussion of the purpose served by each assessment.

**TABLE 1.2.  Primary Skills Developed by Each Exercise**

| Chapter | Working in a Team | Public Speaking | Negotiating Skills | Research Skills | Creative Writing | Math Reasoning Skills | Analytic Writing |
|---|---|---|---|---|---|---|---|
| **2** Constructing a New American Government | yes | yes | yes | yes | | | |
| **3** The Mighty Dorito Cartel | yes | | yes | | | yes | |
| **4** Letting the Bulls Run | | | | yes | | yes | yes |
| **5** Forging a Lasting Middle East Peace | yes | yes | yes | yes | | | |
| **6** Choosing a President | | | yes | | | yes | yes |
| **7** A Whirlwind American Tour | | | | yes | yes | yes | |
| **8** Passing a Crime Bill | | yes | yes | | | | yes |
| **9** Living on a Paycheck | | | | yes | | yes | yes |
| **10** The Delicate Balance of Power | yes | | yes | | | yes | yes |
| **11** Making the United Nations Work | | yes | yes | yes | | | yes |

# REFERENCES

Alpert, Bracha (1991). "Students' resistance in the classroom." *Anthropology and Education Quarterly, 22*: 350–366.

Dobkin, William, Joel Fischer, Bernard Ludwig, & Richard Koblinger (1985). *A handbook for the teaching of social studies (2nd ed.)*. Boston: Allyn and Bacon.

Lazerson, Marvin, Judith McLaughlin, Bruce McPherson, & Stephen Bailey (1985). *An education of value*. Cambridge: Cambridge University Press.

Ornstein, Allan, & Francis Hunkins (1993). *Curriculum foundations, principles, and theory*. Boston: Allyn and Bacon.

Raffini, James (1996). *150 Ways to increase intrinsic motivation in the classroom*. Boston: Allyn and Bacon.

Sizer, Theodore (1992). *Horace's compromise*. Boston: Houghton Mifflin Company.

Slavin, Robert (1994). *Education psychology*. Boston: Allyn and Bacon.

# CHAPTER 2

# Constructing a New American Government

*Students are thrust into the political, regional, and economic conflicts that faced the delegates who drafted the U.S. Constitution in Philadelphia. Students must hammer out a new government for the thirteen colonies, while taking care to defend the material interests of their respective state. Each student or group represents a colony and is guided by simple incentives constructed to reflect that state's economic needs and political demands. This simulation is a flurry of negotiations, backroom agreements, and deadlocked votes that usually culminates in a compromise that resembles the U.S. Constitution. Moral and idealistic concerns conflict with the practical necessity of winning over nine colonies (including both Virginia and New York), introducing students to the challenges of state-building and to the political concerns that shaped the 1787 Constitutional Convention.*

## TEACHER'S NOTE

This exercise simulates the 1787 Constitutional Convention in Philadelphia, at which delegates from 12 of the 13 American colonies gathered to write the U.S. Constitution.[1] The exercise requires students to successfully construct a new government among colonies with conflicting interests and needs. Students are forced to address the issues that shaped the formation of the United States. This lesson was originally designed for an American Civics class, but it has worked equally well in American History classes. It takes between one and two classes to run the actual simulation, although teachers will find the exercise more valuable if students are first introduced to the suggested background material.

Students representing the 13 colonies are charged with forging a workable and broadly supported compromise that addresses the major points of contention. The crucial lesson for students is that the Constitution was not a utopian document dreamed up by philosophers, but rather was a pragmatic document drafted in the midst of intense political conflict. Students learn that politics was not once a pristine art that has fallen on hard times, but that politics is always about compromise, power, and making the best of the hand one is dealt.

This exercise works best when used to enliven student interest in the Convention *prior* to teaching what actually transpired in Philadelphia. The actual nuts and bolts of what occurred in Philadelphia and the agreement that emerged should *not* be covered before the exercise. This encourages students to be more creative, forces them to rely more heavily on their own wits, and rewards students who bother to research how the Convention progressed. It also helps to greatly increase student interest in finding out how the Founding Fathers resolved their compromises on the key issues. The teacher should cover events up until the spring of 1787 prior to the exercise, and should then plan on picking up with the actual Convention after the simulation is completed.

The simulation is relatively simple because students are given specific directives as to what their stands are on the key issues. While these stands are vastly oversimplified from the actual convention, having been shaped primarily in accord with regional and small-state versus big-state pressures, the result is student negotiation that approximates the central arguments at the Constitutional Convention. The simplification helps to keep the game manageable, reducing stress for the

---

[1]An interesting historic note is that only 12 of the colonies sent representatives to the actual Constitutional Convention. Rhode Island chose not to send anyone.

teacher and making the game accessible to a wide range of students. Some students pursue the negotiations on a relatively sophisticated level, while some students with less background still get interested in the power-play aspects of negotiation.

At the Constitutional Convention, all delegates realized that it was crucial for both Virginia and New York to accept the final document if the new government was going to work. To replicate that dynamic, ratification requires that both of these colonies, each with extremely different interests, accept the Constitution that students write. This adds a second dimension to the negotiations, and helps to ensure that the exercise does not devolve into an easy and slipshod general consensus.

# BACKGROUND ON THE CONSTITUTIONAL CONVENTION

The Constitutional Convention was called in 1787 to rectify problems in the Articles of Confederation. The Articles, which had governed relations among the colonies since 1781, had been drafted in an effort to coordinate essential tasks during the Revolutionary War. The Continental Congress had touched off the war against Great Britain by issuing the Declaration of Independence in 1776. The war did not conclude until 1783.

The impotence of the Continental Congress, an informal assembly lacking significant powers, had given rise to calls for a more effective central government. The Continental Congress's lack of resources and power frustrated those responsible for governing the colonies' wartime efforts. These frustrations culminated in the adoption of the Articles of Confederation in 1781, after the Articles had been ratified by all 13 colonies. Between 1777, when the Continental Congress drafted the Articles, and the final approval of the Articles the colonies had been forced to fight a revolution without an effective central government to raise money, troops, or supplies for the wartime effort.

The colonies drafted the Articles with a jealous regard for their individual sovereignty. The Articles were designed to ensure that the revolt against Great Britain did not result in the colonies simply paying homage to a new master. Section II of the Articles specifically stated that, "Each state retains . . . every power, jurisdiction, and right, which is not by the Confederation expressly delegated to the United States in Congress assembled."

As a mechanism for operating a central government, the Articles were particularly crippled by four measures. First, the national government did not possess the ability to raise taxes. Second, the Articles created no executive to direct the government or execute its policies. Third, the Articles did not allow the national government to regulate interstate or foreign commerce. Fourth, the Articles could not be modified without unanimous consent.

A loose framework intended to coordinate politics among 13 sovereign governments, the Articles essentially established a loose alliance of 13 countries. All states had an equal vote in the one-house Congress and any change in the Articles required a unanimous vote of all 13 colonies. Under the Articles, the national government provided little direction of monetary, trade, or military policy. After the Treaty of Yorktown brought a victorious conclusion to the Revolutionary War in 1783, the colonies no longer had a common enemy to unite them. The result was severe conflict between the colonies on trade and other issues, and little willingness to maintain a strong national defense.

The dangers of the weak provisions for common defense in the Article were brought home by a 1786 crisis in Massachusetts. In 1786, Daniel Shays, a Revolutionary War veteran, led 1,500 armed supporters in a march on a western Massachusetts courthouse. Battered by the currency problems that had troubled the new central government, the marchers wanted to close the courthouse in order to stop creditors from foreclosing on their farms. Congress was so terrified by this upheaval that it appropriated $530,000 to establish a national army. The weakness of the Articles became transparent, however, when every state except Virginia refused to supply the money needed to actually fund the army.

Also in 1786, Virginia had invited states to attend a convention at Annapolis in order to consider amendments to the Articles for the purpose of improving commercial regulation. Only five states sent delegates to the meeting. Capitalizing on the angst sparked by Shays' Rebellion, the delegates to the Annapolis Convention used the occasion to call for a much broader meeting in Philadelphia in 1787. The Philadelphia meeting was charged with considering fundamental revisions to the Articles. This proposal attracted wide support and representatives convened in Philadelphia in 1787. At that point in time, Philadelphia was the nation's capital. Washington, DC, was then an unnoticed and undeveloped swamp.

Twelve of the 13 colonies sent a total of 74 delegates to the convention. Rhode Island, nicknamed "Rogue Island" by a Boston newspaper, refused to participate because it feared the meeting was a Trojan Horse designed to create a stronger national government. After weeks of delay caused by an inability to raise a quorum, the delegates finally convened on May 25, 1787. Although 55 of the 74 delegate showed up at some point, no more than 30 delegates were at the Convention at any one time.

The illustrious company at the Convention included George Washington, Benjamin Franklin, future President James Madison, Alexander Hamilton, and many of the nation's other leading political figures. However, between the sweltering Philadelphia spring and summer, the massive problems posed by extended travel, and the uncertain nature of the enterprise, more than a quarter of the delegates to this gathering of "demi-gods" never even bothered to attend.

When it convened, the Convention was not heralded as the historic body that it later proved to be. In the summer of 1787, it was a collection of men in three-piece wool suits and wigs sitting in a closed room during the sweltering heat of the Philadelphia spring and summer. The windows were kept closed so that the discussions would remain confidential. The delegates proved to be adept at secrecy. During the convention's seven months in session there were almost no leaks.

The meeting had been touted as an assembly that would consider necessary modifications to the Articles of Confederation. That relatively tame aspiration kept the affair from receiving too high a profile. In the 1780s, there was considerable opposition among the colonists to a strong national government. As a result, the Convention got underway amid significant amounts of apathy and distrust. Almost immediately the initial modest proposal to modify the Articles was jettisoned in favor of a stronger, national government model proposed by Virginian James Madison. Madison's proposed national government, where power would no longer reside strictly with the colonies, became the framework for the Convention.

The Convention was marked by sharp sectional disputes over the desirability of tariffs and the institution of slavery. The North favored high tariffs to protect its manufacturing and commercial interests, while the agricultural South rejected high trade barriers because it relied more heavily on foreign imports and on overseas sales. The North generally opposed slavery, while the South defended it as integral to its culture, social order, and economy.

There were also sharp splits between the small states and the large states. The large states argued that the states ought to have influence in the new government proportional to their share of the new nation's population. The smaller states, having just fought a war to secure their independence, insisted that the new government be a partnership of equals. Arguments about representation were complicated by questions of taxation, where the positions of the large and small states were reversed. Small states wanted the government to collect revenue in proportion to state wealth or population, while large states wanted each state to contribute an equal share of government revenues.

## The Convention

On May 29, four days after the start of the Convention,[2] Edmund Randolph of Virginia presented the *Virginia Plan* for a strong national government. Drafted by fellow Virginia delegate (and future President) James Madison, the Virginia Plan was not a revision of the Articles but was a proposal for an entirely new central government. The proposal included measures calling for a strong central government with three distinct branches, a bicameral (two-house) legislature, and proportional representation.

[2]Present this material after the simulation.

Fearful of the power that the large colonies would wield under the proportional emphasis of the Virginia Plan, the small states rallied behind New Jersey delegate William Paterson's New Jersey plan. The *New Jersey Plan* proposed eliminating the Virginia Plan's proposed proportional representation and a bicameral legislature in favor of a one-house Congress in which all states would have an equal vote. To resolve this conflict, a special committee was formed. The committee, consisting of one member from each state, worked through the July 4 recess and eventually reached a workable compromise. The Great Compromise, passed by the Constitutional Convention on July 16, dictated that there would be a bicameral Congress in which each state would have an equal vote in the upper chamber, while votes in the lower chamber would be apportioned according to population.

The Constitution that emerged from the Convention in the fall of 1787 was not even loosely based on the Articles, but envisioned a national government that would share power with the states. Within the government, states would no longer each have an equal voice. Instead, the delegates adopted a scheme of proportional representation for the lower chamber of the House of Representatives.

The delegates had to finesse the issue of slavery with a compromise that eventually brought their handiwork to the brink of ruin. A strong national government required that Northerners and Southerners compromise on the issue of slavery. In 1787, 18 percent of the nation's population was slaves. The 697,000 slaves were almost entirely concentrated in the Southern states, which were absolutely not willing to sign onto a new government that threatened their slave-holding culture. The Southern states were unwilling to accept strict restrictions on slavery. They also wanted to have slaves counted as inhabitants for purposes of determining the number of votes that states would have in the House of Representatives (and in the electoral college for President). The Northern states did not want to count slaves for purposes of representation, because their inclusion would give the Southern colonies more votes and therefore serve to increase the relative strength of the Southern voice in national affairs. The Northern colonies did, however, want to count slaves for purposes of taxation.

The result was the *three-fifths compromise*. Using a formula that the Congress under the Articles of Confederation had used for financial assessments in 1783, the convention agreed that slaves would be counted as three-fifths of a person both for purposes of taxation and representation. This agreement meant that in the House of Representatives, which was apportioned according to population, the slave states would hold 47 percent of the votes. This figure was agreeable to both sides. Additionally, the Convention agreed to let the importation of slaves continue for 20 years and to mandate that all fugitive slaves—regardless of the state they were in—be returned to their masters. Slave states did not object to the eventual cut-off date for slave importation because it meant the slaves owned by slave-holders would become that much more valuable.

Because the Constitutional Convention had been called as a meeting to amend the Articles of Confederation, enacting the changes envisioned in the Constitution would require a unanimous vote among the 13 colonies. The recalcitrance of Rhode Island alone ensured that any amendments along the lines of the proposed Constitution would fail. To ensure that their handiwork would have an opportunity to pass into law, the delegates crafted Article 7 of the Constitution. Article 7 supported a new protocol for ratification. Utterly disregarding the fact that they had been sent to Philadelphia to amend the Articles, the Founders devised a ratification process that specified that the Constitution would take effect when it had been ratified by nine—rather than 13—colonies. Additionally, to bypass the state governments who feared losing power to the new national government, the delegates required the states to call a special ratifying convention to determine whether to endorse the new Constitution. These measures sidestepped the problems presented by the unanimity requirement of the Articles and ensured that state government officials threatened by the new Constitution would not be deciding whether to ratify the document.

During the period preceding the crucial ratification conflict in New York, three pro-Constitution advocates penned a collection of newspaper articles on behalf of the Constitution. Collectively known as the *Federalist Papers*, the 85 essays written by Alexander

Hamilton, James Madison, and John Jay have been enshrined as the holy writ of American democracy.

The Constitution officially took effect when it was ratified by the ninth state, New Hampshire, on June 21, 1788. However, the two key states—Virginia and New York—did not ratify the document until August 1788. After ratification by Virginia and New York, the new government became a reality.

When the New York convention followed Virginia's in August 1788 and narrowly ratified the Constitution, by a 30 to 27 margin, the last significant hurdle to the formation of the new government was overcome. The first U.S. national elections were held in late 1788, and the new American government came into being on March 4, 1789, highlighted by the inauguration of the nation's first President, George Washington.

# USING THIS SIMULATION

## Purpose of the Exercise

Substantively, the simulation was designed as a tool to deepen student understanding of the writing of the Constitution and about the issues that defined the times. The lesson is intended for use as part of an American history class, but works equally well in a civics, American government, or political science class. The lesson introduces students to some of the political conflicts that marked the period of the Constitutional Convention, requires them to research the political needs of one state in depth, and then forces them to articulate and defend that state's position in a legislative forum.

The exercise is intended to introduce students to the issues that shaped the period of the founding, to the Constitutional Convention itself, and to the compromises that have shaped the fundamental tapestry of American government. Students learn about the political and social situation that confronted the colonies in the 1780s and do some research on the conditions in one state. The actual exercise instructs students in the nature of political negotiation and illustrates how particular incentives can make it very difficult for politicians to agree on a definition of what "good policy" is.

I especially like that the exercise helps students see why American government and American political institutions took the shape they have. The moral dimension of some of the issues addressed, such as questions of representation and slavery, also offer students an opportunity to weigh self-interest against more amorphous concepts of the "general good" and "the right thing to do."

## Skills Developed

The simulation helps to develop teamwork, negotiating, public speaking, and research skills. The object is for students to negotiate their way around explicit conflicts, developing the arts of argument and discussion. Because different blocs of colonies have different demands, and because these sets of demands are cross-cutting, students must learn how to split the difference in order to produce workable compromises. The key issues at stake broach both moral and philosophical questions, giving students an opportunity to develop their capacity for debate and moral reasoning. Each group's performance depends on the ability of students to forge alliances, prioritize issues, and cooperate in achieving a common goal. As a result, the game rewards and encourages both strategic thinking and interpersonal skills.

## Logistics

*Constructing a New American Government* is relatively simple, but the exercise is aided by some preparation on the part of the *students*. About a week before the exercise is to begin, the teacher should assign the colonies to 13 groups of students. Because each of the 13 colonies is represented by a student or a group of students, the exercise can easily handle a class ranging in size from 13 to 39 students. Each group is to prepare a two-page briefing that compiles basic facts about their state in the 1780s and an analysis of their state's political situation prior to the convening of the Constitutional Convention. Each group also prepares a one-page brief on the condition of the United States in the 1780s. Students should have the briefings prepared before the day of the exercise.

The exercise can be conducted in one or two 40-minute classes. However, because the game's length depends in large part on the students' ability to forge workable compromises, no precise time estimates are possible. All the materials necessary for the simulation are included in this chapter's Appendix—Materials. Once a teacher has read this chapter, preparation for the simulation should take no more than 20 to 30 minutes. Once the State Needs sheets and the Key Issues sheet have been copied, the only real preparation necessary is organizing groups and preparing explanatory remarks.

## HOW THE SIMULATION WORKS

### Student Groups

Students are grouped into 13 colonies, with each group of roughly equal size. In a class of 25 or 30 students, each state delegation will consist of two or three students. Having more than three students representing any state does not work well, since it tends to leave some group members without much to do.

### Object

The object is for the class to construct a Constitution that resolves the seven crucial issues presented to students. Each group also has incentives to forge an agreement that successfully addresses the demands of their particular state. The political demands of each state are represented in the summary sheet that each state's students are issued (see Appendix). Each state has three issues that are considered "major" concerns and two or three that are considered "minor" concerns. In their two-page essay discussing the exercise, students explain and defend their success at obtaining their state's objectives.

There is no arbitrary way to determine "winners," even though teachers can certainly assign bonus points based on how successfully a group achieves its major and/or minor objectives. The problem with using points in this exercise is that state objectives have been designed so that student compromises, which split the difference, are likely to emerge. (For instance, large states want proportional representation and small states want equal representation. The most likely result is a bicameral legislature, which accords with the objectives of neither side.) Students are assessed based on their ability to make the case that they were effective advocates for their state.

### Length of Game

The exercise runs until students have resolved the seven key issues. If students rapidly reach agreements on those elements, the class should certainly be encouraged and rewarded for constructing a more elaborate document. Because the game's length depends in large part on the students' ability to forge workable compromises, no precise time estimates are possible. I give the students about 30 minutes to bask in the process of negotiating without any time limits, and then announce how much longer the students have (usually another 20 to 30 minutes) to forge an agreement. I suggest waiting to make this announcement because, once they are under the gun, students sometimes proceed to forge relatively rapid agreements.

### How the Game Is Played

Students are assigned their colonies a few days before the game. Each group is to prepare a two-page background document on their state. This brief should provide useful and well-organized information about their state's economy, politics, and social situation in the 1780s. Each group is also to prepare a one-page summary on the condition of the United States in the 1780s. Students are to use these materials as a reference and negotiating tool during their convention.

About a week before the Convention, students should be permitted to meet as a group to plan out the briefing materials. They should then receive small amounts of time during one or two additional classes to help them prepare for the convention.

When each group is assigned their state, they are given the state's "Needs" sheet and a copy of a "Key Issues to Be Resolved" sheet (see Appendix). The Needs sheet presents a simplified set of convention demands for each state, while the Key Issues sheet summarizes the seven issues students have to resolve in their constitution. The broad objectives for each state are generally historically accurate because they reflect regional affiliation and state size. However, the objectives have been massaged to ensure that conflict occurs in a way conducive to extended negotiation and compromise, and to minimize the headaches for the teacher actually using the exercise. Each group attempts to emerge from the convention having successfully won on its major, and to a lesser extent, its minor objectives. Because different colonies had directly contradictory demands, it is the interplay of these demands which drives the exercise.

When the convention convenes, students should be grouped by state. Ideally, the 13 groups will sit in a large circle, although the actual arrangement will depend on the size of the class and the classroom. At this point, the teacher reiterates the issues the constitution must resolve, charges the students with electing a chair, and tells the students to get started. The teacher can then step out of the way. Whether students want to handle each issue by secret ballot or by a show of hands, whether they want to tackle issues in order or all at once, whether they want to create a strong chair or a weak chair—any and all of those decisions should be left in the hands of the class. Part of the point of the exercise, after all, is to teach students what it was like to negotiate a constitution and what it is like to effectively manage a meeting.

***The Key Issues*** Students must resolve the following seven key issues in their constitution, and must draft the constitution so that it is endorsed by at least nine colonies (including Virginia and New York). (The seven issues list in the Appendix is reproducable for classwide distribution.)

1. Whether or not slavery ought to be legal in the nation.
2. Whether or not states that do not recognize slavery are still expected to return escaped slaves to their owners in slave-holding states. (This provision was known as "the fugitive slave law.")
3. Whether representation in the national legislature ought to be proportional (according to each state's population) or whether each state ought to have an equal vote. If representation is based on population, how should slaves (who are not citizens) be counted?
4. Whether national taxes ought to be based on each state's population or whether each state ought to pay an equal amount. If taxes are based on population, how should slaves (who are not citizens) be counted?
5. Whether the nation's executive ought to be powerful or whether the executive ought to have carefully limited powers.
6. Whether the executive ought to be elected directly by the people or whether the executive should not be directly elected. If the executive is not to be directly elected, should he or she be chosen by the states, the legislature, or in some other fashion?
7. Whether the new government ought to have strong powers to tax and regulate trade or carefully limited powers.

Additionally, students are free to come up with other provisions, but debate on those provisions is often less gritty because there are no historic incentives shaping and guiding behavior.

***Must Win Support From 9 of the 13 Colonies***   Students must forge an agreement that wins backing from 9 of the 13 colonies, two of which must be New York and Virginia. Students win additional credit if they are able to forge a document that draws unanimous support. (This point is interesting, because classes that take unanimity seriously give each state a de facto veto.)

***The de facto Veto of Virginia and New York***   An unspoken understanding of the Convention was that the new colonial government could not survive unless it included the two oversized and strategically located colonies of New York and Virginia.

---

**SUMMARY TEACHER INSTRUCTIONS**

*Prior to the day the simulation begins*
- Objective is for students to construct a constitution that resolves critical issues presented to the students.
- Assign colonies about two weeks in advance, handing out the State Needs Sheets, copies of the Key Issues to Be Resolved sheet, and copies of the map.
- Students prepare a background briefing on their state and on the condition of the United States during the 1780s.

*The day the simulation begins*
- Explain exercise and key issues that the constitution must address.
- Students elect a chair and commence negotiations.
- Exercise continues until students design a constitution that wins the backing from 9 states, including Virginia and New York.

*After the simulation*
- Assess activity using briefing paper, observed participation, analytic essay, and quiz.
- Use second half of background material to explain to students how the decisions at the Convention actually turned out.

---

## COMMENTS FROM EXPERIENCE

The single most important thing the teacher needs to do is to pick the appropriate students to represent New York and Virginia. The veto power of these states is crucial because it teaches students about the inequity of power and helps ensure that a herd mentality won't allow students to storm through the convention too easily. For these reasons, the teacher needs New York and Virginia students who will not be afraid to stand up to a majority of their classmates. The unusual influence of these states also means, however, that they must play a disproportionate role in leading the convention to workable compromises. Consequently, while these students should not be pushovers, neither should they be stubborn or seekers of conflict. That can be a recipe for sure deadlock.

It is important to ensure that students have adequately prepared ahead of time for the convention. While the conflicting state demands compel students into the desirable conflicts and help to ensure rough authenticity, the negotiations become much more satisfying and interesting when students are more aware of the context and complexity of the questions they are arguing. More class preparation helps to make the simulation more engaging, as will higher expectations for group briefing papers. The teacher can expect two major conflicts to define the negotiations.

### North versus South

The first is the regional conflict between the four New England states and the four Southern states over the questions of slavery and the government's power to regulate trade.

Southern states want slavery to be legal, they want a fugitive slave law requiring escaped slaves to be returned, and they are opposed to extensive government power over trade. The New England states oppose slavery and the fugitive slave law, and advocate strong governmental power over trade. The five Mid-Atlantic states are split on these issues.

### Big versus Small States

The North–South conflict is aggravated by a second conflict between the big states and the small states that cuts cleanly across the regions. The four big states—New York, Virginia, Pennsylvania, and Massachusetts, which include the two states with veto ability—want proportional representation but also want states to be taxed equally. The nine smaller states, including a majority of states from each region, demand that all states have an equal vote while insisting that taxes be accorded by population.

## POSSIBLE MODIFICATIONS

This game has been used effectively with students at grade levels 9 through 12. However, it is possible to make the game simple enough for it to be appropriate for junior high students, or even for sixth graders, or to make it sufficiently challenging for an introductory collegiate American Government course.

### Advanced Students

To make the game more challenging for advanced students, the most effective approach is probably to disregard the simplified and stylized State Needs sheets in the Appendix. Instead, require students to research and determine their own major and minor objectives prior to convening the convention; give students about two or three weeks to complete the assignment. Require the students to write a five- to seven-page briefing paper (rather than the two-page briefing document discussed before) that sets out their state's objectives and supports these objectives with empirical evidence relating to the condition of their state in the late 1780s. In the postgame assessment, require students to justify their effectiveness at pursuing the goals they have outlined in their briefing paper.

### Junior High and Less Advanced Students

To accommodate lower-level students, the teacher has a couple of options. One is to do away with the requirement that students justify their performance in their post-simulation essay and permit students to simplify their briefing sheets. Another is to do away with the requirement that students prepare a two-page factual brief on their state and a one-page brief on national conditions. Doing away with these elements makes the exercise into much more of a free-flowing game in which students are permitted to debate and play-act without too many restrictions or too much work.

## ASSESSMENT

Four kinds of assessment are suggested here, each offering feedback on different elements of the activity. Students should be informed about all assessments when the simulation is being explained to them, *before* the simulation begins. By requiring students to pay attention throughout the exercise, the assessments increase student participation and make the exercise more productive. Prior notice encourages students to pay attention to the substance and the dynamic of the exercise.

First, students in each state are to compose a two-page briefing paper on the status of their state in the 1780s, with an additional page summarizing the condition of the United States. Students should plan on using the briefing papers during the Convention for reference purposes and as ammunition for their arguments. The papers should focus on their state's political, economic, and social situation. Each group should turn its paper in at the conclusion of the Convention. I evaluate the papers based on the quality and usefulness of information and the clarity of organization.

Second, I evaluate students based on my observations of their participation in the exercise. In particular, I look for students who attempt to make some concrete contribution to their state. At the end of the exercise, I also have each student fill out the standard simulation feedback form (see Chapter 12, Final Thoughts), which asks them to assess the contributions of their teammates. Using my observations and the group evaluations, I assess students based on their contribution to their team and to the group. The feedback form takes about five minutes to fill out, so this assessment is completed by the day after the exercise.

Third, students are asked to write a two-page first-person essay that analyzes the simulation. First and foremost, they are asked to explain and evaluate their success at achieving their targeted objectives. They are also to explain how they would act differently if the exercise were conducted again and discuss any particulars they found interesting or significant. Finally, students are asked to compare the course of the exercise to what they know thus far about the real Constitutional Convention. Knowing about this assignment ahead of time helps motivate students to pay closer attention throughout the exercise, increasing student interest and attentiveness. Students write the paper the night after the exercise, and the teacher collects it the next day.

Fourth, students are quizzed on the rules of the game, the substance of the agreement, and the major events that took place during the negotiations. This short quiz should be administered the day after the exercise ends and will take somewhere between 15 and 30 minutes. The purpose of the quiz is to ensure that students paid attention to what took place around them during the game and to encourage students to participate by ensuring that they know the rules and the nature of the exercise. Questions should emphasize factual matter, the rules of the exercise, and student observations about the nature and outcome of the exercise.

All assessments are turned in by the day after the simulation. Together, they offer a well-rounded view of student participation and performance.

# APPENDIX—MATERIALS

## List of Materials

- Key Issues to Be Resolved sheets (for each student)
- Map of the Colonies (for each student)
- State Needs Sheets (for each group)

---

### Key Issues to Be Resolved

1. Whether or not slavery ought to be legal in the nation.

2. Whether or not states that do not recognize slavery are still expected to return escaped slaves to their owners in slave-holding states. (This provision was known as "the fugitive slave law.")

3. Whether representation in the national legislature ought to be proportional (according to each state's population) or whether each state ought to have an equal vote. If representation is based on population, how should slaves (who are not citizens) be counted?

4. Whether national taxes ought to be based on each state's population or whether each state ought to pay an equal amount. If taxes are based on population, how should slaves (who are not citizens) be counted?

5. Whether the nation's executive ought to be powerful or whether the executive ought to have carefully limited powers.

6. Whether the executive ought to be elected directly by the people or whether the executive should not be directly elected. If the executive is not to be directly elected, should he or she be chosen by the states, the legislature, or in some other fashion?

7. Whether the new government ought to have strong powers to tax and regulate trade or carefully limited powers.

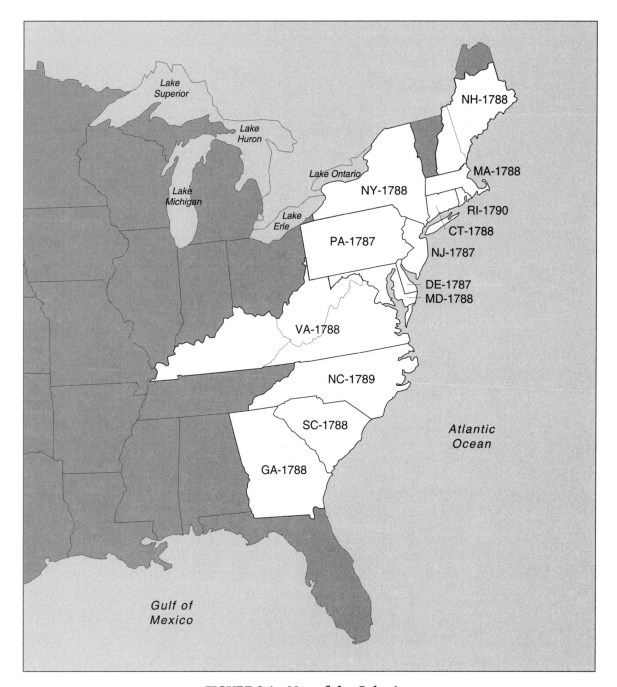

**FIGURE 2.1   Map of the Colonies**

**State Needs Sheet 1   CONNECTICUT**                    Region: New England
                                                         Size: Small

### Major Concerns

All states should have equal representation in the legislative branch.

Taxes should be based on population. Slaves should be counted as a full person for purposes of deciding the taxable population.

The new government should outlaw slavery in all states.

### Minor Concerns

The new government should be given strong powers to regulate international and interstate trade and to make internal improvements.

There should be a weak executive in the new government. The executive's term should run no more than two years, he or she should not be able to serve twice, and the executive should have to get legislative approval before acting.

The executive should not be elected directly by the people, but should be selected by a majority vote of the 13 state governors.

### Remember the Following Conditions

Nine states, including both Virginia and New York, must ratify the Constitution for it to take effect.

If all 13 states ratify the Constitution, all state delegations are treated as if they have successfully won an extra "Major Concern."

States need to reach agreement on at least seven key issues: representation, taxation, slavery, the status of a "fugitive slave" law, the strength of the executive, how to select the executive, and the government's control of trade.


**State Needs Sheet 2   RHODE ISLAND**                   Region: New England
                                                         Size: Small

### Major Concerns

There should be no independent executive branch in the government, because there is too great a risk of monarchy. Executive functions should be handled by the legislative branch.

All states should have equal representation in the legislative branch.

The new government should be given strong powers to regulate international and interstate trade and to make internal improvements.

### Minor Concerns

There should be no "fugitive slave" law. Escaped slaves who make it to Rhode Island should not have to be sent back to their owners in the Southern states

Taxes should be based on population. Slaves should be counted as a full person for purposes of deciding the taxable population.

### Remember the Following Conditions

Nine states, including both Virginia and New York, must ratify the Constitution for it to take effect.

If all 13 states ratify the Constitution, all state delegations are treated as if they have successfully won an extra "Major Concern."

States need to reach agreement on at least the seven key issues: representation, taxation, slavery, the status of a "fugitive slave" law, the strength of the executive, how to select the executive, and the government's control of trade.

### State Needs Sheet 3   MASSACHUSETTS

Region: New England
Size: Large

#### *Major Concerns*

The new government should be given strong powers to regulate international and interstate trade and to make internal improvements.

Representation in the legislative branch should be based on the population of each state. Slaves, who the Southern states say are *not* citizens, should not count at all for purposes of deciding how many representatives each state will have.

Each state should pay an equal share of the total tax burden for the country.

#### *Minor Concerns*

The new government should outlaw slavery in all states.

There should be a strong executive in the new government. The executive's term should run for six or seven years, and he or she should be able to do whatever is necessary to provide for the "general welfare," unless the legislative branch specifically forbids an act.

The executive should be elected directly by the people, according to the popular vote of the majority.

#### *Remember the Following Conditions*

Nine states, including both Virginia and New York, must ratify the Constitution for it to take effect.

If all 13 states ratify the Constitution, all state delegations are treated as if they have successfully won an extra "Major Concern."

States need to reach agreement on at least seven key issues: representation, taxation, slavery, the status of a "fugitive slave" law, the strength of the executive, how to select the executive, and the government's control of trade.

### State Needs Sheet 4   GEORGIA

Region: South
Size: Small

#### *Major Concerns*

Taxes should be based on population. Since they are property and not citizens, slaves should not be counted for purposes of deciding the taxable population.

All states should have equal representation in the legislative branch.

The new government should have no power to regulate or outlaw slavery. Allowing the government to abolish slavery would destroy the state's economy and way of life, and would leave tens of thousands of slaves without food, shelter, or employment.

#### *Minor Concerns*

The government should have only weak power to regulate trade or commerce, because a government that aggressively controls trade will make it harder for Georgia to export its agricultural products to Britain.

There should be a strong executive in the new government.

The executive should be elected directly by the people, according to the popular vote of the majority.

#### *Remember the Following Conditions*

Nine states, including both Virginia and New York, must ratify the Constitution for it to take effect.

If all 13 states ratify the Constitution, all state delegations are treated as if they have successfully won an extra "Major Concern."

States need to reach agreement on at least seven key issues: representation, taxation, slavery, the status of a "fugitive slave" law, the strength of the executive, how to select the executive, and the government's control of trade.

### State Needs Sheet 5   NEW JERSEY

Region: Mid-Atlantic
Size: Small

#### Major Concerns

All states should have equal representation in the legislative branch.

The new government should outlaw slavery.

Each state should pay a share of the national taxes based on its population, with slaves counting for at least one-half of a person.

#### Minor Concerns

The new government should be given strong powers to regulate international and interstate trade and to make internal improvements.

There should be no independent executive branch in the government, because there is too great a risk of monarchy. Executive functions should be handled by the legislative branch and there should be no "commander-in-chief" of the military other than the leading military officer appointed by the legislature.

#### Remember the Following Conditions

Nine states, including both Virginia and New York, must ratify the Constitution for it to take effect.

If all 13 states ratify the Constitution, all state delegations are treated as if they have successfully won an extra "Major Concern."

States need to reach agreement on at least seven key issues: representation, taxation, slavery, the status of a "fugitive slave" law, the strength of the executive, how to select the executive, and the government's control of trade.

### State Needs Sheet 6   NORTH CAROLINA

Region: South
Size: Small

#### Major Concerns

Taxes should be based on population. Since they are property and not citizens, slaves should not be counted for purposes of deciding the taxable population.

The new government should have no power to regulate or outlaw slavery. Allowing the government to abolish slavery would destroy the state's economy and way of life, and would leave tens of thousands of slaves without food, shelter, or employment.

Any slave who escapes from his or her plantation must be returned, whether the slave escapes to a free or a slave state. This "fugitive slave" law is necessary to protect the personal property of slaveowners from Northern attempts to assist runaway slaves.

#### Minor Concerns

All states should have equal representation in the legislative branch.

The government should have only weak power to regulate trade or commerce, because a government that aggressively controls trade will make it harder for North Carolina to export its products to Britain.

#### Remember the Following Conditions

Nine states, including both Virginia and New York, must ratify the Constitution for it to take effect.

If all 13 states ratify the Constitution, all state delegations are treated as if they have successfully won an extra "Major Concern."

States need to reach agreement on at least seven key issues: representation, taxation, slavery, the status of a "fugitive slave" law, the strength of the executive, how to select the executive, and the government's control of trade.

**State Needs Sheet 7    SOUTH CAROLINA**                    Region: South
                                                            Size: Small

### *Major Concerns*

The new government should have no power to regulate or outlaw slavery. Allowing the government to abolish slavery would destroy the state's economy and way of life, and would leave tens of thousands of slaves without food, shelter, or employment.

Taxes should be based on population. Since they are property and not citizens, slaves should not be counted for purposes of deciding the taxable population.

All states should have equal representation in the legislative branch.

### *Minor Concerns*

The government should have only weak power to regulate trade or commerce, because a government that aggressively controls trade will make it harder for South Carolina to export its agricultural products to Britain.

There should be a weak executive, with very limited powers, in the new government. After escaping from the British monarchy, there is no reason to run the risk of having another strong executive. It would be good to have a multiple-person executive, with three or five co-Presidents sharing the office.

### *Remember the Following Conditions*

Nine states, including both Virginia and New York, must ratify the Constitution for it to take effect.

If all 13 states ratify the Constitution, all state delegations are treated as if they have successfully won an extra "Major Concern."

States need to reach agreement on at least seven key issues: representation, taxation, slavery, the status of a "fugitive slave" law, the strength of the executive, how to select the executive, and the government's control of trade.

**State Needs Sheet 8    VIRGINIA**                    Region: South
                                                        Size: Large

### Major Concerns

The new government should have no power to regulate or outlaw slavery. Allowing the
    government to abolish slavery would destroy the state's economy and way of life, and
    would leave tens of thousands of slaves without food, shelter, or employment.

Representation in the legislative branch should be based on the population of each
    state, with each slave counted as one person for purposes of determining population.

Each state should pay an equal share of the total tax burden for the country.

### Minor Concerns

The government should have only weak power to regulate trade or commerce, because
    a government that aggressively controls trade will make it harder for Georgia to
    export its agricultural products to Britain.

There should be a strong executive in the new government. The executive should serve
    for at least four years and should have relatively broad powers.

The executive should be chosen by the national legislature to ensure that the executive
    and legislative branches can work together.

### Remember the Following Conditions

Nine states, including both Virginia and New York, must ratify the Constitution for it to
    take effect.

If all 13 states ratify the Constitution, all state delegations are treated as if they have
    successfully won an extra "Major Concern."

States need to reach agreement on at least seven key issues: representation, taxation,
    slavery, the status of a "fugitive slave" law, the strength of the executive, how to select
    the executive, and the government's control of trade.

**State Needs Sheet 9    DELAWARE**          Region: Mid-Atlantic
                                             Size: Small

### Major Concerns

There should be no independent executive branch in the government because there is
   too great a risk of monarchy. Executive functions should be handled by the legislative
   branch, and the legislature should choose someone to work as "acting President" for
   just one year at a time.

All states should have equal representation in the legislative branch.

Each state should pay a share of taxes based on its population.

### Minor Concerns

The new government should be given strong powers to regulate international and
   interstate trade and to make internal improvements.

There should be no "fugitive slave" law. Escaped slaves who make it to Delaware should
   not have to be sent back to their owners in the Southern states.

### Remember the Following Conditions

Nine states, including both Virginia and New York, must ratify the Constitution for it to
   take effect.

If all 13 states ratify the Constitution, all state delegations are treated as if they have
   successfully won an extra "Major Concern."

States need to reach agreement on at least seven key issues: representation, taxation,
   slavery, the status of a "fugitive slave" law, the strength of the executive, how to select
   the executive, and the government's control of trade.

**State Needs Sheet 10    MARYLAND**          Region: Mid-Atlantic
                                              Size: Small

### Major Concerns

All states should have equal representation in the legislative branch.

Each state should pay a share of taxes based on its population.

The new government requires a strong executive. The executive should serve at least a
   four-year term, should be eligible for reelection, and should be the commander-in-
   chief of the military.

### Minor Concerns

The new government should have very limited powers to regulate international and
   interstate trade. Otherwise, the New England states that do so much shipping will
   import British goods that will put local tradesmen out of work.

Respect for property dictates that there should be a "fugitive slave" law requiring that
   escaped slaves should be sent back to their owners, no matter where the slaves are
   captured.

### Remember the Following Conditions

Nine states, including both Virginia and New York, must ratify the Constitution for it to
   take effect.

If all 13 states ratify the Constitution, all state delegations are treated as if they have
   successfully won an extra "Major Concern."

States need to reach agreement on at least seven key issues: representation, taxation,
   slavery, the status of a "fugitive slave" law, the strength of the executive, how to select
   the executive, and the government's control of trade.

## State Needs Sheet 11    NEW HAMPSHIRE

Region: New England
Size: Small

### Major Concerns

All states should have equal representation in the legislative branch.

Taxes should be based on population. Slaves should be counted as a full person for purposes of deciding the taxable population.

The new government should be given strong powers to regulate international and interstate trade and to make internal improvements.

### Minor Concerns

There should be no "fugitive slave" law. Escaped slaves who make it to New Hampshire should not have to be sent back to their owners in the Southern states.

The executive should not be elected directly by the people, but should be selected by a majority vote of the 13 state governors.

### Remember the Following Conditions

Nine states, including both Virginia and New York, must ratify the Constitution for it to take effect.

If all 13 states ratify the Constitution, all state delegations are treated as if they have successfully won an extra "Major Concern."

States need to reach agreement on at least seven key issues: representation, taxation, slavery, the status of a "fugitive slave" law, the strength of the executive, how to select the executive, and the government's control of trade.

## State Needs Sheet 12    PENNSYLVANIA

Region: Mid-Atlantic
Size: Large

### Major Concerns

Slavery should be outlawed by the new government. The strong Quaker population in Pennsylvania is very serious about this.

Representation in the legislative branch should be based on each state's population.

Each state should pay an equal share of the total tax burden for the country.

### Minor Concerns

The central government should have strong powers to regulate trade and commerce, and to oversee internal developments in the West.

The power of the executive should be limited (as under the Pennsylvania constitution) by having multiple people serve as co-Presidents. Five or seven would be a good number, with one of the executives being replaced each year.

The executives should be selected by a majority vote of the 13 state governors.

### Remember the Following Conditions

Nine states, including both Virginia and New York, must ratify the Constitution for it to take effect.

If all 13 states ratify the Constitution, all state delegations are treated as if they have successfully won an extra "Major Concern."

States need to reach agreement on at least seven key issues: representation, taxation, slavery, the status of a "fugitive slave" law, the strength of the executive, how to select the executive, and the government's control of trade.

## State Needs Sheet 13    NEW YORK

Region: Mid-Atlantic<br>Size: Large

### *Major Concerns*

Each state should pay an equal share of the total tax burden for the country.

Representation in the legislative branch should be based on the population of each state. Slaves, who the Southern states say are *not* citizens, should not count at all for purposes of deciding how many representatives each state will have.

There should be a strong executive in the new government. The executive's term should run for at least four years, the executive should be "commander-in-chief" of the armed forces, and he or she should be able to veto legislative laws.

### *Minor Concerns*

The new government should be given strong powers to regulate international and interstate trade and to make internal improvements.

There should be a single, strong executive in the new government. The executive's term should run for six or seven years and he or she should be able to do whatever is necessary to provide for the "general welfare," unless the legislative branch specifically forbids an act.

The executive should be elected directly by the people, according to the popular vote of the majority.

### *Remember the Following Conditions*

Nine states, including both Virginia and New York, must ratify the Constitution for it to take effect.

If all 13 states ratify the Constitution, all state delegations are treated as if they have successfully won an extra "Major Concern."

States need to reach agreement on at least seven key issues: representation, taxation, slavery, the status of a "fugitive slave" law, the strength of the executive, how to select the executive, and the government's control of trade.

# CHAPTER 3

# *The Mighty Dorito Cartel*

*Students govern eight nations seeking to maximize revenues from a rare natural resource. Students struggle to cooperate in order to control the marketplace, while facing the temptation to gain a private advantage by overproducing. The resulting tension between the urge to cooperate and the temptation to "cheat" leads to a brisk session of negotiating, double-crossing, monitoring, and occasional altruism. This exercise illustrates the "free rider syndrome," an age-old economic dilemma in which individual incentives impede cooperation and lead to suboptimal outcomes. Students receive an accessible introduction to some fundamental economic concepts. The lesson can also be used to teach the role of OPEC in the 1970s and 1980s, or as a thematic introduction to examine the role of trusts in nineteenth-century America.*

*Groups of students represent the nations of the Organization of Dorito Exporting Countries (ODEC), and the groups seek to earn enough from Dorito exports to meet their budgetary needs. Because price levels depend on the total number of Doritos exported, and because the game's incentives urge groups to pursue both high price-per-barrel performance and high total sales, the class seeks to restrict production even as individual groups benefit by maximizing production. As the simulation develops, students are allowed to design and attempt to implement enforcement mechanisms that will ensure cooperation and allow the whole class to profit.*

## TEACHER'S NOTE

*The Mighty Dorito Cartel* is designed to simulate the problems encountered by the OPEC cartel in the 1970s and 1980s as the cartel sought to capitalize on its dominance of global petroleum resources. Groups with different levels of Dorito reserves and needing to generate different amounts of Dorito revenues are forced to cooperate in order to maximize productivity and achieve their mutual goals. Students are required to calculate their needs and self-interest against the effects their selfish behavior will have on the entire organization's ability to maintain a productive framework. The result is a boisterous and intrigue-filled session of economic cooperation, confrontation, and chaos. Students learn some basic economic concepts and why it can be so hard for a group of individuals to do the sensible thing, even as they acquire insights on how to make it easier for groups to work together.

This lesson was initially developed for a ninth-grade World Geography class, but has also been used in American History, Economics, and World History classes. The exercise allows students to experience the concept of "free rider" syndrome, a concept that is crucial to understanding international relations and economic behavior, as well as other issues in the social sciences. The exercise itself is designed as a one-day affair, although it will work best if the students are first taught background material about the relevant economic concepts and/or the rise and fall of OPEC.

All too frequently, students do not learn about certain crucial social science concepts in high school history and social studies. This is especially problematic because some of these concepts are both interesting and relatively easy to teach. The simulation is designed to teach students about the classic free rider problem, a concept central to both economic and political science analysis. It is also an opportunity to teach students about Middle East politics, the effect of uneven resource distribution on international relations, the role of OPEC in world affairs, and the oil politics of the 1970s and 1980s. Because the exercise simulates the decisions made by the Organization of Petroleum Exporting Countries (OPEC) when OPEC was at its height in the 1970s and early 1980s, it also provides an effective introduction to the oil crises that so dramatically impacted American politics in the 1970s.

Students represent the multiple members of the Organization of Dorito Exporting Countries (ODEC). The essence of the game is quite simple: The objective of ODEC members is to charge as much money as possible for their Doritos.

Money earned for Doritos is a function of two factors, the value of the Doritos and the number of Doritos sold. Ideally, students would like their nations to sell as many Doritos as possible at as high a price as possible. However, the law of supply and demand dictates that a larger supply of Doritos will reduce the price. This trade-off is precisely what confronts members of any cartel, and what particularly hobbled the nations of OPEC in the mid-1980s as oil consumption dipped and the worldwide oil supply grew. When times grew tight, the more affluent nations, particularly oil-rich Saudi Arabia, which tended to be more friendly with the Western powers, attempted to negotiate a path of sustained export growth and moderate price increases. Other OPEC members, more strapped for cash, wanted to rapidly increase the price of oil. Some of these same cash-strapped nations, however, were then tempted by the high prices into dumping as much of their oil onto the market as possible. These free riders, who used the restraint of their cartel partners to pad their own earnings, undermined the ability of OPEC to govern cartel earnings.

The groups have very unequal Dorito resources and the production requirements and rewards have been structured to take this into account. Even though it may appear at first glance like some groups are in a vastly superior position, the reality is that all groups have a roughly equal opportunity to do well. The major advantage inherent in the varied level of resources is that it makes efforts at forging cooperation much more interesting and realistic. After all, overproduction by a country with few Doritos is a much smaller problem than overproduction by a country with huge reserves.

## BACKGROUND ON THE FREE RIDER SYNDROME, OLIGOPOLIES, AND OPEC

One of the most basic, and important, concepts in the social sciences is the free rider problem. A *free rider* is someone who refuses to shoulder a fair share of the collective burden, but then enjoys benefits that are made available to the entire group. Every group, whether it is a group of people, organizations, communities, or nations, sometimes must band together to address certain common needs or problems. The free rider reaps the benefits of this cooperation without pitching in. The result is that those who do cooperate must work that much harder to compensate for the free rider. The free rider problem emerges in issues as global as world trade and arms reduction, and as personal as a roommate's refusal to help clean the bathroom.

In a situation in which there are many actors, and in which it is hard to exclude any of them from sharing the benefits of cooperation, it becomes very difficult to compel cooperation. Cooperation is much more likely when there are fewer parties because the participants are more likely to know each other, are better able to keep an eye on each other, and have more of an opportunity to forge a personal relationship.

When there are just a few powerful producers involved in producing a commodity or a service, the industry is described as an *oligopoly*. An oligopoly represents a midpoint on the continuum between a *monopoly* (in which one actor dominates a market) and a *competitive market* in which no one producer has significant influence. For instance, until foreign competition threatened the position of General Motors, Ford, and Chrysler in the 1980s, the U.S. automobile industry had been an oligopoly. Monopolies are economically problematic because the dominant position of one producer means that it is able to overcharge customers and that it lacks incentives to improve its efficiency or the quality of its product. The lack of competitors means that customers have nowhere else to turn, so they are forced to pay what the monopoly demands for its product. Oligopolies are less problematic, because there is some competition, as long as the various producers are in competition with one another. The problem is that when there are only a few producers it becomes much easier and much more rewarding for them to cooperate in order to approximate the privileged position of a monopoly.

When the leading producers in an oligopoly organize, they are collectively considered to be a *cartel*. When producers organize a cartel, they can effectively create a

---

**EXPLAINING THE FREE RIDER SYNDROME**

One of my favorite ways to illustrate the free rider problem is to talk about four friends who have season tickets to watch a basketball team. Three of the friends take turns driving to and from the games. Then there's the fourth friend, the moocher, who always claims to be short of cash and never pitches in. He doesn't have a car and he never offers money for gas. The moocher, who is (quite literally) "riding free," takes advantage of the fact that his friends have already taken care of supplying the car and the gas. He is the "free rider," enjoying the fruits of their efforts without having to contribute. He is taking advantage of the fact that there is space in the car anyway, and his friends are too nice to hassle him.

The result is that the first three guys split the cost of transportation three ways, even though four people enjoy the benefits. At first this doesn't seem like too large a problem. Adding the fourth person doesn't add any extra expenses, so the three contributors come out the same as if the fourth friend had not joined them. However, the incentive to also be a "free rider" can encourage the first three guys to start finding ways to avoid driving or paying for the gas. If two more friends follow the free rider's example and also stop paying for gas, then it comes down to a situation where one guy either has to pay for all of their transportation—or none of them will be able to attend the games.

When dealing with three friends, the problem is small and relatively simple to solve. The three friends could always exclude the moocher, if they were sufficiently provoked. The free rider problem becomes much thornier when it is not so easy to exclude the free rider and when the actors do not share a personal relationship. For instance, if a community decides to clean up its main highway, everyone who uses the road will benefit. However, there is no way for the community to compel all the beneficiaries to give up their Saturday afternoon in order to pitch in, or to keep them from enjoying the improved scenery. As a result, there is an incentive for people to avoid pitching in, because they will enjoy the same benefits without having sacrificed their time.

---

monopoly situation in which they are freed from the discipline of competition. The few powerful companies in a given industry are able to cooperate to keep prices artificially high, to restrain competition, and to pad their profits at the expense of consumers. The power of cartels to reap excessive profits in several industries in the late nineteenth and early twentieth centuries eventually prompted the U.S. government to establish trust-busting regulatory agencies, such as the Federal Trade Commission (established in 1914). Because there are no such trust-busting agencies in the international arena, there is no way to limit such profit-maximizing cooperation on behalf of a group of countries. Therefore, if a group of countries is able to wield a great deal of control over a critical resource or product, it can use its position to extract oversized profits and influence.

## OPEC

In 1971, oil-importing nations paid about $2 a barrel for oil produced by the 13 members of OPEC. Ten years later, in 1981, the price had jumped to about $35 a barrel—an increase of roughly *1,700 percent*! Oil is the lifeblood of the world's industrial economies. The skyrocketing price of oil changed the nature of international trade, the status of more than a dozen formerly undeveloped countries, and the behavior and policies of the major industrial powers. Massive oil price increases in 1973, and in 1978 to 1979, pushed the industrialized nations into prolonged recessions.

In the 1980s, roughly two-thirds of the world's known oil and gas reserves were in the Middle East. Middle Eastern oil also enjoys advantages over oil drilled in the rest of the world because it is relatively inexpensive and simple to produce. OPEC is not simply a Middle East organization; however, it also includes nations from South America, Africa, and Asia. The 13 members of OPEC are: Saudi Arabia, Iran, Venezuela, Indonesia, United Arab Emirates, Nigeria, Libya, Kuwait, Iraq, Ecuador, Qatar, Algeria, and Gabon.

From the end of World War II through the early 1970s, Western oil companies controlled the flow of the world's oil. The ascendance of OPEC marked a dramatic change in the world order. It meant that a bloc of less-developed and previously marginal nations now controlled the world's oil supply. Control of the industrialized world's most critical resource had passed from the pillars of the Western world to nations with an agenda of their own.

***History of OPEC***   During the first half of the twentieth century, the Western oil companies that developed the oil fields in the Middle East played a dominant role in their relations with Middle Eastern governments. Agreements with the local rulers generally required only that the foreign oil companies pay a nominal royalty—an average of just 21 cents a barrel—to the oil-producing countries. In addition, the oil-producing countries exempted the oil companies from taxes and gave the companies complete control over prices and production. Those agreements may have seemed fair to local governments when demand was low, prices were erratic, oil discovery was uncertain, and the nations of the Middle East had not entered post-World War II modernization. During and after the war, however, such arrangements were no longer passively accepted. The Venezuelan government rang in the new order in 1945 when it demanded a 50–50 split of profits with the oil companies.

In 1948, four giant American oil companies formed the Arabian American Oil Company (ARAMCO) to develop the Saudi Arabian concession. Huge amounts of oil were discovered shortly thereafter, and Exxon, Texaco, Socal, and Mobil were assured an immense source of low-cost oil. This spurred the beginnings of the massive development of Middle Eastern oil production. By the early 1950s, all oil-producing countries had negotiated a 50–50 split similar to Venezuela's with the oil companies. Meanwhile, new companies were entering the oil production business in the 1950s. These companies created instability in the oil markets and increased competition, resulting in lower prices and profits for both the established companies and the oil-producing countries. Responding to this instability, in 1959 the Eisenhower administration imposed quotas on how much oil could be imported into the United States. Already buffeted by falling profits and a shrinking market for their oil, the oil-producing countries were hit again in 1960 when Exxon's price cuts triggered another round of price-cutting by the major oil companies.

In September 1960, Iraq called a meeting of oil-producing countries to discuss the common problems they faced with falling prices. The result of the session, which included Venezuela, Saudi Arabia, Iran, and Kuwait, was the decision to create OPEC. The initial goals for OPEC were for the member nations to work cooperatively to get prices back up to earlier levels and to promote consultation about future price decisions. Membership grew during the 1960s. Qatar, Libya, and Indonesia were the next three countries to join. They were eventually followed by the five other members, bringing OPEC's total membership to 13.

OPEC was unsuccessful in its early efforts to restore prices to previous levels or to increase prices by limiting members' production. At a 1968 meeting in Vienna, OPEC nations agreed to a document that declared the cartel's right to control world oil production and prices. At the time, the industrialized nations did not take this agreement very seriously. The West saw little evidence that OPEC would be able to translate this declaration into policy, viewing the document as unrealistic. By the early 1970s, however, a combination of the 1969 revolution in Libya, mishaps in oil production, and more militant behavior by OPEC members (including price increases, nationalization of Western assets, and increasing equity in the oil companies) made those objectives much more serious. OPEC's control of two-thirds of the world's oil reserves gave the cartel the ability to nearly cripple the economies of major industrial powers.

***The First Oil Crisis***   As a result of the 1973 Arab–Israeli War, the Arabs imposed an oil embargo on the United States. The U.S. economy depended on cheap and plentiful oil, with domestic consumption having tripled from less than 6 million barrels per day in 1949 to more than 17 million barrels per day in 1974. OPEC price increases and the Arab embargo produced a U.S. gas shortage and a 500 percent jump in the price of oil between 1973 and 1974. These shocks pushed the U.S. economy into recession while buffeting it with savage inflationary pressures.

The first oil crisis was provoked in 1973 when the oil-producing nations imposed an embargo on petroleum exports to the Western industrialized nations (primarily the United States and Europe). The embargo was a response to Western support for Israel during the 1973 Arab–Israeli War. Representatives of the major oil-exporting countries were scheduled to meet with the world's major oil companies in Vienna in October 1973. Just days before the scheduled meeting the Arab-Israeli War erupted.

In this milieu, the OPEC representatives demanded a doubling in the price of oil from $3 to $6 per barrel. The companies and OPEC were unable to reach a compromise and the meeting broke up. In a mid-October meeting, the OPEC nations decided to unilaterally set the price of oil at $5.12 per barrel, for the first time enacting the principles voiced in Vienna in 1968. When Arab demands that the United States cease supplying arms to Israel and that Israel withdraw from occupied Arab territories were not met, most Arab producers dramatically cut back on their oil production and participated in an embargo against the United States.

The world oil markets panicked, and two months later at a December meeting, OPEC ministers set a new posted price of $11.65 a barrel. Previous Arab attempts at embargoes during crises in 1956 and 1967 had failed, due to lack of organization and the world's lower level of oil consumption. By 1973, however, the circumstances had changed due to the cooperation of the OPEC nations and the world's increased thirst for oil. The excess American production capacity that had answered previous embargo attempts was gone, and the Arab nations were producing nearly 40 percent of the non-Communist world's oil.

The recession of 1974–1975 dampened demand for oil, and the OPEC nations responded cautiously by working to reduce oil production. For instance, Saudi Arabia cut production from 8.5 million barrels per day in 1974 to 7.1 million in 1975. Arguing that the world economy was too fragile to risk more price increases, the Saudis used their dominant position within OPEC to hold prices steady through most of 1976. The Saudis were able to do this because their position as OPEC's leading producer enabled them to function as a "swing producer," increasing or decreasing production to keep supply stable. However, by the end of 1976, other member nations were demanding price increases. In 1978, this internal conflict was brought to an end by the second oil crisis, which quickly drove oil prices to new heights.

***The Second Oil Crisis***   The second oil crisis erupted during the 1978 through 1980 period, when a revolution in Iran replaced Western ally Shah Mohammed Reza Pahlavi with a fundamentalist Islamic regime headed by Ayatollah Ruhollah Khomeini. The ensuing regional turmoil and the new Iranian government's policies significantly reduced oil production, resulting in shortages and sharply higher oil prices. In late 1978, OPEC members decided to end an 18-month freeze on prices and set a new price of $14.54 a barrel. However, the revolution in Iran caused Iranian oil production to drop from 5.5 million barrels per day to less than 1 million. Even though Saudi Arabia and other member nations increased production, the shortfall could not be fully covered. The result was a shortage that quickly served to drive prices up, with spot oil prices of $30 a barrel reported in some places.

For the first time since the 1974 crisis, Americans were forced to line up at gas stations. Prices rocketed upward, sparking inflation and slowing economic growth, while individuals found their daily routines impeded by an inability to buy gas for their cars. Gas stations sometimes closed by midday, purchases were limited, and daily routines were adjusted accordingly. President Jimmy Carter pushed a comprehensive energy policy that sought to advance conservation and encourage the development of alternative energy sources. In 1979, leaders from the major industrial powers met in Tokyo and agreed to work to cut imports by specific amounts and to work together to increase the use of coal and to develop alternative energy supplies.

Prices continued to climb during 1979 and 1980. By late 1980, OPEC's prices ranged from a high of $41 per barrel to Saudi Arabia's low price of $32 per barrel. Even the relatively "cheap" Saudi price was more than double the price OPEC had set just two years before. The tensions within OPEC over price levels were reflected in disputes over production limits, and these conflicts were exacerbated when war erupted between Iraq and Iran in late 1980. At a 1980 meeting in Geneva, all the OPEC members, except Saudi Arabia, voted to cut production and raise prices. The Saudis refused to cut their production from a record 10.3 million barrels per day (more than one-third of all OPEC's production) until other members agreed to change the price structure. The other members refused the Saudi demand and decided on a new price structure among themselves.

Another OPEC meeting in early 1981 ended with more bitterness. For the first time in OPEC's history, the oil ministers called on the heads of the OPEC governments to resolve the standoff. The heads of government failed and the meeting ended with the members even more fragmented about pricing policy. In 1983, for the first time ever, OPEC was forced to agree on overall production quotas. OPEC cut prices to about $30 per barrel and instituted a collective production ceiling of 17.5 million barrels per day.

For over a year these measures stabilized prices, until a worldwide economic slump and warm winter weather depressed demand even further. Meanwhile, some OPEC members were exceeding their quotas and then dumping oil at discounted prices. To maintain a price in the $30 per barrel range, member nations agreed to cut back production by another 1.5 million barrels per day. By the mid-1980s, OPEC nations were producing at less than half of their maximum sustainable capacity while oil prices stagnated. One massive problem for OPEC members was that non-OPEC members were free riding on OPEC's restraint by selling as much of their oil as they could. The result was that these nations were able to take advantage of the inflated per barrel prices, while forcing OPEC members to cut production even more if they wanted to maintain price levels.

Squeezed by the Iran–Iraq War, the conflicting needs of its members, political instability in member nations, and disagreements among members about whether to "manage" demand or to maximize short-term revenues, OPEC found it increasingly difficult to coordinate price and production policy. No longer blessed with a situation of high demand and weak supply, OPEC nations found it difficult to cooperate. Saudi Arabia, rich, stable, and blessed with immense reserves and production capacity, consistently pushed for a moderate approach that sought to keep markets stable. Smaller and less prosperous OPEC members were much more concerned with maximizing revenues, even if it required violating production caps or price agreements.

***The Decline of OPEC***　One of the biggest effects of the price increases in the 1970s was a substantial shift of wealth from the industrialized powers to the 13 nations of OPEC. The nations of OPEC were no longer cash-poor third world nations; many were now able to initiate massive construction projects intended to foster economic development. Huge trade surpluses with Europe, Japan, and the United States meant that the major oil-producing countries had accumulated roughly $400 billion in foreign assets by 1983. The stage appeared to be set for the resource-rich OPEC nations to raise themselves to a prominent place on the world stage.

By the 1980s, OPEC was swamped by falling international demand for oil, a world oil glut, and a steady downward march of petroleum prices. Efforts by OPEC to manage prices by carefully controlling the production of oil kept prices stable during 1983 and 1984, but the supply of oil soon started to outstrip demand. World oil production dropped from 62.5 million barrels per day in 1979 to 53 million in 1983, before gradually beginning to recover. Not only did high prices help to reduce oil consumption, but the prices also prompted the industrialized nations to pursue research on new fuels and to expand alternative sources of energy. For instance, the amount of worldwide electricity generated by atomic power grew by 33 percent between 1982 and 1984. U.S. consumption of oil dropped from more than 18 million barrels per day in 1977 to less than 16 million barrels per day in 1984.

OPEC's efforts to prop up the price of oil by further reducing production were generally unsuccessful. Some OPEC members covertly broke the agreements and dumped additional amounts of oil on the world market. The collapse of OPEC's price-setting power occurred even as the OPEC nations' massive petroleum reserves continued to assure them a strong position for the long-range future.

# USING THIS SIMULATION

## Purpose of the Exercise

Substantively, the lesson introduces students to the oil politics and Middle East relationships that helped define world politics, economics, and living conditions in the 1970s and 1980s. Thematically, students are introduced to the fundamental social science concepts of free riding and the "prisoner's dilemma," and the dilemmas of cooperation. The simulation helps to make clear just why it is that countries, states, and communities sometimes have so much trouble cooperating to do the "right thing." Students learn something about the politics and geography of the Middle East and underdeveloped nations, the energy industry, the impact of conservation, and the principles of supply and demand. Additionally, students receive some background on how domestic American policy was shaped during the 1970s and 1980s.

## Skills Developed

The exercise helps to develop teamwork, negotiating, analytic, and math reasoning skills. Students within each ODEC nation together must determine their optimal strategy and production levels, and then the eight groups must cooperate as they struggle to set and enforce limits on Dorito production. The temptations to overproduce and to free ride ensure that students will be thoroughly challenged. Negotiation skills and the ability to cultivate trust are at a premium.

Analytic and computational skills are also developed as students analyze their collective situation and use that knowledge to set production targets for each country. Taking into account the resources and needs of each country makes this a tricky analysis that demands both calculation and compromise. Calculating the effects of various production levels on each individual group and on the general price of Doritos makes careful computation a useful and visible skill.

## Logistics

The entire exercise can be conducted in one 40-minute class, although I find it a richer experience if the teacher devotes one to two 40-minute classes to playing the game thoughtfully. The exercise can be conducted fruitfully a second time, even though the second time tends to zip by—because the advantages of cooperation tend to become clear during the first go-round.

Because each of the members of ODEC is played by a group, the exercise can handle a class of any size. I have found that groups of two to four students work best, meaning that classes of 16 to 32 will be the easiest to manage.

All the materials necessary for the simulation are located in this chapter's Appendix. After having read this chapter, a teacher should be able to prepare the simulation in well under an hour. The preparation requires the teacher to become familiar with the rules, photocopy the materials at the end of the chapter, reproduce the Price Chart on a chalkboard, and prepare to arrange student desks in eight clusters.

# HOW THE SIMULATION WORKS

## Student Groups

Students are grouped in the eight nations that comprise ODEC. The class should be split roughly evenly among the eight countries, with each of the eight groups of desks clustered and separated from the other clusters. The idea is to provide each group with as much privacy as possible, so as to maximize strategic deception, deal-making, and quiet negotiation. A group of three students should be organized into a prime minister, an oil minister, and a finance minister. Additional group members should function as general ambassadors.

## Object

Students in each country seek to ensure that they earn the money their country needs through their annual Dorito production. The amount of revenue a country needs to generate is displayed on each country information sheet in the Appendix. Additionally, countries are rewarded for preserving and reasonably managing their Dorito reserves for future use, rather than simply exhausting them during the course of the game.

Countries get 1 point every time they hit their annual revenue target. They get 5 bonus points if they hit their target production in at least 9 out of 10 turns. Countries also earn bonus points for the amount of Dorito reserves they have left at the end of play and for exceeding their earnings target in a turn by 50 percent or more.

A country receives 1 point for a given quantity of Doritos left at the end of the exercise. Because countries start with different amounts of Doritos, the bonus is different for each country (i.e., it may be 1 point for each 10,000 barrels left in country A and 1 point for each 40,000 barrels left in country B). The appropriate bonus for each country is indicated on each Country Sheet and on the Teacher's Master Sheet in the Appendix. This bonus system rewards conservation.

The temptation to maximize current earnings is present due to the bonus which gives a country an extra point each time it exceeds its earnings target for a year by 50 percent or more. Each country's earnings target, its reserves, and its maximum rate of production are indicated on each Country Sheet and on the Teacher's Master Sheet.

Three features make the exercise particularly challenging. One, students have a limited Dorito production. Two, as the supply of Doritos in the market goes up, the price falls. Therefore, students don't want other countries to produce a large amount of Doritos. Three, as the price of Doritos increases, the nations that consume Doritos are encouraged to find ways to cut back on their Dorito purchases, so students want to keep prices within a reasonable range.

## Length of the Game

The game is composed of 10 turns, each representing one year of Dorito production. Because the length of the exercise depends on the care with which students play it and the pace at which the teacher chooses to manage it, no precise time estimates can be offered. I have had fellow teachers conduct the exercise in as little as 15 or 20 minutes, and I have taken as long as 50 or 60 minutes to play it.

## Key Elements of the Game

***Dorito Reserves and Production*** Each country has a total supply of Dorito reserves, lying deep underground in massive Dorito fields. Each country also has a somewhat lower amount of Dorito production capacity—the total amount of Doritos it is able to produce each year. The figures for the total Dorito reserves and for Dorito production capacity of each country can be found on the Teacher's Master Sheet and on each Country sheet in the Appendix. Unless groups opt to share this information, each group knows about *only their country's* reserves and production limits. Each year, the groups earn money by producing and selling Doritos. That much is simple. Other things being equal, the more Doritos they sell, the more money they make.

**Price per Barrel**    The crucial complication is that increased Dorito production increases the total supply of Doritos, driving down the price per barrel. The result is that a Dorito glut hurts all the ODEC countries. The price per barrel is determined by the total amount of Dorito production in the world, and the price countries will receive at any given level of total Dorito production is presented on the Price Chart in the Appendix. The price per barrel is fixed, and depends entirely on the total amount of Doritos produced in a year by the eight ODEC countries.

**Determining Price per Barrel**    At the end of each turn, after all negotiations and discussions among students are completed, each group secretly turns in a slip of paper revealing their Dorito production for that year. By adding together these production levels, the teacher determines worldwide Dorito production. This figure is put on the chalkboard and used to determine the per barrel price of Doritos for that year. Each country then determines its revenue for that year by multiplying the number of barrels it produced by that price.

## How the Game Is Played

After explaining the simulation, the teacher should break the class into eight groups, arranging the groups so that each has some degree of privacy. The simulation consists of ten rounds. Each round represents one year of Dorito production.

Each of the eight ODEC nations sits as a group. The nations are free to negotiate whatever agreements they wish and to make whatever formal group decisions they choose. Students may meet in private for negotiations (access to an empty nearby classroom can enrich these dealings) or they may negotiate en masse. The class has the freedom to determine voting procedures, sanctions, bylaws, and enforcement mechanisms.

After an initial round of negotiation, the teacher should call for first year production decisions. Each group should turn in a slip of paper that lists the group's identification (see information on Country Sheets), the number of Doritos the group is producing for that year, and the amount of Dorito reserves the group has left. The teacher should have an assistant (presumably a student who is not playing) tally up the total production on a calculator and put the total level of Dorito production on the chalkboard. The assistant should also track the earnings each round for each country, to minimize possible disputes. I strongly recommend that the teacher use an assistant, the "United Nations Director of Productivity Estimation" to speed up the game, minimize confusion, and help the teacher stay focused on the exercise. Otherwise, the teacher will need to tally total production and track each group's earnings.

The Price Chart (see the Appendix) should be posted or copied onto the chalkboard so that students can calculate their earnings per barrel. Each group should then multiply the appropriate price by the group's production to determine its earnings for the round. The teacher's assistant needs to confirm these calculations in order to avoid cheating and confusion.

After each group has recorded its earnings from the first turn, and after the class has seen how actual total production stacked up to negotiated production, the teacher should permit the class to engage in another round of negotiation. This process should be repeated for the game's ten turns.

The class can see whether total Dorito production actually matched the negotiated production level. If it did not, then the class will know that there are one or more free riders, but will not know who they are. The class's attempts to police this situation provide an excellent opportunity to cultivate cooperation in a challenging environment.

All countries do not approach the negotiation of production ceilings from a common perspective, nor do all countries have the same incentive to free ride. In OPEC, some nations were in need of immediate cash, while other nations were better-situated to take the long view. Similarly, the objectives for the various countries in ODEC have been designed so that all countries will not want to behave in similar ways.

The goal is for students to realize how the situation countries face can reduce or increase the likelihood that they will cooperate. Depending on their individual interests, some countries have an incentive to act as deal-makers, while other countries are squeezed to be less magnanimous.

---

**SUMMARY TEACHER INSTRUCTIONS**

*The day the simulation begins*
- Objective is for students in each country to seek to ensure that they earn the money their country needs through their annual Dorito production.
- Review background material with the students.
- Break the class into eight groups, assigning each group one Country Sheet and a Price Chart.
- The teacher should be prepared with the Teacher's Master Sheet.

*During the simulation*
- Nations are free to negotiate agreements and to produce as they see fit.
- Nations turn in production decisions on paper.
- The teacher puts the class's total production on the board after each turn.
- The appropriate price for a level of production should be determined on the Price Chart and the teacher should record the earnings for each country for each turn. (The teacher should use a "Director of Productivity Estimation" to review calculations.)
- Repeat the process for ten turns.

*After the simulation*
- Assess by using classroom observation of participation, quizzing students on what transpired, group evaluation, and an analytic essay.

---

## COMMENTS FROM EXPERIENCE

I recommend that the teacher use a student assistant to collect and calculate the production figures at the end of each turn. This keeps the teacher from getting bogged down in doing all the calculations by himself or herself each turn (which lends the simulation a frustrating slowness). It is important that calculations on each country's total revenues be replicated and not left solely to each group to ensure that students are not worried about cheating or mistakes affecting national productivity. If you choose not to use an assistant, move more slowly and make sure you calculate each nation's earnings each year (number of barrels produced times the appropriate price) for each country yourself.

It will make a dramatic difference if the teacher mentions that the groups are able to inspect each other's production levels or to impose sanctions if they all agree to do so. On their own, students in some classes will come up with sanctions and some kind of mutual inspection, but they will do so infrequently. If the teacher makes it a point to mention these policing mechanisms, and to explain them, students will generally find it much easier to perform well. It is really a question of how much assistance the teacher wants to offer. The teacher should step gingerly in deciding when to explain these policing mechanisms, because the lesson is intended to illustrate just how hard it can be to cooperate.

## POSSIBLE MODIFICATIONS

### Advanced Students

This game can be further complicated for advanced students in at least two ways. The first is to introduce *calamities*—the teacher can randomly (or selectively) visit problems on the countries. For instance, countries might suddenly lose a portion of their Dorito reserves to natural disasters or have their production capacity limited by domestic unrest. The teacher might want to look at the Special Occurrence in the Appendix of Chapter 6, Choosing a President, to see how this approach might be used.

Second, a teacher with a highly advanced class may want to have consumption shrink in response to situations where the cartel chokes back the levels of production *too* far. This is an interesting wrinkle, because it forces the cartel to walk a fine line between over-producing and underproducing. It makes the calculations critical. The easiest way to do this is to announce that future world consumption of Doritos will drop by some set per-centage any time the cartel produces fewer than x Doritos a year. For instance, if the floor is 50,000 barrels and the class only produces 45,000, the teacher can announce that con-sumption the next year drops by 10 percent. The result is that the price that could be pre-viously charged at 80,000 barrels per year can now only be charged at 72,000 (80,000 − 10 percent) per year, with similar price changes all the way up and down the Price Chart. These new prices should be permanent (reflecting changes in consumer tastes) and can be marked on the Price Chart on the chalkboard to avoid confusion.

### Junior High or Less Advanced Students

It is possible to dramatically simplify the exercise. In the game, the countries vary in their resources and in the number of Doritos they need to produce to fare well. This wrinkle, and the fact that no group really knows the amount of any other group's resources, helps to replicate the stresses of an actual cartel situation. However, it also complicates the game and may cause conflicts over "fairness" in some rare classes. Teachers can simplify the exercise and remove these concerns by simply giving each group an identical set of resources and incentives. If the teacher elects to do this, I recommend issuing the profile of Country C to all groups. Doing this permits the teacher to use the same Price Chart and to run the game by all the normal procedures. Don't worry, the Country C parameters were set up to make this modification run smoothly.

## ASSESSMENT

Three kinds of assessment are recommended for this simulation. Each assessment is de-signed to offer feedback on a different set of skills, including student participation, stu-dent knowledge, and the student's ability to analyze the exercise. By requiring the students to pay attention to what is taking place throughout the exercise, the assessments increase student participation.

First, I evaluate students based on student feedback and my observations of their par-ticipation in the exercise. In particular, I look for students who attempt to make some concrete contribution to their country. At the end of the exercise, each student fills out the standard simulation feedback form (see Chapter 12, Final Thoughts) which asks them to assess the contributions of their classmates. The feedback form takes about five min-utes to fill out.

Second (and students are told before the exercise commences that this will be com-ing), the students are given a short written quiz on what transpired during the simulation. The quiz ensures that all students will be paying attention to the rules, as well as to the course of events during the game. The heightened attention produced by this approach makes it much easier to point out the historic parallels the game is designed to illustrate. This short quiz will take roughly 20 or 25 minutes and should be administered the day after the exercise ends.

Third, students are asked to write a two-page first-person essay that analyzes the sim-ulation. First and foremost, they are asked to total the number of points they scored and to explain how that total was achieved. This will force students to demonstrate an un-derstanding for the incentive-driven nature of the exercise. Students are then expected to explain why they think that the simulation weighted the points in this way. Students also recount what actually happened, explain why the exercise worked out as it did, and explain how they would act differently if the exercise were conducted again. Students are particularly asked to explain what methods can help to make cooperation more likely. Students write the paper the night after the exercise and it is collected the next day.

All assessments are completed by the end of the day after the simulation ends. Informing the students of these assessment devices *before* the beginning of the simulation encourages students to pay attention to what is going on within their group and across the class. The result is that students are much less likely to tune out, because doing so hurts their group evaluation, their knowledge for the quiz, and their ability to write the essay.

# APPENDIX—MATERIALS

## List of Materials

- Teacher's Master Sheet
- Teacher's Master Tracking Table (reproduce on a chalkboard)
- Price Chart (for each student)
- Eight Country Sheets (for each group)

## Teacher's Master Sheet

| Country | Barrels of reserves | Maximum production per turn | Earnings target (1 point) | Earnings target + 50% (1 point bonus) | XX Barrels still in reserve at end (1 point for each) |
|---|---|---|---|---|---|
| A-Alonk | 100,000 | 20,000 | $2,000 | $3,000 | 10,000 |
| B-Bardak | 150,000 | 25,000 | $3,000 | $4,500 | 12,000 |
| C-Carnotem | 300,000 | 40,000 | $6,500 | $9,750 | 20,000 |
| D-Dokeland | 200.000 | 25,000 | $5,000 | $3,750 | 12,000 |
| E-Entebbo | 600,000 | 100,000 | $9,000 | $13,500 | 40,000 |
| F-Fizdog | 100,000 | 10,000 | $1,500 | $2,250 | 8,000 |
| G-Glumbo | 500,000 | 90,000 | $10,000 | $15,000 | 32,000 |
| H-Hackem | 350,000 | 50,000 | $7,500 | $11,250 | 20,000 |
| **Total** | **2,300,000** | **360,000** | | | |

## Teacher's Master Tracking Table (put on chalkboard)

| Turn | 1 | 2 | 3 | 4 | 5 | 6 | 7 | 8 | 9 | 10 | Total |
|---|---|---|---|---|---|---|---|---|---|---|---|
| Total Barrels Produced | | | | | | | | | | | |
| Price per Barrel | | | | | | | | | | | |

## Price Chart

| Total Barrels of Doritos Produced | Price per 1,000 Barrels |
|---|---|
| less than 80,000 | $500 |
| 80,000 to 100,000 | $400 |
| 100,001 to 120,000 | $350 |
| 120,001 to 140,000 | $300 |
| 140,001 to 160,000 | $200 |
| 160,001 to 180,000 | $150 |
| 180,000+ | $100 |

### Country Sheet A   CAIRO

Number of untapped barrels of Doritos that exist under Cairo: 100,000

Maximum barrels of Doritos that can be produced per year: 20,000

Earnings target for each turn: $2,000

*Points:*

1 point each year that you earn at least as much money as your earnings target
5 points if you earn your earnings target in at least 9 out of the 10 turns
1 point for each 10,000 barrels of Doritos still on reserve when the game ends
1 point for each turn when your earnings exceed your target by at least $1,000

*Remember:*

The game runs for 10 turns

The price of each barrel of Doritos can range from $500 to $100, depending on how
many total barrels are produced during in a turn

### Tracking Table

| | Turn | | | | | | | | | | Total |
|---|---|---|---|---|---|---|---|---|---|---|---|
| | *1* | *2* | *3* | *4* | *5* | *6* | *7* | *8* | *9* | *10* | *Total* |
| Number of barrels produced | | | | | | | | | | | |
| Price per barrel | | | | | | | | | | | |
| Total earnings | | | | | | | | | | | |
| Reach earnings target? | | | | | | | | | | | |
| Points earned | | | | | | | | | | | |

### Country Sheet B   AMMAN

Number of untapped barrels of Doritos that exist under Amman: 150,000

Maximum barrels of Doritos that can be produced per year: 25,000

Earnings target for each turn: $3,000

*Points:*

1 point each year that you earn at least as much money as your earnings target
5 points if you earn your earnings target in at least 9 out of the 10 turns
1 point for each 12,000 barrels of Doritos still on reserve when the game ends
1 point for each turn when your earnings exceed your target by at least $1,500

*Remember:*

The game runs for 10 turns

The price of each barrel of Doritos can range from $500 to $100, depending on how
many total barrels are produced during a turn

### Tracking Table

| | Turn | | | | | | | | | | Total |
|---|---|---|---|---|---|---|---|---|---|---|---|
| | *1* | *2* | *3* | *4* | *5* | *6* | *7* | *8* | *9* | *10* | *Total* |
| Number of barrels produced | | | | | | | | | | | |
| Price per barrel | | | | | | | | | | | |
| Total earnings | | | | | | | | | | | |
| Reach earnings target? | | | | | | | | | | | |
| Points earned | | | | | | | | | | | |

### Country Sheet C    TEHRAN

Number of untapped barrels of Doritos that exist under Tehran: 300,000

Maximum barrels of Doritos that can be produced per year: 40,000

Earnings target for each turn: $6,500

*Points:*

1 point each year that you earn at least as much money as your earnings target
5 points if you earn your earnings target in at least 9 out of the 10 turns
1 point for each 20,000 barrels of Doritos still on reserve when the game ends
1 point for each turn when your earnings exceed your target by at least $3,250

*Remember:*

The game runs for 10 turns

The price of each barrel of Doritos can range from $500 to $100, depending on how
    many total barrels are produced during a turn.

### Tracking Table

| | Turn | | | | | | | | | | Total |
|---|---|---|---|---|---|---|---|---|---|---|---|
| | *1* | *2* | *3* | *4* | *5* | *6* | *7* | *8* | *9* | *10* | *Total* |
| Number of barrels produced | | | | | | | | | | | |
| Price per barrel | | | | | | | | | | | |
| Total earnings | | | | | | | | | | | |
| Reach earnings target? | | | | | | | | | | | |
| Points earned | | | | | | | | | | | |

### Country Sheet D    DORITOLAND

Number of untapped barrels of Doritos that exist under Doritoland: 200,000

Maximum barrels of Doritos that can be produced per year: 25,000

Earnings target for each turn: $5,000

*Points:*

1 point each year that you earn at least as much money as your earnings target
5 points if you earn your earnings target in at least 9 out of the 10 turns
1 point for each 12,000 barrels of Doritos still on reserve when the game ends
1 point for each turn when your earnings exceed your target by at least $2,500

*Remember:*

The game runs for 10 turns

The price of each barrel of Doritos can range from $500 to $100, depending on how
    many total barrels are produced during a turn

### Tracking Table

| | Turn | | | | | | | | | | Total |
|---|---|---|---|---|---|---|---|---|---|---|---|
| | *1* | *2* | *3* | *4* | *5* | *6* | *7* | *8* | *9* | *10* | *Total* |
| Number of barrels produced | | | | | | | | | | | |
| Price per barrel | | | | | | | | | | | |
| Total earnings | | | | | | | | | | | |
| Reach earnings target? | | | | | | | | | | | |
| Points earned | | | | | | | | | | | |

## Country Sheet E    RIYADH

Number of untapped barrels of Doritos that exist under Riyadh: 600,000

Maximum barrels of Doritos that can be produced per year: 100,000

Earnings target for each turn: $9,000

*Points:*

1 point each year that you earn at least as much money as your earnings target

5 points if you earn your earnings target in at least 9 out of the 10 turns

1 point for each 40,000 barrels of Doritos still on reserve when the game ends

1 point for each turn when your earnings exceed your target by at least $4,500

*Remember:*

The game runs for 10 turns

The price of each barrel of Doritos can range from $500 to $100, depending on how many total barrels are produced during a turn

### Tracking Table

| | | | | | Turn | | | | | | |
|---|---|---|---|---|---|---|---|---|---|---|---|
| | *1* | *2* | *3* | *4* | *5* | *6* | *7* | *8* | *9* | *10* | *Total* |
| Number of barrels produced | | | | | | | | | | | |
| Price per barrel | | | | | | | | | | | |
| Total earnings | | | | | | | | | | | |
| Reach earnings target? | | | | | | | | | | | |
| Points earned | | | | | | | | | | | |

## Country Sheet F    BAHRAIN

Number of untapped barrels of Doritos that exist under Bahrain: 100,000

Maximum barrels of Doritos that can be produced per year: 10,000

Earnings target for each turn: $1,500

*Points:*

1 point each year that you earn at least as much money as your earnings target

5 points if you earn your earnings target in at least 9 out of the 10 turns

1 point for each 8,000 barrels of Doritos still on reserve when the game ends

1 point for each turn when your earnings exceed your target by at least $750

*Remember:*

The game runs for 10 turns

The price of each barrel of Doritos can range from $500 to $100, depending on how many total barrels are produced during a turn

### Tracking Table

| | | | | | Turn | | | | | | |
|---|---|---|---|---|---|---|---|---|---|---|---|
| | *1* | *2* | *3* | *4* | *5* | *6* | *7* | *8* | *9* | *10* | *Total* |
| Number of barrels produced | | | | | | | | | | | |
| Price per barrel | | | | | | | | | | | |
| Total earnings | | | | | | | | | | | |
| Reach earnings target? | | | | | | | | | | | |
| Points earned | | | | | | | | | | | |

## Country Sheet G   KUWAIT CITY

Number of untapped barrels of Doritos that exist under Kuwait City: 500,000

Maximum barrels of Doritos that can be produced per year: 90,000

Earnings target for each turn: $10,000

*Points:*

1 point each year that you earn at least as much money as your earnings target
5 points if you earn your earnings target in at least 9 out of the 10 turns
1 point for each 32,000 barrels of Doritos still on reserve when the game ends
1 point for each turn when your earnings exceed your target by at least $5,000

*Remember:*

The game runs for 10 turns

The price of each barrel of Doritos can range from $500 to $100, depending on how many total barrels are produced during a turn.

### Tracking Table

| | Turn | | | | | | | | | | Total |
|---|---|---|---|---|---|---|---|---|---|---|---|
| | *1* | *2* | *3* | *4* | *5* | *6* | *7* | *8* | *9* | *10* | |
| Number of barrels produced | | | | | | | | | | | |
| Price per barrel | | | | | | | | | | | |
| Total earnings | | | | | | | | | | | |
| Reach earnings target? | | | | | | | | | | | |
| Points earned | | | | | | | | | | | |

## Country Sheet H   BAGHDAD

Number of untapped barrels of Doritos that exist under Baghdad: 350,000

Maximum barrels of Doritos that can be produced per year: 50,000

Earnings target for each turn: $7,500

*Points:*

1 point each year that you earn at least as much money as your earnings target
5 points if you earn your earnings target in at least 9 out of the 10 turns
1 point for each 20,000 barrels of Doritos still on reserve when the game ends
1 point for each turn when your earnings exceed your target by at least $3,750

*Remember:*

The game runs for 10 turns

The price of each barrel of Doritos can range from $500 to $100, depending on how many total barrels are produced during a turn

### Tracking Table

| | Turn | | | | | | | | | | Total |
|---|---|---|---|---|---|---|---|---|---|---|---|
| | *1* | *2* | *3* | *4* | *5* | *6* | *7* | *8* | *9* | *10* | |
| Number of barrels produced | | | | | | | | | | | |
| Price per barrel | | | | | | | | | | | |
| Total earnings | | | | | | | | | | | |
| Reach earnings target? | | | | | | | | | | | |
| Points earned | | | | | | | | | | | |

# CHAPTER 4

# Letting the Bulls Run

*There's something magical about the sound of the closing bell on the New York Stock Exchange on a day when you've earned thousands of dollars. As a teacher, there's also something wonderful about seeing two students high-five because IBM jumped 1 5/8 the previous day. In this exercise, students are given a chance to dive into the world of high finance, armed with only $50,000 and their own savvy. Students choose their investments, decide when to cut their losses or cash in their winnings, decide how many different investments to hold, all while learning about the nature of the equity markets. This exercise can be run productively for 8 or 12 weeks, with only a modest incursion into class time.*

*Students are required to purchase at least 3 initial stocks or mutual funds, and are limited to no more than 6 holdings. Students track their daily performance on log sheets and are permitted to buy and sell shares at the conclusion of each week (so long as they stay in the 3-to-6 stocks range). All purchases and sales must be registered with the broker (the teacher) and the students must pay standard commissions on each trade. Students can design a Big Board on which to record daily or weekly totals, prompting friendly competition. Besides providing an exciting subtext for the class, the lesson vividly illustrates how equity markets work, the effect of commissions, and how economic ideas operate in the real world.*

## TEACHER'S NOTE

This exercise was designed to get students comfortable with the equity markets. I have always found it fascinating that the vast majority of my students have heard of the stock market and know it exists, but don't much more than that. This knowledge gap presents an incredibly fertile teaching opportunity. Student curiosity is easy to pique because the teacher is about to explain something relevant but mysterious. Also, the market is about making money, which I find to be a big help in stirring student interest. Finally, although the adult population is increasingly aware of investment-related issues, it is likely that a student with some grasp of the market will be the reigning stock market expert in their family. Talk about giving students an opportunity to take home a self-esteem building skill! I don't believe I've ever seen my students as excited about school as when they tell me that a parent had asked them to answer an investment question. When relating those instances, students seem to glow.

The lesson was originally designed for a free-enterprise (economics) course for tenth graders, but I have had one colleague who ran a four-week exercise in conjunction with an American History unit on the Great Depression. My colleague reported that she found the exercise useful. The exercise could also be used quite effectively with a Contemporary Issues class. I suspect that a large number of teachers out there are familiar with someone who has had the students play a mock stock market, in which case this exercise probably looks familiar. I have tried more intricately constructed exercises to teach this material, but have found this design to be effective, manageable, and quite enjoyable.

The simulation itself only takes a day to actually set up and get underway, but the teacher will find that the exercise runs more smoothly if the students are first taught some of the relevant background material. It is particularly useful to let the students know that the exercise is coming so that they can start thinking about the stocks or mutual funds they will want to purchase when the exercise begins.

At the school where I originally devised this exercise, I was fortunate because the local newspaper shipped us a free set of 30 newspapers daily. I was able to keep several copies of the paper in my classroom each day, which consistently produced one of my favorite moments as a teacher. A class of students would bustle into the classroom and then huddle in noisy little clumps around the business sections to see how their stocks had fared. Students would be stomping and high-fiving. The students who had registered good numbers would bolt to their desks and pull out their calculators to see how much money they had made. The energy that students bring to a class after the market has recorded a good day is fantastic.

During the course of the game, many students pay more attention to the news and learn to think about things through a market-based interpretive lens. This lends an extremely practical and hands-on contribution to the course of classroom discussions. For instance, I remember the student who decided to buy stock in Hanes and in an ice cream company as spring began. He figured that people were more active in the spring, thus needing more undershorts, and that they eat more ice cream as the weather warms up. This kind of critical interest made it much easier to teach potentially dull concepts of economic theory and practice.

## BACKGROUND ON THE EQUITY MARKETS

My greatest concern in this exercise was communicating to the students an understanding about what stocks actually are, how the stock markets operate, and the advantages and disadvantages of investing in stocks. The purpose of the exercise is not to teach students about these matters in intimate detail, but to acquaint them and make them comfortable with these issues.

Stocks represent pieces of ownership in a company. A share of stock represents partial ownership of a company. Of course, because most large companies have issued millions of shares, one share of stock represents only a tiny piece of that company. In most cases, a share of stock gives the holder a vote in major company decisions (particularly in the selection of the board of directors, which governs the company on a day-to-day basis). Additionally, in companies that pay out *dividends* (shares of company profits), shareholders are normally entitled to a set amount of dividends for each share they own. There are particular instances that involve "preferred" and nonvoting stock when shareholders do not have a vote in company affairs, but these cases are the exception.

Stock markets operate by coordinating the buying and selling of the pieces of different companies. The value of a share in a given company can rise or fall over time, depending on the overall economy, on the fate of a particular company's industry, on the performance and future prospects of that company, and on numerous other factors. The change in value depends on how much interest there is in purchasing the stock relative to the number of people who want to sell the stock at a given time. The value of a given company's shares can move erratically or remain stable for years.

Buyers and sellers, whether they are looking to sell a million shares or to buy 100 shares, contact a securities dealer to make their transactions. These brokerage firms then match up buyers and sellers. If there is more interest in buying the stock, the price will rise. If there is more interest in selling, the price will fall.

Depending on the actual stock being traded, brokerage firms make transactions in different ways. There are roughly 5,000 actively traded stocks in the United States. If the stock is traded on a physical exchange, such as the New York Stock Exchange, then the broker contacts a representative on the "floor" and the transaction is conducted there. If the company is listed with the National Association of Securities Dealers Automated Quotation System (NASDAQ), which exists as a linked computer network of securities brokers, the transaction is simply conducted in cyberspace.

Stock brokers make their money by taking a "commission" on each trade. These commissions were once a significant expense for shareholders purchasing stock, often totaling upwards of 3% of the price of a stock purchase. However, discount brokers and Internet trading have helped to make broker commissions extremely reasonable for investors who do not need hand-holding or counseling. In 1998, commissions for Internet and discount trades were as low as $8 per trade.

**FINANCING A NEW COMPANY**

I traditionally use one particular example to illustrate the three ways in which a company obtains cash. Presume that Sally has just finished college and wants to open a used guitar shop in town.

She needs $50,000 to accumulate inventory, pay initial costs, rent the store space, and keep herself going for the 12 months she expects it will take until she starts to make money. If Sally were wealthy, or had a wealthy family, the $50,000 would not present a problem. She would have the money she needed to put into the company. Unfortunately, that's not an option for Sally.

A second approach would be to take out a loan. She could borrow the money, with the understanding that she would repay the $50,000 as well as an additional amount of interest. Obtaining a loan requires that Sally be comfortable that she will be able to pay back the money and the interest. In order to receive the loan, Sally will have to secure it with *collateral*—property that is worth $50,000. Since Sally doesn't have anything worth $50,000, she would probably have to ask her parents or family to use a house to guarantee the loan. If Sally was unable to pay back the loan, the house would be taken over by the bank. If Sally cannot find someone willing to put up the collateral, she will probably be unable to get a loan.

The third approach a new business can use is to sell shares of stock. Sally could, after proceeding through the appropriate legal niceties, decide to sell 1,000 shares of stock in "Sally's Guitars, Inc." Each share of stock would give its holder ownership of 1/1000 of the company. To raise $50,000, Sally would sell the shares at $50 apiece (if we ignored the expenses of taking a company public). Those shareholders would now be the company's owners.

If Sally sold all 1,000 shares, she would have no voice in running her own company. If people controlling 501 shares decided to dismiss Sally as president and fire her from the company, she would have no recourse. What Sally will probably do is issue herself 1,001 shares of stock and then sell 1,000 shares, although first she needs to convince potential investors that those shares are each worth the $50 they will be asked to pay. In fact, if the company will be worth about $50,000 when it is launched, a fair value for each of the 2,001 shares would be about $25 ($50,000 divided by 2,001 shares). (There are also issues of preferred and common shares here, but that needlessly confuses matters.) The point is that shares of stock *are*, very simply, pieces of a company.

## Why Issue Stock?

Corporations primarily issue stock to raise money. (They also may issue new stock to compensate employees without having to pay more in salaries.) Companies, large and small, get their hands on money in one of three ways: They either have it, borrow it, or raise it by issuing equity. Companies that are flush with cash, particularly large established companies, can simply buy the things they wish. Other companies, particularly smaller and newer ones, are not so fortunate. They can try to borrow money, which can be difficult if the company does not have an established track record or if the owner does not have enough collateral to secure the loan. Or these companies can convince outsiders to purchase part-ownership in the company. The outsiders are betting that the company will be successful and that their part-ownership will provide a healthy return on their investment.

## The Historic Performance of Equity Markets

Particularly with the growing popularity of equity investments, it is important that students gain some familiarity with the role and value of the equity markets. By the late 1990s, Americans had more money invested in stocks than in their homes. Increased market investment has been encouraged by the growing prevalence of Individual Retirement Accounts (IRAs), 401K plans, and mutual funds. To oversimplify somewhat, IRAs and 401K plans are retirement accounts to which the worker and/or the employer contribute money. Money in these accounts grows tax-free until the employee retires. The employee chooses how to invest the money and, for reasons that will be discussed shortly, young employees tend to fare best if they have most or all of this money in equities.

Mutual funds are an investment tool that allow an investor to spread his or her money across a large number of stocks while not having to worry about which particular stocks to select. Individuals purchase shares in a particular mutual fund. The fund then invests the money in dozens or hundreds of stocks. Different mutual funds invest in different kinds of stocks. Mutual funds make it easy for even small investors to invest in the stock market by reducing the problems associated with investing and by eliminating the worry that an investor will be devastated by making an unfortunate stock selection. Mutual funds began to enjoy massive growth in popularity during the extended market surge of the early 1980s, growth that has continued and has been at least partially sustained by the convenience of mutual funds for IRA and 401K investing.

Historically, over the 1926 to 1996 period, money invested in common stocks grew at almost three times the rate of money held in cash savings and at more than twice the rate of money held in bonds. Between 1926 and 1996, money held in cash grew at a 3.7% annual rate and money held in bonds grew at a 5.1% annual rate. Meanwhile, money held in stocks grew at a 10.7% annual rate. Stocks offer disproportionate rewards because they offer disproportionate risks. Money held in a savings account is pretty safe. Money held in a company's stock is not—its value is subject to the performance of the company, the whims of the broader market, and an infinite number of other considerations outside investors' control.

The fact is that common stocks can present substantial market risk. While a typical savings account might pay 2% or 3% interest a year, stock prices can rise or fall by much more than that amount in a single week—sometimes even in a single day. For instance, in October 1987, stock prices plunged by 20% in just one day. Over time, the quick jolts in the market tend to even out. However, there are no guarantees, and even the experts are never quite sure what the market will do tomorrow or the day after.

In addition to sometimes falling rapidly in a brief time, stock prices can also gradually decline over longer periods. This phenomenon is called a *bear market*. Since 1945, the most notable bear market occurred in 1973–1974, when an oil crisis helped to trigger a broad market decline of nearly 40%. After the bear market, it took nearly four years for many investors to recover the money they had lost in that two-year period. And the bear market of 1973–1974 was relatively mild compared to the famous Great Crash of 1929. After the Great Crash, it took eight years for the typical investor's investments to regain their pre-Crash value.

The opposite of a bear market is a *bull market*, when the value of equities climbs at a brisk pace. The 1995–1998 period produced one of the greatest bull markets in market history, as the major stock indexes increased in value by more than 100% in just that three-year period. Over time, bull markets and bear markets alternate, tending to average out to an annual growth rate of between 10% and 11%.

## The Role of Inflation and Compounding

"What's wrong with a 3.7% return?" a student may ask. (Although they almost never do, because students like to think of investing as a way to make a whole lot of money in a hurry.) There are two factors to consider.

The first complication is the role of inflation. Money, for various reasons, tends to be worth less over time. The rate at which money is falling in value is the *inflation rate*. Inflation reduces the value of investments over time. Historically, during the 1926–1996 period, inflation averaged 3.1%. This means that an investor who kept his or her money in cash averaged only a 0.6% real return over the 1926–1996 period. (A *real return* is how much of the average investment return is left after taking into account the effects of inflation.) Similarly, a bond investor averaged a real return of just 2.0% over the same period. However, a stock investor, during this period, generated an average real return of 7.6%.

A second factor makes these disparities even more significant. This is the nature of *compounding*. The advantages of higher rates of return tend to multiply over time. When the returns on an investment are reinvested, those returns also start to generate future returns. The upshot is that the difference between a 7.6% rate of return and a 2.0% rate of return is even bigger than it appears. How big is it? One easy way to approximate the difference is by using the rule of 72.

The *rule of 72* is a simple principle that can be used to measure the rate at which a given investment will double in value. Simply divide the rate of return into 72, and the resulting figure is the length of time it will take an investment to double in value. Why this little computational short-cut works is not as important for our purposes as the fact that it does. Historically, equity investments (returning 7.6%) have doubled in real value about every 9 to 10 years (72 divided by 7.6). On the other hand, bond investments (returning 2.0%) have taken more than 30 years to double in value. The result? Simple math shows that if equity investments double once a decade, they will have doubled three times within 30 years. Because two times two times two is eight, this means that each dollar invested in equities at the beginning of the 30-year period will have grown by 800% in real value before the money invested in bonds has doubled in real value.

## The Advantage of Long-Term Investing

It is important for students to understand both the long-term rewards of equity investing and the significant risks of investing in common stocks. The key lesson is that while the equity markets can be risky in the short run, the risks of market investment fall dramatically with time. The longer an investor holds a stock (or a bond) investment, the smaller the chance that the investor will lose money and the greater the likelihood of earning a return close to the market's 10.7% long-term average.

Quite simply, short-term investments are very risky, while long-term investments are much less risky. For example, during the 1926–1996 period, the performance of stock holdings over a one-year period ranged from a high of +54.0% to a low of –43.3%. Over ten-year periods, however, returns varied from –0.9% per year for the worst ten-year period to +20.1% per year for the best ten-year period. And over 20-year periods, the returns have ranged from a high of +16.9% to a low of +3.1%. Notice that, with time, both the highs and the lows moderate dramatically.

***Efforts at Market Timing***   One way investors sometimes try to deal with the uncertainty of the market is by out-guessing it; this is known as market *timing*. When it comes time to invest, many people hesitate because they fear market fluctuations. There is nothing more disheartening to a beginning investor than losing money because of a market "correction." To reduce this risk, some investors seek to *time* the market by moving money into stocks when they think the values will go up and out of stocks when they think stocks are overpriced. This approach sounds ideal in theory. The problem is that even professional investors can only rarely foresee the direction of the stock or bond markets.

The difficulty with market timing is that market rallies occur in brief spurts. Because human nature generally causes people to wait for evidence of a rise before they buy, and for evidence of a decline before they sell, market timers are often in the markets at the wrong time. More often than not, market timers are "out of the market" when prices rise, and therefore do not fully benefit from the rally. The out-of-market risk is high. One study, conducted by the Ibbotson Associates in 1996, indicated that during the 1982–1987 period, stocks gained 26.3% per year. But investors who were out of the market on the few days when the largest price advances occurred saw their returns slashed. Investors who missed the 20 best days during that period (or about four days a year), earned only

13.1% per year. Investors who missed the 40 best days probably would have fared better in bonds because they earned just 4.3% per year.

***How Much to Invest in Stocks*** There are three key factors for investors to weigh when deciding how much to invest in equities. The first is their personal financial situation. People should not put money into stocks that they cannot afford to lose. Because stocks are risky in the short term, money the investor is likely to need in the next five years probably should not be invested in equities.

The second issue is risk tolerance. Investors who will panic when their savings plunge in value should be careful about investing in equities and about the kinds of equities in which they invest. Investors who sell when the market falls are sure to miss postcorrection market rallies and will underperform the market. Additionally, people who find investing in equities stressful probably should take that into account when weighing the risks and rewards of their various savings options.

The third issue is asset allocation. Professionals recommend that individuals not put all of their eggs into one basket. Investors should maintain a strategic balance between the money they invest in stocks, bonds, cash, and other assets (for example, real estate). Depending on the life situation and needs of the individual investor, assets can be balanced in varying fashions. For young investors without families to provide for, such as is the case with most students, the balance should be heavily weighted toward the growth potential of equities.

***Which Stocks to Pick*** There are several considerations for stock pickers to contemplate. Most have to do with measures of a company's value, performance, and growth prospects. However, quite frankly, only the occasional student will find the mechanics of price/earnings (P/E) ratios either useful or interesting. Instead, there are a few more general trade-offs for students to consider in constructing a portfolio.

The first is the difference between growth stocks and value stocks. Simply put, the earnings of growth companies are growing more rapidly than are those of value companies. Value stocks tend to be the larger and safer companies, while growth companies tend to be more volatile.

The second is the difference between *small cap* (small capitalization), *mid-cap* (medium), and *large cap* stocks. A company's *capitalization* is the total amount of money that its stock is worth. A small cap company is usually worth only a few hundred million dollars, while a large cap company is worth five billion or more. Small-cap stocks are riskier, but also provide higher returns over the long term.

The third consideration is the difference between economic sectors. Investors can buy stock in financial services companies, software companies, consumer products companies, or any of dozens of other kinds of companies. An investor's opinion as to what kind of companies will fare well in the future can help an individual choose stocks wisely.

The fourth consideration is whether to purchase stocks in domestic or international companies, and whether to invest in stocks that earn much of their revenue overseas. Large multinational companies that do a lot of business overseas, such as Coca-Cola or Ford, are less vulnerable to domestic market conditions but more vulnerable to changes in the economies of other nations.

Finally, there is the issue of how many stocks to invest in. Holding more stocks provides more security, particularly when the stocks are varied in nature. The easiest way to hold a large number of different stocks, without drowning in paperwork, fees, or headaches, is to invest in mutual funds. Because mutual funds invest money for large numbers of investors, they are able to invest in a very broad selection of stocks. Because each mutual fund operates according to specific investment guidelines, it is possible for an investor to invest in hundreds of very different types of stocks by owning just three or four mutual funds.

## USING THIS SIMULATION

### Purpose

The exercise is intended to introduce students to the nature and functioning of the stock market. For a sustained period of time, students are exposed to the operation of the equity markets. In the process of making investment decisions, students learn about the nature of market risk, what shares of stock represent, and the rhythms of corporate America. The lesson can be used as part of an economics or free-enterprise class, or it can be used in an American History class in conjunction with a unit on the Great Depression. The exercise cultivates recordkeeping skills and introduces students to the analytic skills associated with investing in equity markets.

### Skills Developed

The exercise helps to develop research, math reasoning, and analytic writing skills. Students use their mathematical and recordkeeping skills extensively as they track and calculate their investment performance. Additionally, students who get enthusiastic about the exercise get a great deal of practice doing hands-on research. Students who throw themselves into the simulation often wind up spending a fair bit of time surfing the Internet, reading magazines or newspapers, or talking to their parents or parents' friends in order to research different stocks and mutual funds. These are all pleasant side-effects.

### Logistics

Students buy and sell stock and mutual funds during the game. Aside from the class session in which the teacher introduces the exercise, and from occasional slices of time that the teacher may wish to devote to the exercise while it is in progress, the game demands only a small amount of class time. The only required materials are the Student Market Log sheets, the Big Board students produce, the Week's Market Log sheets, and a Teacher's Master Spreadsheet (see Appendix—Materials). The only other considerations are that students need access to the Internet or to a newspaper that lists at least one major stock market. The game need not displace any class time except during the first day.

## HOW THE SIMULATION WORKS

### Student Groups

I would recommend that teachers permit students to play the simulation in groups of two, although there is no strong reason to use or not use student groups. Teachers should make this decision based on their knowledge of their students, their students' needs, and the resources available to the students. For students who will have difficulty accessing the Internet or newspapers, groups clearly become a useful way to reduce student stress. If teachers do use groups, I would advise keeping them to no more than two students per group to prevent slacking. (Obviously, in an odd-numbered class, there will be one group of three. This is not a major problem, although the teacher might want to require that group to invest in four or five holdings, rather than three to ensure that there will be enough work for three students.)

Using teams offers another chance to foster collaboration, offers the camaraderie of working on an extended exercise with a partner, reduces the burden on each student, and can serve to enhance the information students collect. However, it is important to keep teams to no more than two students to minimize the problems of uneven work distribution and inattention by some team members to the details of investing.

## Object

The goal is for students to maximize the returns to their initial stake during the duration of the exercise.

## Length of Game

I generally let the game run for about 8 to 12 weeks. Other teachers have used it for as little as two or three weeks and told me they thought the experience was still quite useful for the students. Personally, I believe it is important to run the game over a period that is long enough for students to experience both ups and downs in the market. I have found that increased exposure, in and of itself, is useful in increasing student's comfort with the market and their understanding of the market.

## How the Game Is Played

Each student (or group) is issued $50,000 with which to invest in the equity markets. I permitted students to invest in the New York Stock Exchange (NYSE) and NASDAQ listed equities, as well as in mutual funds, but it makes sense to restrict the available markets if the daily newspaper does not carry all of these. The balance of student money is held as cash, and is presumed to be invested in a money market fund that pays 5.2% annual interest, or 0.1% per week.

***Stock and Mutual Fund Holdings***   Students are required to purchase at least three stocks and/or mutual funds at the beginning of the exercise. During the course of the exercise they are to always hold at least three. This ensures that all students will spend a set amount of time tracking performance and becoming familiar with the calculations. Students should not be permitted to hold more than five stocks and/or mutual funds at any point to ensure that neither student nor teacher has to spend an exorbitant amount of time tracking issues. For simplicity sake, students are required to purchase shares in blocks of 50 or 100.

***Commissions***   To dissuade students from the bad habit of frantic trading, and to enhance authenticity, students must pay a brokerage commission for each transaction. I charge students a flat brokerage fee of $35 for each trade. Students who sell stock in one company and then buy stock in a second company have completed two trades, each of which should cost $35. Commissions are recorded on the Student's Market Log along with the other transaction information.

***Dividends***   Dividends are not taken into account during the game. Many stocks pay out an annual or quarterly dividend to shareholders. This payment is a distribution of corporate profits. However, these amounts tend to be relatively small—and do not work well in the context of an 8- or 12-week exercise. Dividends should be discussed, but students should be told that they are simply too troublesome to include in the game.

***Stock Splits***   Companies will sometimes split their stocks if they feel that the price has gotten too high. The odds are against this happening even once during the course of a given exercise. What is a stock split? For instance, General Motors may split 3-for-2, meaning that each stockholder will receive 3 shares for each 2 currently held. Someone who owns 100 shares would now have 150. When a company splits its stock, the share price is lowered proportionately. So, if General Motors was previously trading at $90 per share before the split, it will be trading at $60 per share (two-thirds of its previous price) after the split. If GM had split 2-for-1, the price per share would have been reduced to $45 (half the previous price per share).

   If a company splits during the game, the students' shares should be multiplied in the same fashion as those of any other shareholder. Neither the teacher nor student needs to do anything about the company stock price, because that will change in the stock exchange listing. It is possible that a student will not realize his or her stock has split, so the teacher should encourage students to investigate any time a stock price drops by one-third or more in one day. Drops of this size happen *very* infrequently, aside from splits, so this is not likely to be much of a burden. A student needs to have some evidence to document a split if the teacher is not aware of the split. It obviously is not acceptable to have students multiplying their shares on their own say-so.

***Cash Holdings***    Money held in cash is presumed to be invested in a money market fund paying 5.2% interest. This means that the student will receive 0.1% interest each week. The student should multiply his or her cash holdings at the end of each week by 0.1% and then enter the result under the Change in Total Value column on the Week's Log sheet (see Sample Week's Log in the Appendix). The student's daily cash holdings will already be recorded in the Stock Symbol column on the log sheet, so this calculation is as straightforward as can be.

***Starting the Simulation***    The game should begin on a Monday, with students buying their initial holdings based on the final prices from the preceding Friday. Students should record and turn in their selections on the first day, at which time the teacher should create a Master Spreadsheet to record what stocks and how much of each stock the students bought (see Sample Teacher's Master Spreadsheet in the Appendix). The teacher will *not need* to track prices or use this spreadsheet on a daily basis. Instead, it will simply be updated *once* a week to keep track of which stocks students have bought or sold. All the tracking of prices will be handled entirely by *students*.

After the initial purchase, I would only transact buy-and-sell orders at the week's closing price. This vastly simplifies the teacher's life, discourages some of the tracking work associated with a daily flurry of buy-and-sell orders, and does so without significantly modifying the principles the exercise is designed to illustrate. In fact, by slightly tempering the tendency of students to buy and sell on a near-daily basis, this limit helps to impart (in some small way) the discipline of a longer-term perspective.

***The Big Board***    The real *Big Board* on Wall Street tracks the minute-by-minute performance of stocks on the New York Stock Exchange. The presence of a Big Board in the classroom can add a little more atmosphere to the ongoing exercise and serves as a visual reminder that the game is ongoing, while helping to ensure that students track the daily performance of their holdings. A student volunteer constructs a Big Board using a large sheet of posterboard. The student creates a matrix on which each student (or group) tracks the total daily performance of their holdings. The volunteer should list the class along the left-hand axis and the days of the week along the top of the sheet. I require students to update the total value of their holdings on the Big Board at least two or three days a week.

During the course of the simulation, we would go through about one Big Board per week, permitting a number of students with a flair for artistry to integrate their skills into the class and to earn extra credit for doing so. Some of the boards that students designed have been so pretty that it almost seemed a shame to actually write on them. I always found that the students got a kick from watching the weekly results. Additionally, the presence of a Big Board for each class permits students to check up on how their friends in other classes are doing, which can give rise to some good-natured competition.

***Buying and Selling***    After the initial purchase day, students can bring trade orders to the teacher at any point during the week. As previously mentioned, the date does not matter because all transactions occur at the stock price listed at next Friday's close. The consequence of this policy is that almost all students wait until Friday to make any trades, because this way they know where the stocks stood on Thursday. This behavior allows the teacher to manage buy-and-sell logistics in a compact time window.

***Log-Keeping***    Students are required to track their stocks on a daily basis. This means that students keep a log. (The teacher can either photocopy the Market Log sheet in the

Appendix or simply require students to maintain a notebook log using the same format.) Students are required to track each holding, the daily change in the value of each holding, the total change in value of all shares held, and the total change in their net worth on a daily basis. This recordkeeping is important both because it utilizes basic math skills, and because it rubs students' noses in the operations and the nature of the market.

Students should total the performance of their holdings on both a daily and a weekly basis. At the end of the week, students should add in the 0.1% interest they receive on their cash holdings (see Sample Week's Market Log sheet). Also, at the end of the week, students should record any transactions they wish to make. They should record the number of shares bought or sold, the total cost paid or amount received for the shares, and the commission paid. Students should then update their cash holdings accordingly. After about a week of this recordkeeping, it will become second-nature for students.

---

**SUMMARY TEACHER INSTRUCTIONS**

*The day the simulation begins*
- Objective is to introduce students to the nature and functioning of equity markets.
- Explain background material on stocks and stock market.
- Explain the rules of the exercise.
- Pair students up, either by assigning teams or letting them choose teammates.
- Pass out Student Market Log and Sample Week's Log sheets, and inform each pair of students they have $50,000 to invest.
- Require teams to purchase three to six stocks and/or funds to begin the exercise.
- Have students select stocks and record their purchases on the Student Market Log sheets.
- Create a Teacher's Master Spreadsheet to record student holdings.
- Select a student volunteer to create the first week's Big Board.

*During the simulation*
- Students may buy and sell stocks on Fridays by notifying the teacher.
- Students will record all weekly transactions, weekly interest earned, and weekly net worth on their logs.
- Students will post their daily results on the Big Board at least 2–3 times per week.
- A different student volunteer will produce a new Big Board for each week of the game.

*After the simulation*
- Students turn in their project paper.
- Assess simulation using classroom observations of participation, class evaluations, and a quiz.

---

## COMMENTS FROM EXPERIENCE

If the teacher wishes to make the exercise competitive, or to reward high-market performance, then it is necessary to track the performance of each student's holdings to ensure that there is no cheating. For two reasons, I strongly recommend that teachers *not* try to reward students based on the performance of their holdings. First, making the exercise noncompetitive relieves the teacher of the burden of ensuring that students are accurately tracking stock performance. Second, not rewarding portfolio performance keeps students whose holdings perform poorly from getting too frustrated and students whose picks do well from overinterpreting or getting overly caught up in a couple of lucky breaks. It is important to emphasize that a large element of stock performance—particularly in the short term—is due to factors beyond the investor's control. Far more important than the performance of student holdings is that students get used to the functioning and rhythm of the equity markets and learn to appreciate the concept of long-term investing.

It is possible for students to slack off on their recordkeeping, and then go back through newspapers or use the Web or other sources late in the project to fill in all of the missing entries. There are strategies to address this problem, depending on how concerned the teacher is about this kind of behavior. One labor-intensive approach is to check the logs on a frequent basis, either by having students bring their logs to the teacher's desk or by circling the classroom and checking logs. A second approach, one I prefer, is to have students turn in logs at the conclusion of each week. One problem in requiring daily tracking is that students need to have access to either a daily newspaper with the appropriate business listings or to the Internet. If students cannot check the listings on a daily basis, but must check multiple outcomes on one or two days a week, that obviously calls for the teacher to show some flexibility in terms of expectations.

## POSSIBLE MODIFICATIONS

This game has been used effectively, as is, with high school students of various ages. However, it is an easy task to simplify the exercise, if teachers of younger students believe it will be productive. To simplify the management of the game, the teacher may want to modify the rules on how many stocks students can hold, how often they can trade, whether they are permitted to purchase mutual funds, and how much money students are given to invest. Reducing the scope in any of these ways will also make it an easier exercise for a teacher to run.

### Advanced Students

To make the game more challenging for advanced students, it is possible to make the exercise more complex. Unfortunately, this means more work for the teacher. As it stands, the exercise has been designed to provide a reasonable level of sophistication without overburdening the teacher. Some complications teachers may want to add are to permit daily trading; require daily tracking; require students to offer a one-page analysis that explains any particular decision to buy or sell; or even expand the scope of the game and permit students to trade in commodities, futures, or bonds. I would suggest that teachers be cautious when considering any of these modifications.

### Junior High and Less Advanced Students

To accommodate lower-level students, the teacher can do away with many of the restrictions, making the exercise into an easier and more free-flowing game. First, teachers may want to eliminate mutual fund investing. They may also want to restrict students to using one stock exchange (either the NYSE or the NASDAQ). Second, teachers may want to do away with weekly interest payments on cash holdings. This simplifies bookkeeping and encourages students to invest all of their money. Third, teachers may want to limit students to making no more than a few trades (maybe three or four) during the course of the exercise. Finally, teachers may want to do away with the Big Board and with the expectation that students will track market outcomes daily. Teachers may want to require only that students report weekly results, which means that students only have to check the newspaper or Internet once a week. (For those teachers who use this option, it is helpful to remember that most daily papers run composite weekly results in the Sunday business section.)

## ASSESSMENT

Three assessments are suggested for this exercise. Students should be informed of all assessments *before* the simulation begins. By requiring students to pay attention throughout the exercise, the assessment devices make the exercise more productive.

The most significant assessment is the final project that students will prepare. The project should include the outcomes of the exercise, the trading strategy the team used, what the students would do differently if they could start all over again, and what advice the students would offer to friends or parents who are thinking about investing in equities. The suggested target length for this paper is 8 to 12 pages, supplemented by graphs depicting portfolio performance and the day-to-day records tracking the securities that students held.

The players are permitted to divvy up the job of actually tracking each stock, but, in the final project, both members of a team are responsible for turning in materials that track the performance of *all* of the team's stocks. Additionally, in their final project, each team member should indicate which stocks they specifically tracked and researched during the simulation. Because the students operate in two-person teams, they are not asked to fill out a group assessment sheet. Instead, I recommend using the Nongroup Assessment Sheet (see Chapter 12, Final Thoughts) to get feedback from students about the general tenor of the simulation and their perception of which of their classmates performed exceptionally.

Second, students should be given a long quiz or short test at the conclusion of the simulation. I would also recommend that the teacher administer two or three brief quizzes during the course of this extended simulation. Quizzing students on the essentials of market operations helps teams to operate cooperatively by encouraging all students to pay attention to the trivia of share transactions, the rules of the exercise, and the general contours of the market. Questions should measure the students' factual knowledge of the market and their understanding of the rules of the simulation. Students need to understand the differences between bonds, stocks, and cash assets; the fact that stock is part ownership of a company; the increased risks and *long-term* rewards associated with stock ownership; the basic mechanics of stock-trading and stock-holding; and how market transactions operate.

Finally, during the course of the simulation, I make it a point to pay attention to how energetically students participate in the exercise. Students are informed up front that they are expected to maintain their daily logs and regularly track their performance on the Big Board. I will occasionally conduct spot-checks of student logs to check on participation. Large numbers of students are likely to be enthused about the whole exercise, and these measures will be superfluous for them. For students less enthused about the exercise, however, this policing can prompt them to participate enough so that they will learn the intended knowledge and skills.

# APPENDIX—MATERIALS

## List of Materials

- Students will require access to market listings in newspapers and/or on the World Wide Web
- Teacher's Master Spreadsheet (based on Sample Teacher's Master Spreadsheet)
- Student Market Log sheets (for all students)
- Sample Week's Market Log sheets (for all students)
- Sample Big Board (reproduced by students)

## Sample Teacher's Master Spreadsheet

| Students | Account balance | Stocks bought | Shares | Prices | Date | Amount paid | Stocks sold | Shares sold | Amount received |
|---|---|---|---|---|---|---|---|---|---|
| J Adams | $50,000 | | | | | | | | |
| D Smith | | AMSY | 300 | $60½ | 11/17 | $18,150 | | | |
| | | FDX | 100 | $120¼ | 11/17 | $12,025 | | | |
| | | CSTO | 500 | $30 | 11/17 | $15,000 | | | |
| | $4,825 | | | | | | | | |
| | | | | $40 | 11/31 | | CSTO | 200 | $8,000 |
| | $12,825 | | | | | | | | |
| | | IBM | 100 | $105¼ | 11/31 | $10,525 | | | |
| | $2,300 | | | | | | | | |

## Sample Big Board

| Name | Previous week's total | Monday | Tuesday | Wednesday | Thursday | Friday | Weekly total |
|---|---|---|---|---|---|---|---|
| J Adams | | | | | | | |
| D Smith | | | | | | | |
| T Brenton | | | | | | | |
| W Hart | | | | | | | |
| F Carrol | | | | | | | |
| J Jackson | | | | | | | |
| U Dent | | | | | | | |
| E Mecham | | | | | | | |

**Sample Week's Market Log**

| Date (day) | Stock symbol | Shares held | Closing price | Previous closing price | Price change | Change in total value | Net holdings |
|---|---|---|---|---|---|---|---|
| 12-3-97 M | IBM | 100 | 105⅝ | 105¼ | +⅜ | +37.50 | $10,562.50 |
| 12-3-97 M | AMSY | 200 | 32 | 30¾ | +1¼ | +250.00 | $6,400.00 |
| 12-3-97 M | AMEX | 200 | 61 | 62 | −1 | −200.00 | $12,200.00 |
| 12-3-97 M | Cash | $20,000 | | | | | $20,000.00 |
| 12-3-97 M | **Total** | | | | | **+87.50** | **$49,162.50** |
| 12-4-97 T | IBM | 100 | 105 | 105⅝ | −⅝ | −62.50 | $10,500.00 |
| 12-4-97 T | AMSY | 200 | 32½ | 32 | +½ | +100.00 | $6,500.00 |
| 12-4-97 T | AMEX | 200 | 61 | 61 | 0 | 0 | $12,200.00 |
| 12-4-97 T | Cash | $20,000 | | | | | $20,000.00 |
| 12-4-97 T | **Total** | | | | | **+37.50** | **$49,200.00** |
| 12-5-97 W | IBM | 100 | 105 | 105 | 0 | 0 | $10,500.00 |
| 12-5-97 W | AMSY | 200 | 32¼ | 32½ | −¼ | −50.00 | $6,450.00 |
| 12-5-97 W | AMEX | 200 | 62 | 61 | +1 | +200.00 | $12,400.00 |
| 12-5-97 W | Cash | $20,000 | | | | | $20,000.00 |
| 12-5-97 W | **Total** | | | | | **+150.00** | **$49,350.00** |
| 12-6-97 T | IBM | 100 | 107 | 105 | +2 | +200.00 | $10,700.00 |
| 12-6-97 T | AMSY | 200 | 32½ | 32¼ | +¼ | +50.00 | $6,500.00 |
| 12-6-97 T | AMEX | 200 | 59 | 62 | −3 | −600.00 | $11,800.00 |
| 12-6-97 T | Cash | $20,000 | | | | | $20,000.00 |
| 12-6-97 T | **Total** | | | | | **−350.00** | **$49,000.00** |
| 12-7-97 F | IBM | 100 | 107 | 107 | 0 | 0 | $10,700.00 |
| 12-7-97 F | AMSY | 200 | 34 | 32½ | +1½ | +300.00 | $6,800.00 |
| 12-7-97 F | AMEX | 200 | 59 | 59 | 0 | 0 | $11,800.00 |
| 12-7-97 F | Cash | $20,000 | | | 0.1% Int[1] | +20.00 | $20,020.00 |
| 12-7-97 F | **Total** | | | | | **+320.00** | **$49,320.00** |
| 12-7-97 | Sell IBM | 100 | 107 | weekly close | −$35 Com[2] | To cash | +$10,665.00 |
| 12-7-97 | Buy CLDF | 300 | 23 | weekly close | −$35 Com | From cash | −$6,935.00 |
| 12-7-97 | New cash | $20,000 | | | | +$3,750 | $23,750.00 |

[1]Students receive the 0.1% interest on their cash at the end of each week.
[2]Students pay their $35 broker commission for each trade they transact.

**Student Market Log**

| Date | Stock symbol | Shares held | Closing price | Previous closing price | Price change | Change in total value | Net holdings |
|------|------|------|------|------|------|------|------|
|  |  |  |  |  |  |  |  |
|  |  |  |  |  |  |  |  |
|  |  |  |  |  |  |  |  |
|  |  |  |  |  |  |  |  |
|  |  |  |  |  |  |  |  |
|  |  |  |  |  |  |  |  |
|  |  |  |  |  |  |  |  |
|  |  |  |  |  |  |  |  |
|  |  |  |  |  |  |  |  |
|  |  |  |  |  |  |  |  |
|  |  |  |  |  |  |  |  |
|  |  |  |  |  |  |  |  |
|  |  |  |  |  |  |  |  |
|  |  |  |  |  |  |  |  |
|  |  |  |  |  |  |  |  |
|  |  |  |  |  |  |  |  |
|  |  |  |  |  |  |  |  |
|  |  |  |  |  |  |  |  |
|  |  |  |  |  |  |  |  |
|  |  |  |  |  |  |  |  |
|  |  |  |  |  |  |  |  |
|  |  |  |  |  |  |  |  |
|  |  |  |  |  |  |  |  |
|  |  |  |  |  |  |  |  |
|  |  |  |  |  |  |  |  |
|  |  |  |  |  |  |  |  |
|  |  |  |  |  |  |  |  |
|  |  |  |  |  |  |  |  |
|  |  |  |  |  |  |  |  |
|  |  |  |  |  |  |  |  |
|  |  |  |  |  |  |  |  |
|  |  |  |  |  |  |  |  |
|  |  |  |  |  |  |  |  |
|  |  |  |  |  |  |  |  |
|  |  |  |  |  |  |  |  |
|  |  |  |  |  |  |  |  |
|  |  |  |  |  |  |  |  |
|  |  |  |  |  |  |  |  |
|  |  |  |  |  |  |  |  |

# CHAPTER 5

# Forging a Lasting Middle East Peace

*The class is convened as a region-wide summit on Middle Eastern conflicts and has been granted authority by the regional governments to write binding agreements. The time is the early 1980s. Buffeted by deep-rooted cultural, political, economic, and natural resource conflicts, students struggle to construct workable agreements while fending off the specter of military conflict. This lesson can easily accommodate a class of any size. It is an effective introduction to issues of ethnic strife, religious tolerance, economic underdevelopment, and international conflict in one of the world's most sensitive regions.*

*Students represent Middle Eastern governments, as well as influential outside nations. Each nation has a set of economic, political, and social incentives, ranging from issues of religious conflict to water access. Students sit as a conference of equals, with each regional actor possessing an absolute veto in a format modeled on the UN Security Council. Efforts by students to attain their objectives produce a conflict-ridden exercise that eventually slides toward consensus as the incentives to reach **some** agreement become dominant late in the conference.*

## TEACHER'S NOTE

*Forging a Lasting Middle East Peace* is designed to simulate an inclusive Middle East peace conference during the sustained period of tension that marked Arab–Israeli relations in the late 1970s and early 1980s. The simulation requires students to manage the sensitive economic, political, cultural, and social issues that characterize one of the world's most significant and most unstable regions.

The exercise was designed for a ninth-grade World Geography class, but colleagues and I have also used it successfully in American History classes. The exercise was intended to introduce students to the complex issues that have made the Middle East a perpetual tinderbox. The simulation itself takes between one and two classes to run, but the teacher will find it more rewarding if students have been previously taught background material on the politics, geography, and economic situation of the Middle East.

Although no classroom exercise can replicate the deep-rooted religious and cultural conflicts that complicate Middle East relations, it is possible to confront students with the practical conflicts that have proved so nettlesome. Questions of territory, military and economic aid, the pursuit of peace, nonrecognition, the supply of oil, and water access provide sufficient issues to fill an extensive negotiating menu. By having students confront the practical issues that aggravate Middle East tensions, it becomes easier to help them understand the cultural and religious tensions that frame the conflicts.

The exercise is set in the early 1980s, which offers a couple of additional advantages. First, it helps to fill in some of the contemporary history that often receives short-shrift in social studies. Second, it catches Middle East politics at one of its most interesting and complex points—a period when Egyptian–Israeli ties had brought hopes of peace, but when the Iran–Iraq conflict and the rumblings of the still-potent Soviet military meant that the region was a tinderbox with massive international implications. Third, the nature of these simultaneous conflicts means that there are a slew of interesting roles for students to play in this simulated general conference. The same exercise set in the 1990s would have many fewer interesting roles, as the end of the Cold War, the emergence of Iraq as a rogue state, and the beginnings of an Israel–PLO settlement reduced the number of significant actors in the Middle East.

My initial experiences with this activity were pretty frustrating because I had trouble getting the framework and the incentives right. The biggest problem was student ignorance of the context and relevant history. However, extensive fine-tuning and much more emphasis on prepping students on the relevant history have turned this into a frequently fascinating and highly enjoyable exercise. I find it rather profound when students, steeped in the roiling international waters of the early 1980s, culminate two days of negotiations by finally devising a comprehensive pact for Middle East peace. During the exercise, students often seem to acquire this same appreciation for the significance of the chore. I can recall at least two occasions when the classroom was silent, when there was actually a tinge of solemnity, as the students finalized the treaty. It is an amazing experience to look around at a bunch of 13-year-olds as they seriously and attentively cheer the ratification of a well-crafted—if imaginary—compact.

## BACKGROUND ON MIDDLE EAST CONFLICT

The roots of contemporary Middle East conflict can be traced back to the destruction of the Second Temple in 70 A.D., when the Jews were forced from Palestine in the Diaspora. From that point until the twentieth century, the Jews were a people without a homeland, frequently encountering oppression as they established communities in Europe and Russia. During that period, Islam was founded. Muhammad, the founder of Islam, was born in Mecca in 570 A.D. By the time of his death in 632 A.D., Muhammad had founded a religion that would dominate Middle Eastern culture into the twentieth century.

When Jews started to return to Palestine in the early twentieth century, Palestinian–Israeli rivalry and the cultural schism between the Muslim and Jewish faiths fueled the tensions. Jews claimed Palestine as their homeland, but Arabs argued that the this claim was illegitimate because nearly 2000 years had elapsed since the Jews had departed Palestine. The issues were complicated by the presence of colonial European powers, primarily Britain and France, which controlled the Middle East at the dawn of the twentieth century.

Support for construction of a Jewish homeland in Palestine coalesced in the fledgling Zionist movement in the 1890s. The Zionists began pushing for international support for a Jewish homeland at an 1897 conference in Basel, Switzerland. After 20 years, those efforts resulted in Britain's 1917 Balfour Declaration, which pledged support for a "national home" for the Jews in Palestine. Initially the Arabs, dominated by the colonial European powers, demonstrated some willingness to consider the proposal.

By 1937, however, Arab opposition to a Jewish state in Palestine had grown and solidified. Arabs rioted in protest. In response to the rioting, the British sought to work out a compromise between the Arabs and the Jews. First the British proposed partitioning Palestine into two countries, one for the Jews and one for the Palestinians. The Jewish leaders accepted the proposal, which gave them the homeland they fervently desired, but the Palestinians rejected it. The British then invited all concerned parties for a 1939 conference in London. However, the conference went nowhere when the Arab delegation refused to sit in the same room with the Jewish delegation. Efforts to reconcile the conflict were interrupted by the outbreak of World War II in 1939.

In 1947, after the end of World War II, the United Nations voted to partition Palestine. Relieved to be freed from the turmoil, the British withdrew from Palestine in May of 1948. After the UN vote, and before the British withdrew, a bloody civil war broke out between the Jews and Arabs in Palestine. At first the more numerous Arabs were winning, but the superior unity, organization, and preparation of the Jews turned the tide. Shortly after Britain pulled out, the Jews declared the new nation of Israel on May 14, 1948. In ensuing fighting, the Israelis managed to defeat both the Palestinian Arabs and forces from the adjacent Arab nations.

The state that the UN had envisioned for the Palestinian Arabs never came into being. The land that had been set aside for the Palestinians was annexed by Israel, Egypt, and Transjordan. The Palestinian people were left without a homeland, and Arab unity was undercut by mutual suspicion and blame for the Arab League's inability to defeat Israel.

The 1948 war resolved nothing. Instead, it was only the first in a sequence of Arab–Israeli wars that would scar the next quarter century. After the 1948 war, the Arabs refused to recognize the existence of Israel and maintained the publicly stated goal of destroying Israel. The United States, in large part due to guilt fueled by revelations about the attempt of Nazi Germany to exterminate the Jewish people, assumed the role of Israel's protector and benefactor. U.S. aid, rigorous training and discipline (which included mandatory military service for men and women), inter-Arab conflict, and superlative military performance permitted Israel to survive against its combined enemies.

## Arab–Israeli Conflict

In 1956, the Suez Canal crisis provoked the second Arab–Israeli War. The new ruler of Egypt, Colonel Gamal Abdel Nasser, nationalized the British-owned Canal. This threatened Europe's access to oil and to Asian trade. Meanwhile, Nasser attempted to choke off Israel by blockade. In response, Israel forged a secret alliance with the French and the British aimed at retaking the Suez. The Israelis launched an attack on Egypt that reached the Canal faster than even France and Britain had anticipated. However, the nature of the Israeli–British–French agreement quickly became clear. Scared of provoking international conflict with the Soviet Union, which was supplying Nasser with arms, the United States demanded that its allies retreat. After the Suez crisis, Nasser was careful not to provoke Israel. He called for pan-Arabic organization and argued that the Arabs needed to bide their time until they were organized enough to defeat Israel.

New Arab–Israeli troubles erupted in 1964 when Syrian and Lebanese engineers started trying to divert the waters of the Jordan River so that their nations—rather than Israel—would be able to use the precious water. The project would have left Israel without necessary water. Israel responded with artillery attacks, the project was not completed, and tensions escalated yet again.

A series of small conflicts between Egypt and Israel in early 1967 led to an Egyptian embargo of Israel and coordinated war preparations among Egypt, Jordan, Syria, and Iraq. Fearing that its neighbors were finally going to mount a unified invasion, Israel launched a surprise first strike on Egypt and initiated the third Arab–Israeli War. This war lasted only six days, and ended with Israel capturing the Sinai Peninsula and Gaza Strip from Egypt, the West Bank from Jordan, and the Golan Heights from Syria.

The Six-Day War of 1967 was a humiliating defeat for the Arabs and an immense triumph for Israel. The war left Israel with important bargaining chips, particularly the West Bank and Sinai Peninsula. Further, the possession of the Sinai gave Israel an important buffer zone against Egypt—its most feared opponent. Meanwhile, the brief war had turned Nasser from a heroic Arab leader into an object of ridicule. Nasser died in 1970, to be replaced by the less dynamic Anwar al-Sadat. The UN Security Council responded to the War's outcome by passing Resolution 242, which called for territorial concessions by Israel in return for a guarantee of peace from the Arabs.

The Israelis relaxed after their overwhelming 1967 victory, though Egyptian guerillas continued to provoke border violence into 1969. During this period, Sadat used a public façade of peaceful intentions to cover up his preparations for another assault on Israel. Sadat arranged for the necessary cooperation from Syria and Jordan and launched a surprise attack during the Jewish observance of Yom Kippur on October 6, 1973. Lulled into complacency by the outcomes of the 1967 war, and attacked on the day of the Jewish religion's most sacred holiday, the Israelis were initially driven back. However, the Israelis righted themselves, eventually driving deep into Egyptian and Syrian territory.

The United States convinced the Israelis to pull back and brokered a peace. However, the Arabs responded to Western support for Israel by imposing an oil embargo on the Western powers in 1973 and 1974. The embargo imposed massive costs on the oil-reliant companies and consumers of the United States and Europe. The oil embargo that the Arabs imposed on the West in 1973 dramatically increased the influence of the Arabs in world affairs. Meanwhile, the psychological benefits of having threatened the Israelis bolstered Sadat's status in Egypt and the Arab world, while the near-death experience of their early defeats left the Israelis more willing to negotiate with their hostile neighbors.

## From 1973 Through the Early 1980s

The 1973 war provoked a shift in the superpower roles in the Middle East. After 1973, the Soviet Union was largely excluded from the Middle East peace process. During the 1973 war, a nuclear showdown had nearly been provoked when American President Richard Nixon put American forces on worldwide alert in case the Soviets intervened on behalf of the Arabs.

After the war, the United States and Egypt started to make the first steps toward establishing a relationship. By 1977, it was clear that the United States was the key outside participant in the Middle East peace process. In fact, Sadat repeatedly said that "the U.S. holds 99 percent of the cards." Sadat had expelled Soviet military advisers in 1972, bringing a deep chill to Egyptian–Soviet relations. The gradual warming of U.S.–Egyptian relations meant that the United States was the only superpower on good terms with both Egypt and Israel.

A civil war broke out in Lebanon in 1975, leading to Israeli attacks on Arab forces in southern Lebanon in 1978. Frustrated by Palestinian attacks on the northern Israeli border, and angered that Palestinian terrorists were using war-torn Lebanon as a base of operations, Israel invaded Lebanon in 1982. Israel claimed it only intended to create a 25-mile buffer zone from terrorist attacks, but its real intention was to wipe out the Palestinian armed forces. U.S. efforts to maintain peace in the region suffered a grievous setback in October 1982 when a terrorist bombing killed 241 Americans in the Marine headquarters in Beirut, Lebanon. American President Ronald Reagan responded by quickly slashing the number of U.S. troops in harm's way.

In 1979, the Shah of Iran was overthrown by the radical Muslim leader Ayatollah Khoemeini. The Shah had been the key U.S. ally in the region. His fall, coupled with the embarrassing year-long seizure of U.S. embassy personnel by Iranian revolutionaries, struck a great blow to U.S. influence in the region. Soon after Khoemeini came to power, Iraq invaded Iran. The Iraqi invasion initiated a drawn-out and costly war, which presented only disturbing outcomes for the international community. An Iraqi victory threatened to make the unstable aggressor the dominant country in the region, while an Iranian victory would encourage extremist leaders to stir up fundamentalist Muslims throughout the region. By the early 1980s, Middle East countries were spending more than $15 billion a year to purchase foreign arms and military products. From the Vietnam War to the end of the Cold War, the Middle East led all areas of the world in the amount of imported arms.

The lone successful peacemaking effort during these decades of conflict was the Camp David Accord reached between Israel and Egypt in 1979. In 1977, early in his presidency, American President Jimmy Carter had laid out the outlines of a peace plan in which Israel would pull back to roughly its 1967 borders, the Arabs would establish a permanent peace with Israel, and a Palestinian homeland would be created (probably in the West Bank and the Gaza Strip). Later in 1977, Sadat had made a dramatic visit to Jerusalem, where he addressed the Israeli parliament. Sadat's unprecedented visit to Israel kicked off negotiations that ended in a 1978 stalemate.

Frustrated by the standoff, Carter took the dramatic step of bringing Begin and Sadat to the Camp David presidential retreat for 13 days of talks in mid-1978. The risky gamble by the unpopular President paid off fabulously when the private talks allowed the leaders to break new ground. The Israelis agreed to return the Sinai Peninsula to Egypt, the Egyptians agreed to sign a peace treaty with Israel, and all parties agreed to a "framework" for settling the future of the West Bank and Gaza Strip. Additionally, the United States agreed to provide large amounts of aid to both countries. The agreements of 1978 were enacted as a formal Accord in 1979. In Israel and Egypt, there were large segments of the population that regarded Begin and Sadat—respectively—as traitors to their nations. Sadat was widely reviled by his fellow Arabs and was assassinated by militants during a 1981 parade.

### The Palestinians

About 500,000 Palestinians were left homeless after the 1947–48 war that established Israel. They wound up in dreary United Nations refugee camps in Syria, Jordan, and Lebanon. Over time, these camps grew into permanent communities of the displaced. The refugees were left without land or property and were given no compensation for what they had left behind. Attempts to work out an agreement to return these people to Israel broke down when Israel would only agree to accept a small number back, while the Arabs opposed any refugee settlement that recognized Israel.

The frustration of the refugees led to the formation of Arab terrorist groups in the 1950s, and eventually to the founding of the Palestinian Liberation Organization (PLO). In the 1950s, Arab governments started to provide money to train Palestinian guerillas who would attack Israel. In 1964, at a meeting in Cairo, the heads of the Arab states supported the creation of the PLO. The PLO was formed with the understanding that the Palestinian problem could only be resolved "in Palestine and by the force of arms." The PLO was initially allied with Egypt, and did not emerge as an autonomous entity until after the organization's guerillas were recognized for their performance in the 1967 war.

The PLO started to gain more influence in the 1970s, when it was recognized by the United Nations in 1974 and the Arab League in 1976. The PLO had few contacts with the United States during that time period, although it received strong support from the Soviet Union. The PLO believed terrorism to be a legitimate means of pursuing its political ends.

The PLO's overriding goal was the creation of an independent Palestinian state. The PLO was receptive to an independent Palestinian nation on the West Bank, although Israel was loath to give up the land—particularly without ironclad guarantees that a smaller and more vulnerable Israel need not fear the new Palestinian nation to its east. Meanwhile, the PLO was loath to submit to Israeli demands that the West Bank homeland be a demilitarized state and that the Palestinians renounce all claims to other parts of Israel.

## USING THIS SIMULATION

### Purpose of the Simulation

The exercise is intended to introduce students to the significance of cultural and social conflict in political relations. It also provides understanding of the latticework of issues that characterize the Middle East, offers insight into the dynamics of the Cold War, and helps contextualize the Gulf War and much contemporary international tension.

### Skills Developed

The simulation helps to develop teamwork, negotiating, public speaking, and research skills. Students are forced to work at negotiating their way through a delicate and conflictual situation. Argument, persuasion, and compromise are all called on at different moments. Because each of the nations has unique and somewhat contradictory needs, students must learn how to split the difference in order to produce workable compromises. The game rewards and encourages both strategic thinking and interpersonal skills.

### Logistics

*Forging a Lasting Middle East Peace* benefits from some preparation on the part of the students. There are groups representing 11 nations in the game. Groups of students should be assigned their nation 1 to 2 weeks before the exercise is to begin. Students are to prepare a three-page briefing on their nation's political, economic, and social situation in the early 1980s (in the case of the United States and Soviet Union, the briefing is to focus on their nation as it related to the Middle East). Each group should have the briefing prepared prior to the beginning of the simulation.

Because the game's length depends in large part on the students' ability to forge workable compromises, no precise time estimates are possible. Depending on the teacher's guidance, the students can be encouraged to make the negotiations more complex or to gloss over conflicts and thereby to accelerate the pace at which they complete the exercise. I generally ran the affair for between one and two 40-minute class periods, making it a practice to announce at some mid-point of the exercise just how much longer students would have to forge an agreement. I would wait to make this announcement because, once given a deadline, students sometimes forge rapid agreements by simply splitting their differences. Although the game is designed to make this difficult, I would initially give the students 20 or 40 minutes to negotiate without a time limit before mentioning the deadline.

Because each of the 11 nations is represented by a student or a group of students, the exercise can accommodate a class ranging in size from 11 to about 40 students. I have the class sit in a large circle for the talks, with the members of each country clustered together. Students are permitted to move to the corners of the room at will for private conferences.

All the materials necessary for the simulation are included in this chapter's Appendix. Once a teacher has read this chapter, preparation for the simulation should take no more than an hour. Once the Country Profile sheets and the Middle East map have been copied, the only real preparation necessary is organizing groups and preparing explanatory remarks.

## HOW THE SIMULATION WORKS

### Student Groups

There are 11 countries, each of which can be represented by a student or a group. It is optimal to have groups of two for most countries, with groups of three for the most significant actors (i.e., the United States, Israel, Jordan, the PLO).

### Object

The overall objective is to forge a peace agreement that resolves all or most of the concerns of the nations involved. The class will actually write down the treaty protocol. The protocol should explicitly list agreements, including the decision of countries to offer diplomatic recognition to others, promises of economic and military aid, peace agreements, offers of land, and guarantees of access to oil production. The protocol will be used by students in each group to compute their score for the exercise.

The political demands of each nation are represented on the Country Profile sheets issued to students in each group (see Appendix). Each nation has objectives to be achieved and outcomes to be avoided. Students score points based on how well they fare on these tasks. The larger goal is for students to produce an intelligent and thoughtful conference in accord with their national demands.

There is no set benchmark for judging victory. Instead, each country finds itself able to score a similar number of points, based on the students' ability to achieve their objectives. Each group can achieve a high score of +10 and a low score of –10, depending on how the conference comes out. Teachers may want to offer these points as bonus points, or simply have students discuss, analyze, and justify their score in the assessment essay when making the case for their group's performance.

### Length of Exercise

The exercise runs until the class has reached a comprehensive settlement, unless it triggers a nuclear holocaust. Because the simulation makes reaching agreement on some points extremely difficult, the students decide just how comprehensive it will be. Each group has an incentive to see its demands met. That generally proves incentive enough to drive a broad and wide-ranging settlement. Because classes move at different speeds and in different fashions, there is no way to predict how long a given conference will take. Additionally, there exists the possibility of a superpower showdown, which could provoke nuclear war and bring an immediate end to the exercise.

## How the Game Is Played

Students are assigned their countries about a week before the conference. At that time they should be issued the Country Profile sheets. Each group is to prepare a three-page national briefing that discusses their nation's economic, political, and social situation in the 1982–1984 period. The U.S. and Soviet Union groups should concentrate their briefs on how the Middle East affected their nations during that time period. Students should prepare the briefs with the intention of enabling themselves to effectively represent their nations, by collecting information that will support their demands, and by finding other issues that they may want the conference to address.

There is no sequence of turns in this simulation. Rather, students are convened in a large circle and are then left to their own devices. It is up to the students to arrange for leadership and to organize deliberations. Representatives of each group are free to get up and move around, permitting them to negotiate in private, as long as at least one member of each country is always in the circle.

Students should use the chalkboard to list the issues that the conference is attempting to resolve and to keep track of progress on each issue. One student can be given this responsibility or it can be shared. Regardless, the list should be continually updated as negotiations proceed. During the course of negotiations, students can either finalize each agreement independently or compile all the agreements into a comprehensive protocol. Wrapping all the agreements and trade-offs into a comprehensive protocol frequently works best, because so many of the issues and countries involved are intertwined.

The class is charged with attempting to resolve a bushel of contentious and intertwined issues. The following are the key international issues students address:

1. The status of Israel—Will the Arab nations recognize Israel's right to exist?
2. The issue of a homeland for the Palestinians. Questions include where it would be located, what its rights would be, and its relationship with Israel.
3. The status of the PLO and how to address its ongoing terrorist activity against Israel.
4. The status of the Israeli-controlled West Bank, which was formerly part of Jordan.
5. The status of the Golan Heights, which were formerly part of Syria.
6. The status of the Gaza Strip, which was formerly part of Egypt.
7. The relationship between Egypt, reviled for its recognition of Israel, and its fellow Arab nations.
8. The issue of control over the Jordan River's water. Lebanon and Syria would benefit greatly from getting control over the river's water supply, but Israel would suffer greatly.
9. Resolving the ongoing Iran–Iraq War.
10. Resolving the ongoing Israeli invasion of Lebanon.
11. Continued U.S. access to nine million barrels of oil per day.

Additionally, there are peripheral issues, including concerns about economic aid, military aid, and the role of the Soviet Union in the region. Each nation scores points based on its ability to achieve certain goals. Countries can also lose points if certain feared results come to pass. Each nation can wind up with a score ranging from +10 to –10 points.

Each country enters the conference with its own set of resources and needs. Some nations, such as the United States, have immense resources but also have extensive demands. Other nations, such as Lebanon, have very few resources, but also have much more modest demands for the conference.

***Military Conflict***   The relative military strength of the nations is pertinent to the conference. The relative military strength of Iran and Iraq is one consideration. The relative military strength of Egypt, Syria, the PLO, and Jordan as compared to the strength of Israel is a second consideration. If one side, either in the Iran–Iraq War in the tense Egypt–Syria–Jordan–PLO–Israel situation, musters twice the military strength of the opponent, that side is able to conquer its opponent. At the start of the conference neither side is in that position, but they may attain sufficient strength with support from either the United States or the Soviet Union. In addition to contributing troops, the United States and Soviet Union are also able to aid countries by giving military aid (in which case the superpowers are not directly involved).

If one nation announces that it is attacking another, the announcement is made in the conference circle. At that point, any allied nations joining in the attack must announce themselves. Once all attacking nations have announced themselves, any nations coming to the defense of the victim should announce themselves. If the attack is repulsed, because the attackers do not have twice the defender's strength, all invading countries lose one-third of their armed forces (round down) while the defending nation emerges unscathed. If the attack succeeds, the defending nation ceases to exist, and its members join the victorious groups.

Only certain countries—Israel, Egypt, Jordan, Syria, Iraq, and Iran—can be attacked in this game. The PLO, United States, and Soviet Union also have military capabilities, but can only use them offensively—these countries cannot be attacked. If the Soviet Union and the United States enter on opposite sides of a conflict, the conflict escalates to nuclear war and the entire exercise is over.

***U.S.–Soviet Conflict***   If the United States and the Soviet Union both get involved—by sending troops, not merely by giving aid—on opposite sides of one of the two Middle East conflicts, everybody loses. A U.S.–Soviet conflict in the Middle East always posed a massive threat of triggering nuclear war. If the two powers both commit troops to opposite sides in one of the conflicts, then the conference ends in a state of utter failure, and everything else becomes irrelevant. (The starkness of this threat, as intended, has prevented a U.S.–Soviet confrontation from ever occurring in one of my classes.)

***Military Aid***   The United States and Soviet Union are able to offer military aid to other nations. Each $1 billion in aid given by the United States or Soviet Union increases the receiving nation's armed strength by one-quarter million soldiers. Military aid does not directly involve the United States or Soviet Union in any conflict.

***Oil Access***   The United States needs continued access to oil from the Middle East, particularly to the reserves of Saudi Arabia. The United States needs to import 9 million barrels of oil per day in this game. The Saudis are able to supply 9 million, while the Soviets, Egyptians, Iranians, and Iraqis are each able to supply 3 million barrels per day. The upshot is that the United States needs to ensure either a continued oil supply from Saudi Arabia or from three of the four other oil exporters.

***Economic Aid***   The United States and, to a lesser extent, Saudi Arabia and the Soviet Union are able to supply economic aid to other nations. The Country Profile sheets indicate which nations are in need of economic aid and how much they need. The teacher should note that there is not enough aid to fulfill every nations' desires.

## COMMENTS FROM EXPERIENCE

If a U.S.–Soviet confrontation were to break out (provoking nuclear war and the conference's immediate end), I would seize on that event as an excellent teaching moment. If that event occurs, the closing essay should be revamped so that students explain what provoked the confrontation, why it was not avoided, and what strategies could avoid a similar result in the future.

---

**SUMMARY TEACHER INSTRUCTIONS**

*Prior to the day the simulation begins*
- Objective is for the class to construct a comprehensive treaty protocol that resolves the slew of concerns characterizing the Middle East.
- Give each group its Country Profile sheet, and each student a copy of the Summary of Key Issues to Be Resolved and the Middle East map. Each group should be assigned their country 1–2 weeks before the simulation begins so that they have time to prepare their three-page brief before the conference.
- Explain the background of the political situation in the Middle East.

*The day the simulation begins*
- Arrange classroom seats in a circle, with representatives from each country sitting together.
- Have students commence negotiations, with at least one member from each country remaining in the conference circle at all times.
- Either the teacher or a student should track the emerging protocol on the chalkboard.
- Students may initiate military conflict at any point during the conference.

*After the simulation*
- Require students to write an analytic essay that tallies and explains the number of points they received, and explains why they were effective representatives in compiling the score they did.
- Assess simulation using country briefing, classroom observations of participation, group assessment form, the written analysis of the simulation, and a quiz.

---

The teacher can expect the Soviet Union to play a more intrusive role than was the norm in the 1975–1985 period. The game was designed that way, both to give students a bit more exposure to the feel of the Cold War and to keep the game more interesting than it was when I first designed it with a largely unchallenged U.S. role.

The exercise has a tendency to break into two or three different negotiating sessions. One is among Iran, Iraq, Saudi Arabia, and the superpowers regarding the Iran–Iraq War. A second is among Israel, Syria, and Lebanon regarding water and the Israeli invasion of Lebanon. The third is among Israel, the PLO, Egypt, Jordan, Syria, and the superpowers regarding Israeli–Arab relations and the Palestinian question. The students playing the superpowers and Israel tend to be the links who tie the disparate negotiations together. I do not interfere in this modular approach. First, it is a fair representation of what happened in the real world. Second, it is valuable for the students to work at fitting the various negotiations together.

I do require that each country have one student posted in the conference circle at all times, even if other teammates are off negotiating in private. The conference circle is charged with keeping all members up to date on various agreements and with keeping the conference moving forward. It is important to have a student from the conference circle keep track of all issues of contention on the chalkboard and to continually update the status of the issues on that list. The chalkboard list helps to keep the conference circle working toward solutions that will integrate all the smaller negotiations taking place.

Having students research their countries is useful not only for the obvious reasons, but also because it tends to increase student interest and give students a greater sense of connection to their country. Most of my students know so little about the actors involved that it can be hard for them to get invested in the fate of their country. By having students research, talk, and think about the country they are representing, the teacher can dramatically elevate the students' attachment to the exercise. This increases enthusiasm, makes for sharper and more interesting negotiating, and produces a more rewarding exercise.

## POSSIBLE MODIFICATIONS

This game has been used effectively with high school students at all levels. The game's explicit incentives offer a structure that can make the game appropriate for younger or older students. Younger students can rely on the clear directives, while older students can use them as an excuse to design devious and pressure-filled negotiating schemes. Similarly, it is no great trick to make the exercise sufficiently challenging for an introductory college course in Comparative Politics or one on the Middle East.

### Advanced Students

To make the game more challenging for advanced students, the most effective approach is probably to disregard the simplified and stylized Country Profile sheets in the Appendix. Instead, teachers should require students to research and determine their own major and minor objectives prior to the conference. Give students about two to three weeks to complete the assignment, and require each group to prepare an eight- to ten-page briefing paper, rather than the three-page briefing document discussed before. The briefing should outline the suggested material, and use that material to outline the nations' key objectives, supporting the objectives with appropriate historical material from the early 1980s. In the post-game assessment, students are expected to defend their performance on achieving the goals they outlined in their briefing paper.

### Junior High and Less Advanced Students

To accommodate lower-level students, the teacher can take one of two approaches. One is to do away with the point scoring and with the requirement that students justify their performance in their post-simulation essay. This permits students to disregard their objectives and the concerns enumerated on the Country Profile sheets. The teacher may also want to do away with the requirement that students prepare research briefs. Doing away with these elements makes the exercise into much more of a free-flowing discussion about the Middle East, in which students are permitted to debate and play-act without too many restrictions or too much work. Teachers with younger students may find this approach a more appropriate way to get the students to interact with the material.

## ASSESSMENT

Four complementary assessments are suggested for this exercise. Students should be informed of all assessments *before* the simulation begins. By requiring students to prepare for and pay attention throughout the exercise, the assessment devices make the exercise more productive and maximize student participation.

First, each group is to compose a three-page briefing on their nation's economic, political, and social situation in the 1982–1984 period. (Students representing the United States and Soviet Union should concentrate on the relevance of the Middle East to their nations.) Students use the briefing papers during the conference for reference purposes and as ammunition for argument. Each group will turn in its briefing paper at the end of the conference. Briefs should be evaluated according to clarity of organization, and the quality and usefulness of the information.

Second, students are evaluated based on the teacher's observation of their participation in the exercise. I particularly look for students who attempt to make some concrete contribution to their nation's case. At the end of the exercise, I also have each student fill out the standard simulation feedback form (see Chapter 12, Final Thoughts). This form asks students to assess the contributions of their teammates, and to reflect on the entire class. Using my observations and the group evaluations, I assess students based on their contribution to their team and to the group. The feedback form takes about five minutes to fill out. This assessment is completed by the day after the exercise.

Third, students are asked to write a two- or three-page first-person essay that analyzes the simulation. Primarily, students are asked to tally up and explain their score, discussing performance in terms of their success at achieving their targeted objectives. Students should explain what their successes were, why they achieved what they did, and why they were unable to achieve what they did not. The requirement that students justify and explain their score helps keep the simulation true to form and motivates students to pay close attention throughout the game. Therefore, this essay should be fully explained ahead of time. Students are also to explain how they would act differently if the exercise were conducted again. Students are to write the paper the night after the exercise.

Fourth, students are quizzed on the substance of the agreement, and major events that took place during the negotiations. This short quiz should be administered the day after the exercise ends, and should take somewhere between 15 and 30 minutes. The purpose is to ensure that students paid attention to what transpired around them during the game and to help ensure that all students are familiar with the rules of the exercise.

All the assessments are finished by the end of the day after the simulation. The approaches offer a well-rounded view of student participation and performance, while cultivating useful skills. By informing students of the multiple assessments *before* the simulation, the teacher encourages students to pay attention to the substance and dynamic of the exercise.

# APPENDIX—MATERIALS

## List of Materials

- Map of the Middle East (for each student)
- Summary of Key Issues to Be Resolved (for each student)
- Country Profile Sheets (for each group)

---

### Summary of Key Issues to Be Resolved

1.  The status of Israel—Will the Arab nations recognize Israel's right to exist?

2.  The issue of a homeland for the Palestinians. Questions include where it would be located, what its rights would be, and its relationship with Israel.

3.  The status of the PLO and how to address its ongoing terrorist activity against Israel.

4.  The status of the Israeli-controlled West Bank, which was formerly part of Jordan.

5.  The status of the Golan Heights, which were formerly part of Syria.

6.  The status of the Gaza Strip, which was formerly part of Egypt.

7.  The relationship between Egypt, reviled for its recognition of Israel, and its fellow Arab nations.

8.  The issue of control over the Jordan River's water. Lebanon and Syria would benefit greatly from getting control over the river's water supply, but Israel would suffer greatly.

9.  Resolving the ongoing Iran–Iraq War.

10. Resolving the ongoing Israeli invasion of Lebanon.

11. Continued U.S. access to nine million barrels of oil per day.

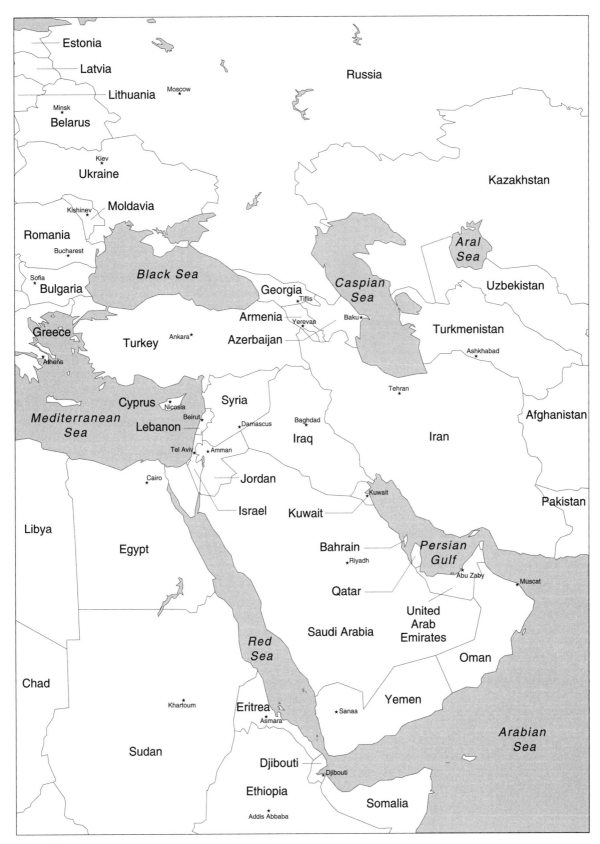

**FIGURE 5.1   The Middle East**

## Country Profile Sheet 1　UNITED STATES

### *Resources*

Military strength: 1 million troops

Military aid to give: $15 billion

Economic aid to give: $12 billion

### *Goals*

1. Guaranteed access to oil production of at least 9 million barrels per day (+5 points)
2. Peace agreement and diplomatic recognition between Israel and PLO, Jordan, Syria (already exists with Egypt) (+3 points)
3. Ensuring that neither Iran nor Iraq wins a victory in the Iran–Iraq war (+2 points)

### *To Avoid*

1. Israel getting conquered (–7 points)
2. Egypt, Jordan, or Israel establishing official ties to the Soviet Union (–1 point each)

### *To Avoid at All Cost*

The United States and Soviet Union committing their military strength (not military aid) on opposite sides of a conflict. If the two superpowers enter on either side of a conflict, the conflict quickly becomes a nuclear war. Everyone receives a final score of –10 points and the exercise comes to an immediate end.

### *Remember*

The group must prepare a three-page briefing on the economic, political, and social conditions of the nation in the early 1980s. How did these conditions shape your nation's needs?

All agreements should be written into the treaty protocol.

### *Military Conflict*

If one side, either in the Iran–Iraq War or in the tense Egypt–Syria–Jordan–PLO versus Israel situation musters twice the military strength of the opponent, that side is able to conquer its opponent. At the start of the conference neither side is in that position, but one side or the other may get strong enough with support from either the United States or Soviet Union. In addition to contributing troops, the United States and Soviet Union are able to aid countries by giving military aid (in which case the superpowers are not considered to be directly involved in the fighting). Each $1 billion in military aid produces one-quarter million more troops. Only certain countries can be attacked in this game. Only Israel, Egypt, Jordan, Syria, Iraq, and Iran can be attacked. The PLO, United States, and Soviet Union also have military capabilities, but they can only be used offensively—these countries cannot be attacked.

　　If one nation announces that it is attacking another, the announcement must be publicly made in the conference circle. At that point, any allied nations joining in the attack must announce themselves. Once all attacking nations have announced themselves, any nations coming to the defense of the victim should announce themselves. If the attack is repulsed, all invading countries lose one-third of their armed forces (round down), while the defender(s) lose nothing. If the attack succeeds, the attacked nation ceases to exist, and its members join the victorious groups.

### Country Profile Sheet 2  SOVIET UNION

#### *Resources*

Military strength: 3 million troops

Military aid to give: $6 billion

Economic aid to give: $3 billion

Oil production: 3 million barrels per day

#### *Goals*

1. Establishing official ties with Egypt, Israel, Jordan, Saudi Arabia, and/or Lebanon (+1 point each)

2. Iraqi victory over Iran in their war (+3 points)

3. Creating a Palestinian homeland on the West Bank which agrees to base 1 million or more Soviet troops (+2 points)

#### *To Avoid*

1. Israeli peace agreement with PLO, Syria, or Jordan if none of those countries will agree to establish ties with the Soviet Union (–5 points)

2. Giving away all $9 billion in available aid (–2 points)

#### *To Avoid at All Cost*

The United States and Soviet Union committing their military strength (not military aid) on opposite sides of a conflict. If the two superpowers enter on either side of a conflict, the conflict quickly becomes a nuclear war. Everyone receives a final score of –10 points and the exercise comes to an immediate end.

#### *Remember*

The group must prepare a three-page briefing on the economic, political, and social conditions of the nation in the early 1980s. How did these conditions shape your nation's needs?

All agreements should be written into the treaty protocol.

#### *Military Conflict*

If one side, either in the Iran–Iraq War or in the tense Egypt–Syria–Jordan–PLO versus Israel situation musters twice the military strength of the opponent, that side is able to conquer its opponent. At the start of the conference neither side is in that position, but one side or the other may get strong enough with support from either the United States or Soviet Union. In addition to contributing troops, the United States and Soviet Union are able to aid countries by giving military aid (in which case the superpowers are not considered to be directly involved in the fighting). Each $1 billion in military aid produces one-quarter million more troops. Only certain countries can be attacked in this game. Only Israel, Egypt, Jordan, Syria, Iraq, and Iran can be attacked. The PLO, United States, and Soviet Union also have military capabilities, but they can only be used offensively—these countries cannot be attacked.

If one nation announces that it is attacking another, the announcement must be publicly made in the conference circle. At that point, any allied nations joining in the attack must announce themselves. Once all attacking nations have announced themselves, any nations coming to the defense of the victim should announce themselves. If the attack is repulsed, all invading countries lose one-third of their armed forces (round down), while the defender(s) lose nothing. If the attack succeeds, the attacked nation ceases to exist, and its members join the victorious groups.

### Country Profile Sheet 3   ISRAEL

#### *Resources*

Military strength: 3 million troops

#### *Goals*

1. Peace agreement with PLO, Jordan, and Syria (+6 points)
2. Get PLO to remove all military personnel from Lebanon (+2 points)
3. Needs $5 billion in military aid (+2 points)

#### *To Avoid*

1. Can't afford to lose access to the Jordan River's water supply (–3 points), although Israel could replace the lost supply with an additional $6 billion in economic aid
2. Creating a Palestinian homeland on the West Bank (–3 points), although it is only minus 1 point if the Palestinian state agrees to have no military
3. Giving up Eastern Jerusalem, the Gaza Strip, or the Golan Heights (–1 point each)

#### *To Avoid at All Cost*

The United States and Soviet Union committing their military strength (not military aid) on opposite sides of a conflict. If the two superpowers enter on either side of a conflict, the conflict quickly becomes a nuclear war. Everyone receives a final score of –10 points and the exercise comes to an immediate end.

Getting conquered means an automatic final score of –10 points.

#### *Remember*

The group must prepare a three-page briefing on the economic, political, and social conditions of the nation in the early 1980s. How did these conditions shape your nation's needs?

All agreements should be written into the treaty protocol.

#### *Military Conflict*

If one side, either in the Iran–Iraq War or in the tense Egypt–Syria–Jordan–PLO versus Israel situation musters twice the military strength of the opponent, that side is able to conquer its opponent. At the start of the conference neither side is in that position, but one side or the other may get strong enough with support from either the United States or Soviet Union. In addition to contributing troops, the United States and Soviet Union are able to aid countries by giving military aid (in which case the superpowers are not considered to be directly involved in the fighting). Each $1 billion in military aid produces one-quarter million more troops. Only certain countries can be attacked in this game. Only Israel, Egypt, Jordan, Syria, Iraq, and Iran can be attacked. The PLO, United States, and Soviet Union also have military capabilities, but they can only be used offensively—these countries cannot be attacked.

If one nation announces that it is attacking another, the announcement must be publicly made in the conference circle. At that point, any allied nations joining in the attack must announce themselves. Once all attacking nations have announced themselves, any nations coming to the defense of the victim should announce them-selves. If the attack is repulsed, all invading countries lose one-third of their armed forces (round down), while the defender(s) lose nothing. If the attack succeeds, the attacked nation ceases to exist, and its members join the victorious groups.

## Country Profile Sheet 4   PALESTINIAN LIBERATION ORGANIZATION

### Resources

Military strength: 1 million troops

### Goals

1. A homeland on the West Bank (+6 points)
2. East Jerusalem being included as part of Palestinian nation (+2 points)
3. Recognition by the United States (+1 point)
4. $3 billion in economic aid (+1 point)

### To Avoid

1. Not being permitted to have armed forces in a West Bank homeland (–4 points)
2. Having Israeli troops remain in Lebanon (–2 points)
3. Being required to pull all military forces out of Lebanon (–2 points)

### To Avoid at All Cost

The United States and Soviet Union committing their military strength (not military aid) on opposite sides of a conflict. If the two superpowers enter on either side of a conflict, the conflict quickly becomes a nuclear war. Everyone receives a final score of –10 points and the exercise comes to an immediate end.

### Remember

The group must prepare a three-page briefing on the economic, political, and social conditions of the nation in the early 1980s. How did these conditions shape your nation's needs?

All agreements should be written into the treaty protocol.

### Military Conflict

If one side, either in the Iran–Iraq War or in the tense Egypt–Syria–Jordan–PLO versus Israel situation musters twice the military strength of the opponent, that side is able to conquer its opponent. At the start of the conference neither side is in that position, but one side or the other may get strong enough with support from either the United States or Soviet Union. In addition to contributing troops, the United States and Soviet Union are able to aid countries by giving military aid (in which case the superpowers are not considered to be directly involved in the fighting). Each $1 billion in military aid produces one-quarter million more troops. Only certain countries can be attacked in this game. Only Israel, Egypt, Jordan, Syria, Iraq, and Iran can be attacked. The PLO, United States, and Soviet Union also have military capabilities, but they can only be used offensively—these countries cannot be attacked.

If one nation announces that it is attacking another, the announcement must be publicly made in the conference circle. At that point, any allied nations joining in the attack must announce themselves. Once all attacking nations have announced themselves, any nations coming to the defense of the victim should announce themselves. If the attack is repulsed, all invading countries lose one-third of their armed forces (round down), while the defender(s) lose nothing. If the attack succeeds, the attacked nation ceases to exist, and its members join the victorious groups.

### Country Profile Sheet 5    SYRIA

#### Resources

Military strength: 1 million troops

#### Goals

1. Retaking the Golan Heights from Israel, either peacefully or by conquering Israel (+4 points)
2. The ability to redirect the Jordan River's water supply away from Israel, although the same effect can be achieved with $6 billion in economic aid for water development (+3 points)
3. $4 billion in military aid (+3 points)
4. Have Egypt withdraw recognition from and break its peace treaty with Israel (+1 point)

#### To Avoid

1. Recognizing and signing a peace treaty with Israel (–3 points)
2. Getting involved in a war (–2 points)

#### To Avoid at All Cost

The United States and Soviet Union committing their military strength (not military aid) on opposite sides of a conflict. If the two superpowers enter on either side of a conflict, the conflict quickly becomes a nuclear war. Everyone receives a final score of –10 points and the exercise comes to an immediate end.

Getting conquered means an automatic final score of –10 points.

#### Remember

The group must prepare a three-page briefing on the economic, political, and social conditions of the nation in the early 1980s. How did these conditions shape your nation's needs?

All agreements should be written into the treaty protocol.

#### Military Conflict

If one side, either in the Iran–Iraq War or in the tense Egypt–Syria–Jordan–PLO versus Israel situation musters twice the military strength of the opponent, that side is able to conquer its opponent. At the start of the conference neither side is in that position, but one side or the other may get strong enough with support from either the United States or Soviet Union. In addition to contributing troops, the United States and Soviet Union are able to aid countries by giving military aid (in which case the superpowers are not considered to be directly involved in the fighting). Each $1 billion in military aid produces one-quarter million more troops. Only certain countries can be attacked in this game. Only Israel, Egypt, Jordan, Syria, Iraq, and Iran can be attacked. The PLO, United States, and Soviet Union also have military capabilities, but they can only be used offensively—these countries cannot be attacked.

If one nation announces that it is attacking another, the announcement must be publicly made in the conference circle. At that point, any allied nations joining in the attack must announce themselves. Once all attacking nations have announced themselves, any nations coming to the defense of the victim should announce themselves. If the attack is repulsed, all invading countries lose one-third of their armed forces (round down), while the defender(s) lose nothing. If the attack succeeds, the attacked nation ceases to exist, and its members join the victorious groups.

### Country Profile Sheet 6   JORDAN

#### Resources

Military strength: 1 million troops

#### Goals

1. Israel relinquishing control of the West Bank, either peacefully or by being conquered (+4 points)

2. The ability to redirect the Jordan River's water supply away from Israel, although the same effect can be achieved with $6 billion in economic aid for water development (+3 points)

3. Israel relinquishing control of East Jerusalem, either peacefully or by being conquered (+2 points)

4. Have Egypt withdraw recognition from and break its peace treaty with Israel (+1 point)

#### To Avoid

1. Recognizing and signing a peace treaty with Israel (–3 points)

2. Getting involved in a war (–2 points)

#### To Avoid at All Cost

The United States and Soviet Union committing their military strength (not military aid) on opposite sides of a conflict. If the two superpowers enter on either side of a conflict, the conflict quickly becomes a nuclear war. Everyone receives a final score of –10 points and the exercise comes to an immediate end.

Getting conquered means an automatic final score of –10 points.

#### Remember

The group must prepare a three-page briefing on the economic, political, and social conditions of the nation in the early 1980s. How did these conditions shape your nation's needs?

All agreements should be written into the treaty protocol.

#### Military Conflict

If one side, either in the Iran–Iraq War or in the tense Egypt–Syria–Jordan–PLO versus Israel situation musters twice the military strength of the opponent, that side is able to conquer its opponent. At the start of the conference neither side is in that position, but one side or the other may get strong enough with support from either the United States or Soviet Union. In addition to contributing troops, the United States and Soviet Union are able to aid countries by giving military aid (in which case the superpowers are not considered to be directly involved in the fighting). Each $1 billion in military aid produces one-quarter million more troops. Only certain countries can be attacked in this game. Only Israel, Egypt, Jordan, Syria, Iraq, and Iran can be attacked. The PLO, United States, and Soviet Union also have military capabilities, but they can only be used offensively—these countries cannot be attacked.

If one nation announces that it is attacking another, the announcement must be publicly made in the conference circle. At that point, any allied nations joining in the attack must announce themselves. Once all attacking nations have announced themselves, any nations coming to the defense of the victim should announce themselves. If the attack is repulsed, all invading countries lose one-third of their armed forces (round down), while the defender(s) lose nothing. If the attack succeeds, the attacked nation ceases to exist, and its members join the victorious groups.

## Country Profile Sheet 7    LEBANON

### *Goals*

1. Israeli army out of Lebanon (+5 points)

2. The ability to redirect the Jordan River's water supply away from Israel, although the same effect can be achieved with $6 billion in economic aid for water development (+3 points)

3. Receiving $3 billion in military aid (+2 points)

### *To Avoid*

1. Having Israeli troops remain in Lebanon (–2 points)

2. Having PLO troops remain in Lebanon (–1 point)

3. Having Israel be recognized by any of its Arab neighbors (–1 point)

### *To Avoid at All Cost*

The United States and Soviet Union committing their military strength (not military aid) on opposite sides of a conflict. If the two superpowers enter on either side of a conflict, the conflict quickly becomes a nuclear war. Everyone receives a final score of –10 points and the exercise comes to an immediate end.

### *Remember*

The group must prepare a three-page briefing on the economic, political, and social conditions of the nation in the early 1980s. How did these conditions shape your nation's needs?

### *Military Conflict*

If one side, either in the Iran–Iraq War or in the tense Egypt–Syria–Jordan–PLO versus Israel situation musters twice the military strength of the opponent, that side is able to conquer its opponent. At the start of the conference neither side is in that position, but one side or the other may get strong enough with support from either the United States or Soviet Union. In addition to contributing troops, the United States and Soviet Union are able to aid countries by giving military aid (in which case the superpowers are not considered to be directly involved in the fighting). Each $1 billion in military aid produces one-quarter million more troops. Only certain countries can be attacked in this game. Only Israel, Egypt, Jordan, Syria, Iraq, and Iran can be attacked. The PLO, United States, and Soviet Union also have military capabilities, but they can only be used offensively—these countries cannot be attacked.

If one nation announces that it is attacking another, the announcement must be publicly made in the conference circle. At that point, any allied nations joining in the attack must announce themselves. Once all attacking nations have announced themselves, any nations coming to the defense of the victim should announce themselves. If the attack is repulsed, all invading countries lose one-third of their armed forces (round down), while the defender(s) lose nothing. If the attack succeeds, the attacked nation ceases to exist, and its members join the victorious groups.

## Country Profile Sheet 8 EGYPT

### Resources

Military strength: 2 million troops

Oil production: 3 million barrels per day

### Goals

1. Work out agreement with Syria and Jordan in which they agree to forgive Egypt for its recognition of Israel (+4 points)
2. Have Israel reach peace treaty with PLO, Syria, and Jordan (+3 points)
3. Receive $5 billion in military aid (+2 points)
4. Receive Gaza Strip back from Israel (+1 point)

### To Avoid

1. Getting less military aid than Israel (–3 points)
2. Having a war break out between Israel and any of its neighbors (–3 points)
3. Having to take military aid from the Soviet Union (–1 point)

### To Avoid at All Cost

The United States and Soviet Union committing their military strength (not military aid) on opposite sides of a conflict. If the two superpowers enter on either side of a conflict, the conflict quickly becomes a nuclear war. Everyone receives a final score of –10 points and the exercise comes to an immediate end.

Getting conquered means an automatic final score of –10 points.

### Remember

The group must prepare a three-page briefing on the economic, political, and social conditions of the nation in the early 1980s. How did these conditions shape your nation's needs?

### Military Conflict

If one side, either in the Iran–Iraq War or in the tense Egypt–Syria–Jordan–PLO versus Israel situation musters twice the military strength of the opponent, that side is able to conquer its opponent. At the start of the conference neither side is in that position, but one side or the other may get strong enough with support from either the United States or Soviet Union. In addition to contributing troops, the United States and Soviet Union are able to aid countries by giving military aid (in which case the superpowers are not considered to be directly involved in the fighting). Each $1 billion in military aid produces one-quarter million more troops. Only certain countries can be attacked in this game. Only Israel, Egypt, Jordan, Syria, Iraq, and Iran can be attacked. The PLO, United States, and Soviet Union also have military capabilities, but they can only be used offensively—these countries cannot be attacked.

If one nation announces that it is attacking another, the announcement must be publicly made in the conference circle. At that point, any allied nations joining in the attack must announce themselves. Once all attacking nations have announced themselves, any nations coming to the defense of the victim should announce them- selves. If the attack is repulsed, all invading countries lose one-third of their armed forces (round down), while the defender(s) lose nothing. If the attack succeeds, the attacked nation ceases to exist, and its members join the victorious groups.

### Country Profile Sheet 9   SAUDI ARABIA

#### Resources

Economic aid to give: $5 billion

Oil production: 9 million barrels per day

#### Goals

1. Receive $7 billion in military aid (+4 points)
2. Having no military conflict break out during the conference (+4 points)
3. Get a homeland for the Palestinians (+2 points)

#### To Avoid

1. Having Iran defeat Iraq in their war (–3 points)
2. Having any more Arab countries recognize and sign peace treaties with Israel (–3 points)

#### To Avoid at All Cost

The United States and Soviet Union committing their military strength (not military aid) on opposite sides of a conflict. If the two superpowers enter on either side of a conflict, the conflict quickly becomes a nuclear war. Everyone receives a final score of –10 points and the exercise comes to an immediate end.

#### Remember

The group must prepare a three-page briefing on the economic, political, and social conditions of the nation in the early 1980s. How did these conditions shape your nation's needs?

#### Military Conflict

If one side, either in the Iran–Iraq War or in the tense Egypt–Syria–Jordan–PLO versus Israel situation musters twice the military strength of the opponent, that side is able to conquer its opponent. At the start of the conference neither side is in that position, but one side or the other may get strong enough with support from either the United States or Soviet Union. In addition to contributing troops, the United States and Soviet Union are able to aid countries by giving military aid (in which case the superpowers are not considered to be directly involved in the fighting). Each $1 billion in military aid produces one-quarter million more troops. Only certain countries can be attacked in this game. Only Israel, Egypt, Jordan, Syria, Iraq, and Iran can be attacked. The PLO, United States, and Soviet Union also have military capabilities, but they can only be used offensively—these countries cannot be attacked.

If one nation announces that it is attacking another, the announcement must be publicly made in the conference circle. At that point, any allied nations joining in the attack must announce themselves. Once all attacking nations have announced themselves, any nations coming to the defense of the victim should announce them-selves. If the attack is repulsed, all invading countries lose one-third of their armed forces (round down), while the defender(s) lose nothing. If the attack succeeds, the attacked nation ceases to exist, and its members join the victorious groups.

## Country Profile Sheet 10   IRAN

### Resources

Military strength: 3 million troops

Oil production: 3 million barrels per day

### Goals

1. Reach peace treaty with Iraq (+4 points)
2. Convince Egypt, Syria, Jordan, and PLO to refuse American military or economic aid (+3 points)
3. Getting $4 billion in economic aid (+3 points)

### To Avoid

1. Having PLO, Syria, and Jordan sign peace treaty with Israel (–3 points)
2. Having Soviet Union give military aid or troops to Iraq (–2 points)
3. Having to accept aid or troops from the United States (–1 point)

### To Avoid at All Cost

The United States and Soviet Union committing their military strength (not military aid) on opposite sides of a conflict. If the two superpowers enter on either side of a conflict, the conflict quickly becomes a nuclear war. Everyone receives a final score of –10 points and the exercise comes to an immediate end.

Getting conquered means an automatic final score of –10 points.

### Remember

The group must prepare a three-page briefing on the economic, political, and social conditions of the nation in the early 1980s. How did these conditions shape your nation's needs?

### Military Conflict

If one side, either in the Iran–Iraq War or in the tense Egypt–Syria–Jordan–PLO versus Israel situation musters twice the military strength of the opponent, that side is able to conquer its opponent. At the start of the conference neither side is in that position, but one side or the other may get strong enough with support from either the United States or Soviet Union. In addition to contributing troops, the United States and Soviet Union are able to aid countries by giving military aid (in which case the superpowers are not considered to be directly involved in the fighting). Each $1 billion in military aid produces one-quarter million more troops. Only certain countries can be attacked in this game. Only Israel, Egypt, Jordan, Syria, Iraq, and Iran can be attacked. The PLO, United States, and Soviet Union also have military capabilities, but they can only be used offensively—these countries cannot be attacked.

If one nation announces that it is attacking another, the announcement must be publicly made in the conference circle. At that point, any allied nations joining in the attack must announce themselves. Once all attacking nations have announced themselves, any nations coming to the defense of the victim should announce themselves. If the attack is repulsed, all invading countries lose one-third of their armed forces (round down), while the defender(s) lose nothing. If the attack succeeds, the attacked nation ceases to exist, and its members join the victorious groups.

## Country Profile Sheet 11  IRAQ

### *Resources*

Military strength: 3 million troops

Oil production: 3 million barrels per day

### *Goals*

1. Conquer Iran (+5 points) or reach a peace treaty with Iran (+3 points)
2. Receive $6 billion in military aid (+3 points)
3. Receive $4 billion in economic aid (+2 points)

### *To Avoid*

1. An unsuccessful attack on Iran (–3 points)
2. Having Iran get military aid or troops from United States or Soviet Union (–2 points)
3. Having PLO, Syria, and Jordan sign peace treaty with Israel (–1 point)

### *To Avoid at All Cost*

The United States and Soviet Union committing their military strength (not military aid) on opposite sides of a conflict. If the two superpowers enter on either side of a conflict, the conflict quickly becomes a nuclear war. Everyone receives a final score of –10 points and the exercise comes to an immediate end.

Getting conquered means an automatic final score of –10 points.

### *Remember*

The group must prepare a three-page briefing on the economic, political, and social conditions of the nation in the early 1980s. How did these conditions shape your nation's needs?

### *Military Conflict*

If one side, either in the Iran–Iraq War or in the tense Egypt–Syria–Jordan–PLO versus Israel situation musters twice the military strength of the opponent, that side is able to conquer its opponent. At the start of the conference neither side is in that position, but one side or the other may get strong enough with support from either the United States or Soviet Union. In addition to contributing troops, the United States and Soviet Union are able to aid countries by giving military aid (in which case the superpowers are not considered to be directly involved in the fighting). Each $1 billion in military aid produces one-quarter million more troops. Only certain countries can be attacked in this game. Only Israel, Egypt, Jordan, Syria, Iraq, and Iran can be attacked. The PLO, United States, and Soviet Union also have military capabilities, but they can only be used offensively—these countries cannot be attacked.

If one nation announces that it is attacking another, the announcement must be publicly made in the conference circle. At that point, any allied nations joining in the attack must announce themselves. Once all attacking nations have announced themselves, any nations coming to the defense of the victim should announce themselves. If the attack is repulsed, all invading countries lose one-third of their armed forces (round down), while the defender(s) lose nothing. If the attack succeeds, the attacked nation ceases to exist, and its members join the victorious groups.

# CHAPTER 6
# *Choosing a President*

*The classroom becomes a political convention charged with selecting a president. Even better, the class is not a modern convention with a predetermined outcome, but is a multicandidate, deadlocked convention with state delegation bosses, special interest leaders seeking to break state delegations, and aspiring governors and senators.*

*Students play all the various roles and the positional incentives are designed so that the students are tugged in different directions. The result is usually a boisterous affair, featuring bandwagons, dark horses, broken delegations, backroom deals, and avaricious special interests. The cast of characters was loosely based on the candidates at the 1988 Democratic convention, which provides a useful overview of some of the key issues and figures in 1980s politics.*

## TEACHER'S NOTE

The game is designed to introduce students to the notion of old-fashioned political power, to politics the way it was played in the years stretching from the rise of the party bosses in the middle of the nineteenth century until the fragmentation of party control in the 1950s and 1960s. The simulation acquaints students with the ins and outs of traditional power politics, and with the fundamental principles and mechanics of presidential conventions. Along the way, students are exposed to political players who interact with the executive branch, and to the role of campaign finances, issues, and "bandwagon" effects.

This is probably the most "political" simulation in this book. I consider it also to be the most exquisitely crafted and most subtle of the simulations, but you should note that this care in crafting has made it the most complicated and difficult to play. The exercise has prompted everything from student poems (one of which began, memorably, "First there was Dukakis, but he had shallow pockets . . .") to frenzied, long-running, caffeine-sustained, after-school negotiating sessions. I still remember the time that the head of the AFL-CIO got the Vice Presidential nod in a deal that took shape while four students were waiting in the main office to fill out tardy slips. The deal apparently included two campaigns, four state bosses, and three interest groups. One of the members of that tardy-slip putsch got so taken with politics that she started subscribing to the *New Republic* the week after the exercise.

Political conventions, at least as practiced in the late nineteenth and twentieth centuries, provided high theater. Scandals, nominations, major legislation, and domestic crises have supplied spectacular moments in contemporary politics—but few of these touch the drama inherent in a contested political convention. Multiple candidates, advocating different visions of their party's future, pulled levers behind closed doors and manipulated mob psychology to win the highest office in the land. *Choosing a President* is designed to allow students to experience the thrills, tactics, and strategy of those conventions, in order to lay bare and let students savor the classic politics of a bygone era.

This exercise was first used to illustrate late nineteenth century presidential politics in an 11th-grade American History class, but I have also used it with even more effective results in 10th-grade American Civics. Colleagues have also reported using the simulation effectively in Contemporary Issues and American Government classes. The actual simulation generally takes about two class periods, but teachers should teach some background material prior to the exercise.

The essence of the game is that five presidential candidates, and a few possible "dark horse" candidates, seek the nomination at a deadlocked convention. Each candidate, depending on the size of the class, has a campaign manager. Other students play bosses of major state delegations, controlling large blocs of votes, or interest group leaders who control pools of campaign cash and chunks of votes within each state delegation. Candidates arrive with a pledged number of delegates that is far short of the number needed for nomination. All the nonpledged votes are initially controlled by the state bosses. However, special interest groups control varying numbers of votes in the states. The special interest leaders are able to break the grip the state bosses have over their delegations by coordinating to claim control of 51% of the votes in a given state's delegation and agreeing on a candidate to back. At that point, when special interests have "broken" some delegations and control blocs of votes while unbroken bosses in other states control their full delegation, broken state bosses control some votes and are negotiating with special interests to regain control of their delegation, and the presidential campaigns struggle to round up votes, the game gets interesting.

The romance of the classic political convention has been largely lost to changes in American politics, communications, and the media. Changes in the rules of political parties and the democratization of the nomination process have ensured that the nominees are now generally known before the convention commences. To bring party conventions to life, it helps to revive the context and rules of the early twentieth-century convention.

Two major elements help to resurrect this ambiance. First, unlike nearly all nomination contests in recent decades, no one arrives at the convention with a majority of delegates. Second, the unit rule, used by the men who controlled state delegations in the nineteenth and early twentieth century to reinforce their dominance, is resurrected. The *unit rule* permits a majority of a state's delegation to vote the entire delegation in a given direction, greatly enhancing the power of state bosses.

Players are motivated to play the game in a realistic fashion. Students are given specific characters and incentives and are evaluated, in part, on their diligence in fulfilling their assigned role. Student incentives serve to foster a chaotic and delicate balance, helping to produce a torrid bout of negotiating and deal-making.

The status of the state delegations is tracked on the chalkboard, helping the students become aware that the class is the scene of two nested, frenzied negotiations. The first is the effort of presidential campaigns to win support from bosses and interest groups. The second is the intricate negotiations between interest group leaders trying to "break" delegations so that they can control blocs of votes and state bosses trying to protect 51% of their delegations so that they retain their power base.

Particularly fun are the game's less savory elements. First is the pressure of campaign finance. Special interest representatives come to the convention with campaign funds that they can contribute to candidates or to state bosses. Second, the *bandwagon effect* encourages bosses and interest group leaders to try and make sure they are backing the nominee (just as in real life). This produces the semicomic, and realistic, effect of students scrambling from one candidate to another as the identity of the frontrunner changes.

I have taken certain liberties in designing this exercise. To contemporize the lesson and add to its usefulness, the cast of characters has been loosely based on the Democratic political convention of 1988. This change makes the key issues and actors easier to grasp and raises some of the late- and post-Cold War substantive issues which often do not receive much attention in history classes.

## BACKGROUND ON POLITICAL PARTY CONVENTIONS

The U.S. Constitution provides for presidential selection by means of a rickety structure known as the Electoral College. Every four years, electors are selected for the purpose of choosing a new president. In the first two presidential elections, the task of the electors was simple, as the college unanimously elected George Washington to the presidency. During Washington's term in office, however, the body politic split into two opposed camps. The new nation's political dialog quickly polarized into a conflict between the Federalists and the Anti-Federalists, giving rise to the two-party system. By the early years of the nineteenth century, the tradition of each party coalescing behind a single nominee for the presidency had become entrenched.

In these early years of the republic, each party selected its nominee with minimal public input. In each party, nominees were chosen by the Party Caucus, which consisted of U.S. Senators and Representatives of each party. The Party Caucus selected the early presidential nominees in closed discussion. The Caucus generally decided on a national figure from among themselves, the vice president, and the president's cabinet. Party caucuses dominated the presidential nomination process until the more inclusive Party conventions emerged in the 1820s and 1830s, spurred by the election of populist Democrat

Andrew Jackson in 1828. Party conventions were gatherings of chosen party members from each state who came together primarily for the purpose of selecting a nominee.

As suffrage was expanded and as the two-party system became entrenched in American political life, the selection of presidential nominees became more inclusive. However, this inclusiveness did not spread to the popular election of delegates to the Party conventions. The idea of selecting delegates in popular primaries would not gain currency until the Progressive era at the dawn of the twentieth century. Even then, primaries were only important because they signaled a candidate's broad appeal. Delegates to the conventions were selected at caucuses that were generally controlled by the leaders of the state political parties. Primaries did not become a significant means of selecting Party convention delegates until the 1970s.

During the 1800s, as the nation spread westward across the continent and as the parties, in turn, became more geographically diffuse, Party conventions became an opportunity for party leaders, officeholders, and organizers to gather and reach common understandings. At the quadrennial conventions, in addition to choosing the party's presidential nominee, these leaders would address necessary issues and administer party business. The men who controlled the politics in each state tended to be big-city mayors or behind-the-scenes operatives, and were often referred to as political *bosses*. Because the two major parties were very much an alliance of state organizations, rather than centrally controlled bodies, the priority for convention attendees was to ensure that decisions made and nominees selected would not hurt their state party. This was particularly true in the nineteenth century, when the state and local governments controlled vast amounts of patronage and public money that could be used to control large blocs of urban voters.

## The Decline of the State Bosses and Political Party Leaders

Until the New Deal Era began in 1932, the federal government remained a less significant and less lucrative concern than the state governments. It was important to win national office and useful to have a strong candidate at the "top of the party ticket," but not so important that state leaders were willing to lose control of their organizations or have a presidential nominee who opposed their stance on a major issue.

One result of this system was that fierce convention battles, deadlocked conventions, and dark-horse (long-shot) candidates were commonplace during the 1860 to 1940 period. Dark-horse candidates would often take the nomination from better-known and more imposing men, precisely because the eventual nominee was less threatening to the independence and power of sectional interests and state leaders.

Reformers fought steadily to change this system, winning the first of a long series of victories in the 1880s. The reformers struck their first serious blow at traditional party systems in 1883, when the Pendleton Act created a federal civil service for the first time. The Pendleton Act was passed by Congress during the furor that erupted after a disappointed political office seeker assassinated President James Garfield. The civil service was intended to fill jobs on the basis of merit, rather than allowing presidents to staff the jobs with their allies or supporters. Over the next 40 or 50 years, the reach of the civil service system gradually expanded until it included almost all federal jobs. This struck directly at the power base of the bosses and party leaders.

During the Progressive movement in the early twentieth century, political reforms helped to democratize the parties and further reduced the power of the party bosses. Changes, such as the direct election of U.S. Senators and the introduction of party primaries, opened up the political process and reduced the power of those who controlled the political machines.

In the 1930s, Franklin Roosevelt's "New Deal" struck even more heavily at the power of party politicians. By dramatically increasing the scope of federal government activity and by shifting services from localities to large national agencies, Roosevelt rendered superfluous many of the services that bosses and state party leaders provided. Now, the poor and unemployed in need of assistance could turn somewhere besides to their local party boss. The growth of various programs, such as the Tennessee Valley Authority, social security, and Aid to Dependent Children, in the years after World War II dramatically eroded the power of local political chiefs.

## The Declining Role of the Party Conventions

The shrinking role of local political bosses was soon matched by declining significance of national party conventions. Advances in communication and transportation during the early twentieth century meant that it was no longer unusual for party leaders to meet and discuss their concerns and needs. The introduction of the telephone, radio, and television meant that sectional leaders were much more familiar with one another and the roster of potential nominees.

Additionally, America's growing international responsibilities and the increased role of the federal government meant that sectional differences became increasingly less significant. Trade-offs among sectional leaders became less problematic, while the president's actual policies and ability to lead the nation became a larger concern for party members. The result was that the selection of presidential nominees became a national concern, shifting the decision from the small coterie of state bosses who had traditionally shaped each party's decisions.

Finally, changes in election rules and campaigning dramatically reworked the role of the conventions in the 1950s and 1960s. Presidential primaries became a standard feature in a handful of states, giving the voters a direct opportunity to register their preferences among the candidates. This marked a dramatic change from the old caucus system, in which state party leaders would confer among themselves and select the state's convention delegation—generally ensuring that the slate was primarily loyal to the state boss. After the reforms of the late 1960s and early 1970s, primaries became the dominant form of delegate selection. Rather than candidates running in a few primaries for show, while primarily winning convention delegates by negotiating with state leaders, the nomination process became a long public campaign in which nominees traveled from one primary state to the next.

The expenses of traveling, opinion polling, and advertising made the presidential primaries into an expensive war of attrition by the late 1970s. By the early 1980s, the first few primaries served to eliminate all but the top two or three candidates in each party. This winnowing mechanism, along with massive attention generated for the front-runner by national television and the national press, ensured that one candidate would arrive at the convention with enough votes to win on the first ballot. In fact, no candidate has failed to win a first-ballot convention victory since World War II.

## USING THIS SIMULATION

### Purpose of the Simulation

*Choosing a President* is intended to increase student interest in politics and government by exposing them to some of the most exciting political theater ever contrived. The exercise introduces students to the hows and whys of executive selection, with an emphasis on a historical perspective. In doing so, it helps to explain why the United States selected the presidents it did during the 1840–1960 era, and how changes in that system continue to influence the presidents we select today.

### Skills Developed

*Choosing a President* develops negotiating, math reasoning, and analytic skills. Students are equipped with different kinds of financial, vote-based, and positional resources, and each of them must marshal these resources and find points of agreement with class-mates who have other resources and other goals. The need to manage delicate negotiations while everyone else in the class is engaging in the same kind of frenetic activity, can produce intense energy and focus.

The exercise also cultivates analytic skills as students seek to position themselves within the constantly evolving milieu of the convention "horse race." To be effective, students need to keep track of who is committed to which candidate, which alliances appear nascent, who controls how many votes, and what other resources are possessed and by whom. Effective analysis requires not just the ability to see the big picture, but also paying careful attention to what classmates are doing and applying basic mathematical and deductive skills.

## Logistics

Introducing and then playing the simulation takes roughly two or three 40-minute classes. The length of the exercise will depend in large part on how the teacher runs the class and the chemistry of the students involved. Students are assigned particular roles to play during the course of the exercise. Roles contain no gender identifiers, maximizing the teacher's flexibility in assigning roles and eliminating concerns about sexist role assignment.

Students play the roles of the 5 candidates (and, in a large class, their 5 campaign managers), 11 state delegation bosses, and 9 special interest leaders. The game was initially designed for a class of 25 to 30. In larger classes, students can be paired to play the roles of special interest leaders, allowing the exercise to accommodate up to 38. In smaller classes, doing away with campaign managers and dropping certain special interest leaders and state delegations means the exercise will work for a class as small as 19 students.

The exercise requires some preparation on the part of the teacher. The teacher needs to photocopy the Student Profile sheets for each student and photocopy the Special Occurrence slips and cut into strips (see Appendix). These strips determine which student will play which role. Then, write the presidential vote chart on the chalkboard (see Exhibit 6.1). Students are given the appropriate profile sheet the day before the exercise begins. On the day of the exercise the teacher should put the Special Occurrence slips into a hat, bowl, or some similar object from which they can be drawn.

---

**SMALLER CLASSES**

For classes of fewer than 25 students the teacher will need to forego some of the special interests and state delegations. Although this causes some slight imbalances in the vulnerability of state delegations and the distribution of power, great care has been taken to ensure that all the major state delegations are vulnerable to being "broken" and that no interest groups or state bosses are tremendously hurt or advantaged by the changes. In smaller classes the teacher should eliminate the following players from the game:

- class of 24 students—don't use business interest group
- class of 23 students—also don't use civil rights interest group
- class of 22 students—also don't use Massachusetts delegation
- class of 21 students—also don't use Washington delegation
- class of 20 students—also don't use North Carolina delegation
- class of 19 students—also don't use Michigan delegation

For classes in which the teacher has to eliminate some of the delegations, it is important for the teacher to recalculate the total number of votes in the game. There are normally 3,900 votes in the full game. Massachusetts, Washington, and North Carolina each control 150 votes. So dropping Massachusetts yields a vote total of 3,750; also dropping Washington lowers the total to 3,600; also dropping North Carolina lowers it to 3,450; and also dropping Michigan (200 votes) lowers it to 3,250. Since the winning nominee needs to claim one vote more than 50%, the winning vote total in the 19-student game drops from 1,951 to 1,626.

**EXHIBIT 6.1 Sample Chalkboard Chart**

|                    | *Harper* | *Jacobson* | *Duke* | *Stiffner* | *Gillespie* |
| ------------------ | -------- | ---------- | ------ | ---------- | ----------- |
| Base votes         |          |            |        |            |             |
| State votes        |          |            |        |            |             |
| Spec interest votes |         |            |        |            |             |
| **Total votes**    |          |            |        |            |             |

After explaining the exercise, the teacher should prominently write the number of votes needed for the nomination on the board and then take an initial ballot. First, the teacher should call out each of the candidates and record their initial levels of support. (Initial votes are noted on the profile sheet of each candidate.) The teacher should then call out the state delegations to see if they are voting for any candidate. The state delegations will mostly be uncommitted at this point. Any votes cast for candidates should be added to candidate support on the board, in order to keep a running tally (see Sample Chalkboard Chart in Exhibit 6.1). If special interests have gained control of any votes, the teacher should call on those interests after the state bosses cast the votes they control. The figures from the initial tally should be left on the board until the second ballot is called, when the initial figures should be erased and the new figures written in as this procedure is repeated.

The most difficult element of this exercise is explaining a couple of the relatively confusing rules to students. The two particularly confusing elements in this game are the notion of "breaking" state delegations and the way points are scored.

This is one of the more complex exercises in the book. It does not necessarily require a long time to explain to students (20–25 minutes should suffice), but it is vital that students pay careful attention to the guidelines. If students do not, they can find the exercise very frustrating.

## HOW THE SIMULATION WORKS

### Student Roles

Except for the presidential candidates, who are normally played by two students (a candidate and a campaign manager), each role is generally played by a single student. The candidates are represented both by the candidate and by a campaign manager, because they are the hub of all the activity. For exceptionally large classes, it is possible to pair up students for the interest group roles.

### Object

The objective is for one candidate to claim the nomination by winning a majority of votes. However, the exercise is constructed so that there are numerous winners, as different students all seek to "win" different things from the convention. Students score points in various ways. One key consideration is that the winning candidate will also need to name a vice president, two members of his or her cabinet, and positions on six key issues. All players have a stake in some or all of those decisions. The multiple incentives have been set up so that all students have a roughly equal chance to score points (with a score of about 10 points typical, and a score over 15 extremely high).

There are six different ways for students to score points. The points are structured to help students concentrate on their objectives. The following are the six ways that points can be scored:

1. *Winning the nomination*: Any player, not just the announced candidates, can conceivably win the nomination. However, the candidates have the advantage of their unchallenged baseline votes and an ability to completely concentrate on the

nomination. Presidential candidates receive 12 points if they win the nomination, state bosses win 10 if they do, and special interest leaders win 6 if they do.

2. *Being the vice president*: Anyone can be named the vice president (VP). It's not the prize of choice, but it is a heck of a lot better than nothing. Presidential nominees win 5 points for being named VP by the winner, bosses win 7 points if they are VP, and special interest leaders win 6 if they are named.

3. *Being named a cabinet secretary*: Candidates often come to implicit under-standings about whom they intend to appoint to their cabinet. At the convention, candidates are allowed to promise two cabinet positions to supporters. These positions are worth a good deal to special interest leaders and a fair bit to bosses, but less to rival candidates. Candidates win 3 points for being given a cabinet post, bosses win 4 points, and special interest leaders win 6 points.

4. *Bandwagon effect*: Everybody wants to be part of the winning team. Bosses and special interest group leaders who vote for the winner on the winning ballot receive 3 points, assuming they control some votes at that point (see the Rules of the Game section for discussion of when students will or will not control votes).

5. *Campaign funds*: Interest groups have campaign funds to donate. Nominees and bosses each get 1 point for every $10,000 they are able to collect in campaign contributions.

6. *Issues*: Finally, politics is, after all, about policy. Each interest group leader, boss, and nominee has issue preferences. There are six issues that the nominee will have to take a stand on in his or her fall campaign. During the game, candidates must indicate what their policies will be in the fall campaign. Candidates are permitted to shift their positions as they negotiate. Points are scored when the winning nominee's final position on an issue matches the player's preferred position. Candidates have four issue preferences, and receive 1 point for each one that matches the nominee's campaign position. Bosses are more focused. They have two issue preferences and receive 2 points for each one that matches the nominee's campaign position. Special interest groups are highly focused, with just two issue preferences. They receive 4 points for each one that matches the nominee's campaign position. *A nominee is free to go against his or her issue preferences to win support from bosses, special interests, or opponents.*

## Length of Game

The teacher should be prepared for this simulation to take about two days. It generally takes a round of balloting or two for students to really get a feel for what's going on. The latter portion of the first class and the first half of the second class are generally the most useful period. Finally, students start to become frustrated and search for ways to resolve the stalemate.

## How the Game Is Played

At the beginning of the simulation each of the presidential candidates enters the con-vention with a predetermined number of votes. The candidates seek to add votes to this total by allying with state delegation bosses, with special interest leaders, and with one an-other (by convincing a challenger to accept the vice presidency or a cabinet post in return for his or her support). The nominee requires a majority vote to win. While candidates are pursuing votes, interest group leaders and state bosses are seeking to influence policy po-sitions and cabinet selections while maximizing their leverage by controlling all the votes they possibly can.

So long as five candidates are in the race it is extremely difficult for a winner to emerge. What happens, often sooner rather than later, is that candidates begin to drop out of the race in return for vice presidential bids. However, the designed fragmentation of votes ensures that even a ticket featuring two presidential candidates still has a great deal of work to do with state delegations and interest groups in order to claim the nomination. The vote totals and incentives have been balanced so that these duos will have trouble assembling the support necessary to put them over the top.

In the midst of all this, the teacher injects special occurrences at his or her discretion. Special occurrences are a series of random events intended to shake up the convention status quo and instill some of the uncertainty characteristic of nominating conventions. The teacher can find these events listed on Special Occurrence slips in the Appendix. These occurrences may entail a shift of votes, a delegation's decision to temporarily leave the convention, or a sudden influx of campaign funds.

The game continues, through alternating rounds of balloting and negotiating, until one candidate claims enough votes to win the nomination.

## Rules of the Game

Each student is either a candidate, a campaign manager, a state delegation head, or an interest group leader. The student's behavior is guided by a set of incentives based on certain objectives (e.g., a cabinet position, more financing for the campaign, ideological directives, being with a winner) and on policy preferences. Of course, students can disregard these incentives, but I find that they generally play along. I have had fellow teachers attempt to run this simulation without the incentives, and the problem there is that students then feel completely free to assist their friends or to do what they think would be cool. That tends to undermine the lessons modeled in the exercise.

***Majority of Delegates to Win***   To claim the nomination, the winning presidential nominee has to win a majority of the votes cast. Since there are 3,900 votes available in the game, that means that the winner needs to claim 1,951 votes to win.

***Vote Breakdown***   There are 3,900 total votes at the convention. At the beginning of the convention, there are a total of 1,600 delegates committed to the five candidates. These supporters never abandon their favored candidate unless a special occurrence indicates that they should. The other 2,300 votes are controlled by the state bosses, at least at the beginning. These 2,300 delegates are also committed to various special interest groups. The leaders of these groups are able to access the delegates' votes if the special interests can break the state boss's unit-rule hold on the delegations.

***The Unit Rule***   Whoever controls 51% of a state's votes is able to control the entire vote of the state delegation. So long as special interests cannot agree on how to control 50% of a state's votes, the boss retains control. If special interests controlling 50% or more of a state's votes can agree on a candidate to support, then they can cast those votes for that candidate and the state boss loses control of those votes. Further, if special interests can agree on whom to support with 51% or more of a state's delegation, then they can use the unit rule to control the entire delegation. The unit rule does not require players to control the entire delegation just because they control 51% of the votes. It is perfectly okay for players to only vote the delegates they control rather than using the unit rule to control 100% of the votes.

When might a student not exercise the unit rule? When the student is sufficiently good-hearted or sufficiently worried about losing a majority, he or she reaches an agreement with others who control part of the state's delegation. For instance, a state boss with a tenuous majority might agree to not exercise the unit rule if special interest leaders with votes in the state delegation agree not to break the delegation.

***Breaking Delegations***   At the beginning of the convention, the 11 state bosses each control their state's delegation. However, most of the members in each state's delegation are also affiliated with one of several interest groups. Those delegates are useless to the interest groups so long as they are controlled by a state boss using the unit rule. To get use of those delegates, the interest groups need to stop the state boss from using the unit rule. This requires one of two approaches. First, the interest group leader or leaders can work out a compromise with the boss. Second, the interest groups with supporters in a

---

**BREAKING DELEGATIONS**

Breaking delegations is easiest to understand, and easiest to explain to a class, through an example. Take Ohio. There are 200 delegates in the Ohio delegation. Seventy members are completely loyal to the boss, and 130 delegates are also members of particular interest groups. Looking at the Teacher's Matrix of State Delegations (see Appendix), you will see that 20 members of the Ohio delegation are members of the business group, 40 are members of the labor group, 30 members are members of the agriculture group, and 40 are members of the social conservative group.

At the beginning of the game, no one except the teacher knows the entire breakdown of the delegations. Students only know about their own delegates, and must talk to their classmates to figure out who else controls delegates and how many they control. Once the special interest leaders realize what they have, there are several ways they could exert control over the Ohio delegates. If the labor, agriculture, and social conservative interests can agree to vote their 110 delegates for one candidate, then they gain control of those votes. By using the unit rule, this alliance could control all 200 Ohio delegates, if they so wished. (They might not wish to do so, for instance, if they thought that the state boss would be motivated to find a way to split their fragile coalition.) Likewise, a four-party alliance that also included business would control 130 votes, and could wield the entire delegation. A labor, social conservative, and business alliance—assuming they were able to agree on one candidate—would control 100 votes, exactly 50% of the delegation. This alliance could vote their 100 delegates for one candidate, and the Ohio boss would still control the other 100 delegates. The key here is that these interest groups, with very different objectives and interests, have to find a way to overcome their differences and cooperate.

---

particular state must cooperate in order to cast their votes for one particular candidate and to break the boss's hold on the delegation.

***Special Occurrences***    The Special Occurrence slips (see Appendix) replicate the kinds of random events that can shake up a convention. A teacher should feel free to pull out a random event at least once per ballot, and perhaps twice per ballot if the teacher thinks it will add to the exercise. Special Occurrence slips are self-explanatory and should take effect immediately. The teacher should be sure to explain to the class ahead of time that special occurrences exist and what their effect will be. Otherwise, student confusion about the occurrences can lead to frustration and charges of unfairness.

***Campaign Funds***    Special interest groups have campaign funds to donate. These funds are valuable to both state bosses and the presidential candidates. Special interest group leaders may use these funds in any way they see fit. To avoid confusion, I strongly recommend that the teacher have players come up and report a transaction each time cash changes hands. The teacher should track these transactions on the Campaign Donation Transaction Sheet shown in the Appendix.

***The Bandwagon Effect***    Bosses and special interest leaders desire to support the winning candidate because the gratitude of a victor can produce great rewards. Earning this gratitude requires voting for the winning candidate on the final ballot. To do this, a boss or interest group leader must control at least some votes during the final ballot. If the student controls no votes, then he or she cannot claim "bandwagon" points.

***Offers of Position***    Some bosses and special interest group leaders want a specific cabinet position for themselves or want one to be given to a particular ally. Although this kind of trading is technically illegal, these kinds of understandings are part of the political fabric. Candidates are expected to promise offices to other players, but those players should be sure to get the promise in writing for purposes of point scoring.

***Balloting***    Balloting should be conducted as the teacher deems appropriate. The teacher should begin the exercise with a first ballot, which helps to clarify matters and

---

**HOW A ROUND OF BALLOTING MIGHT LOOK**

Let's assume it is the third ballot of a game and no one has claimed the nomination yet. Duke had the most votes on the last ballot and has been negotiating furiously. At the beginning of the third ballot, Gillespie announces that she is giving up the campaign to be Duke's vice presidential nominee. With Duke's 400 base votes, Gillespie's 250 bring the ticket's base up to 650. Also, the Duke ticket announces that Harper is dropping his campaign to accept a cabinet post with Duke (and $10,000 in campaign contributions that Duke convinced the urban group to give to Harper). Harper's 225 votes brings the Duke base to 875.

Meanwhile, on the last ballot, candidate Jacobson added Ohio's boss Callahan as his vice presidential running mate, increasing his current vote total to 550. Finally, candidate Stiffner announces at the beginning of the balloting that she has selected Florida's boss Hernandez as her vice presidential running mate, which will bring her a total to 625 votes. Unfortunately for Stiffner and the Florida boss, their announcement is interrupted by the heads of the social conservatives, defense hawks, and urban groups—who announce that they have broken the Florida delegation and will switch the delegation's support from Stiffner to Jacobson. Since the three groups control 130 of Florida's 250 votes they have a majority and are able to swing the delegation. The result is a grievous blow to Stiffner, who is now running with a vice president who can't even bring his own state's votes. Jacobson's vote total goes to 800, while Stiffner remains at 375.

The teacher calls for the votes of the state delegations alphabetically. The teacher starts with California. California's chair Navelson announces that she is declaring herself a candidate, and that the 300 California delegates are voting for her. Stiffner announces she is dumping Hernandez as her vice president and replacing Hernandez with boss Sawbuck from Illinois. Sawbuck brings Stiffner his 200 votes, increasing Stiffner's total to 825. After Massachusetts casts its 150 votes for Jacobson and Michigan casts its 200 votes for Duke. The board shows Duke at 1,075, Jacobson at 950, Stiffner at 575, and Navelson at 300 votes.

New York backs Jacobson, as does North Carolina, bringing his vote total to 1,350. Pennsylvania announces it is voting for Duke (the Pennsylvania boss has gotten Duke to accede to all of Pennsylvania's issue demands). This brings Duke's total to 1,275. Texas announces it will back Jacobson–Callahan. Unfortunately for Jacobson, the agriculture, business, and defense special interest leaders interrupt Texas's announcement and say they have broken the Texas delegation and all delegates are voting for the Stiffner–Hernandez ticket. Since, of the 250 Texas delegates, agriculture has 50, business has 40, and defense hawks have 60, the three control 60% of the delegation. Therefore, they indeed are able to break the delegation and cast its votes for Stiffner–Hernandez. Washington then casts its 150 votes for Jacobson.

The final tally for the third ballot reads: Jacobson 1,500, Duke 1,275, Stiffner 825, and Navelson 300. Since no candidate reached the magic number of 1,951, students are free to negotiate while they prepare for the fourth ballot.

---

gives students a better feel for the game. After the initial ballot, balloting should probably be conducted every 10 to 15 minutes until a candidate wins the nomination.

Balloting should be conducted on the chalkboard while the whole class watches. First, the teacher should tally the pledged delegates for each candidate and for the candidate's vice presidential nominee (if any). Then, the teacher should poll the state delegations in alphabetical order. As the states are being polled, interest group leaders should speak up when the teacher calls on a state where some or all the votes have been wrested from the boss. If a state boss and special interest leaders disagree about whether a state delegation has been broken, the teacher should tally how many votes the special interest alliance controls in the disputed delegation.

***Selecting a Vice President***   A nominee needs a vice presidential running mate. A savvy candidate will get one of the other nominees on board as a running mate, since each of the nominees controls a slew of votes. A candidate may also offer the vice presidential slot to a boss or a special interest group leader.

---

**SUMMARY TEACHER INSTRUCTIONS**

*The day the simulation begins*
- Objective is for one candidate to claim the nomination by winning a majority of votes (1,951 out of 3,900 votes).
- Explain the background on political conventions.
- Explain the five ways that points can be scored.
- Each student is assigned to a position (e.g., presidential candidate, campaign manager, state delegation head, or interest group director).
- Each presidential candidate enters the convention with a predetermined number of votes.
- Explain the "unit rule" (whoever controls 51% of state's votes is able to control the entire vote of the state delegation), "breaking delegations," special occurrences, campaign funds (special interest groups can donate these funds to state bosses and to the presidential candidates), and the "bandwagon" effect (in order to vote for the winner the student must control some votes on the last ballot).
- Explain the balloting process.
- Explain the six issues the nominee must take a stand on in their platform.

*During the simulation*
- Take an initial ballot.
- Announce each of the candidates and record their level of support.
- Call out state delegations alphabetically to determine how they are casting their votes. Interest group leaders speak up when they have gained control of votes in a state.
- If no candidate gets a majority vote, call a special occurrence and give students 5 or 10 minutes to negotiate before calling another ballot.

*After the simulation*
- Have students write an essay that tallies up and explains their score and analyzes the simulation.
- Assess simulation using essay, classroom observations of participation, and a quiz.

---

## COMMENTS FROM EXPERIENCE

The presidential candidates all need be out hustling votes. Well-played presidential campaigns empower the state bosses and the interest group leaders by making them pivotal in the race to assemble a winning coalition.

The total number of votes and the split of vote totals have been designed to produce a relatively gridlocked convention, but not one so gridlocked that it fails to pick a winner. The ideal is to have students go through three or four or five ballots before a candidate finally claims the nomination. Victory generally requires a presidential candidate deciding to accept the vice presidential slot behind an opponent, giving that unified ticket the combined votes of the two candidates. This kind of combination can put the ticket nearly halfway to victory.

The special interest groups tend to start throwing around campaign cash like drunken sailors, especially early in the game when they are flush with cash. Consequently, over time, I have dramatically reduced the amount of campaign cash. The current levels of cash are rather low (in terms of relative point value), but I have found this level to be reasonable. It is important that someone keeps track of the campaign money before players work themselves into a frenzy of confusion.

## POSSIBLE MODIFICATIONS

### Advanced Students

Teachers working with more sophisticated students may want to resurrect the two-thirds rule that was in place at Democratic conventions during the late nineteenth and early twentieth centuries. The *two-thirds rule* provides that a nominee must win the support of two-thirds of nominees. It was used by the Democratic party to give the "Solid South" a veto over the presidential nominees during the period stretching from Reconstruction through the 1930s. The Democrats instituted this during the period in which the Solid South made up the backbone of the national Democratic party and supplied more than one-third of Democratic convention delegates. This rule ensured that any delegate unacceptable to the party's Jim Crow Southern base would not be nominated. Resurrecting this rule makes the exercise particularly combustible and challenging.

### Junior High and Less Advanced Students

It is possible to reduce the complexity of the game by removing the point scoring and simply letting students play. Eliminating the point scoring simplifies the game by doing away with such complications as the bandwagon effect and the need to keep track of campaign funds. While this tends to be a much less effective and less authentic exercise, it still provides young students with an enjoyable introduction to old-fashioned politics.

Another way to simplify the game is to do away with special occurrences, giving the students more complete control over the exercise. This reduces the number of things going on in the classroom and removes the possibility that students will have to deal with unpleasant and unexpected surprises.

## ASSESSMENT

Three kinds of assessment are recommended for this simulation. The assessments take into account student participation, student knowledge, student attentiveness to the simulation, and the student's ability to analyze the exercise.

First, note student interaction throughout the simulation. I particularly look for students who show evidence of strategic thinking and constructive participation. Given the chaos that often transpires during *Choosing a President*, the teacher will have to settle for an imperfect assessment of student performance. The teacher should not be frustrated by this, but should do his or her best and use the other instruments to get a more complete sense of how individual students performed. Indications of constructive student behaviors might include their negotiating and maneuvering, their analysis of the current situation, and their voting behavior. At the end of the simulation students fill out the Student Assessment Sheet for Nongroup Exercises (see Chapter 12), which asks students to assess their classmates' participation. Evaluation of participation is based on observation and student feedback.

Second, the day after the exercise, students are quizzed on the rules of the game, on what actually transpired, and on the historical background of nominating conventions. I do this using a short written quiz. The quiz generally takes 15 to 30 minutes, depending on the class and on the types of questions asked. The quiz encourages all students to pay attention to the rules and the events during the game, which makes it easier to then use the lessons of the simulation for instructional purposes.

Third, students write a two-page, first-person essay that analyzes the simulation. They are to explain and evaluate their actions and to explain what they would do differently if they were to play the exercise again. They are to offer a narrative discussion of what transpired in the larger class and compare the convention to what they have been taught about the functioning of political conventions historically. The knowledge that they will have to write this paper encourages students to jot down some notes during the exercise and helps them to stay focused on the lesson. Students write the paper the night after the exercise. The teacher should collect it the next day just prior to the quiz.

All the assessments are completed by the day after the simulation. They offer a rounded view of student performance, help students cultivate critical skills, and encourage students to pay attention to the exercise unfolding around them.

# APPENDIX—MATERIALS

## List of Materials

- Student Profile sheets (candidates, state bosses, and interest group leaders)

- Special Occurrences listed on separate slips so that they can be randomly chosen

- Chalkboard chart to keep track of votes

- Teacher's Master Point Matrix

- Campaign Donation Transaction Sheet

- Teacher's Matrix of State Delegations and Interest Group Influence

- List of six issues on which candidates must have a position

## Teacher's Master Point Matrix

| Points for | Presidential nominees | State delegation bosses | Interest group representatives |
|---|---|---|---|
| Winning the nomination | 12 points | 10 points | |
| Being the vice presidential nominee | 5 points | 7 points | 6 points |
| Being chosen for a cabinet position by the nominee | 3 points | 4 points | 6 points |
| Voting for the nominee on the winning ballot ("bandwagon") | | 3 points | 3 points |
| Each issue position endorsed in the nominee's platform | 1 point (have 4 issues) | 2 points (have 2 issues) | 4 points (have 2 issues) |
| Each $10,000 in campaign donations | 1 point | 1 point | |

**Confidential: Teacher's Matrix of State Delegations and Interest Group Influence**

| | CA | FL | IL | MA | MI | NC | NY | OH | PA | TX | WA |
|---|---|---|---|---|---|---|---|---|---|---|---|
| **Total state delegation** | **300** | **250** | **200** | **150** | **200** | **150** | **250** | **200** | **200** | **250** | **150** |
| **51% of state delegation** | **151** | **126** | **101** | **76** | **101** | **76** | **126** | **101** | **101** | **126** | **76** |
| Urban group 190 votes | 40 | 40 | 30 | 20 | | | 60 | | | | |
| Agriculture 190 votes | 30 | | | | | 40 | | 30 | 20 | 50 | 20 |
| Business 160 votes | | 30 | 20 | 20 | | | 30 | 20 | | 40 | |
| Labor 190 votes | | | 40 | | 30 | | | 40 | 50 | | 30 |
| Defense hawks 210 votes | 50 | 50 | | | | 20 | 30 | | | 60 | |
| Defense doves 190 votes | 40 | | 20 | 40 | 20 | | 40 | | 30 | | |
| Civil rights group 160 votes | 50 | | | | 40 | 20 | 20 | | | | 30 |
| Social conservatives 200 votes | | 40 | 20 | | 40 | | | 40 | 40 | 20 | |
| Totally free votes | 90 | 90 | 70 | 70 | 70 | 70 | 70 | 70 | 60 | 80 | 70 |

---

**Six Issues the Candidates Must Take a Stand on in Their Platform**

1. Whether to spend more money on cities OR on agriculture

2. Whether to cut taxes OR spend more money on worker training and education

3. Whether to support OR oppose affirmative action

4. Whether to support OR oppose school prayer

5. Whether to increase OR reduce military spending

6. Whether to eliminate OR to continue to maintain nuclear weapons

**Campaign Donation Transaction Sheet**

| Donor | Amount donated | Amount donor has left | Recipient | Amount recipient has collected |
|-------|----------------|-----------------------|-----------|--------------------------------|
|       |                |                       |           |                                |
|       |                |                       |           |                                |
|       |                |                       |           |                                |
|       |                |                       |           |                                |
|       |                |                       |           |                                |
|       |                |                       |           |                                |
|       |                |                       |           |                                |
|       |                |                       |           |                                |
|       |                |                       |           |                                |
|       |                |                       |           |                                |
|       |                |                       |           |                                |
|       |                |                       |           |                                |
|       |                |                       |           |                                |
|       |                |                       |           |                                |
|       |                |                       |           |                                |
|       |                |                       |           |                                |
|       |                |                       |           |                                |
|       |                |                       |           |                                |
|       |                |                       |           |                                |
|       |                |                       |           |                                |
|       |                |                       |           |                                |
|       |                |                       |           |                                |
|       |                |                       |           |                                |
|       |                |                       |           |                                |
|       |                |                       |           |                                |
|       |                |                       |           |                                |
|       |                |                       |           |                                |
|       |                |                       |           |                                |
|       |                |                       |           |                                |

### Student Profile 1  Presidential Nominee Duke, Governor of Massachusetts

Pledged Delegates: 400

Views: Moderate–Liberal

#### Domestic Views

Favors active government. Strong supporter of labor and the cities, but also wants to be able to cooperate with business. Being a New Englander, he has a feel for the northern states, such as New York, Pennsylvania, Ohio, and Michigan.

#### Foreign Views

Wants to redesign America's foreign policy so that we don't rely so heavily on our weapons. Wants to cut defense spending and concentrate on peace through negotiations.

#### Policy Views

1. Supports tax cuts, which means there can be no new spending on worker training

2. Supports affirmative action

3. Wants to cut defense spending

4. Is opposed to prayer in the schools

#### Points Scored

1. 12 points for winning the presidential nomination

2. 5 points for being named vice president by the nominee

3. 3 points for being named to the cabinet by the nominee

4. 1 point for every $10,000 in campaign contributions

5. 1 point for each issue on which the nominee's announced campaign position (whether the nominee is you or someone else) matches your preferences

#### Remember

You need a majority of delegates to win.

You are allowed to offer to make one person your vice president.

You are allowed to offer to make up to two people your cabinet secretaries.

### Student Profile 2   Presidential Nominee Stiffner, Senator from Tennessee

Pledged Delegates: 375

Views: Moderate–Conservative

#### Domestic Views

Favors less government and more reliance on free markets. Is extremely concerned that businesses stay healthy, thereby creating jobs. Thinks that economic growth is more important than having government help workers. From a farming state, Stiffner wants to increase government support for agriculture. As a southerner, Stiffner isn't trusted up north. A running mate from Pennsylvania, New York, Ohio, or Michigan might help calm northern suspicions about him.

#### Foreign Views

Favors a strong American military. Believes in peace through strength—that America should only negotiate when it is militarily superior to its enemies. Wants to continue President Reagan's heavy military spending from the 1980s.

#### Policy Views

1. Supports tax cuts, which means there can be no new spending on worker training

2. Wants to increase spending on agriculture, which means there will be no money to increase spending on cities

3. Wants to increase defense spending

4. Is opposed to getting rid of U.S. nuclear weapons, believing they are a useful deterrent against hostile countries

#### Points Scored

1. 12 points for winning the presidential nomination

2. 5 points for being named vice president by the nominee

3. 3 points for being named to the cabinet by the nominee

4. 1 point for every $10,000 in campaign contributions

5. 1 point for each issue on which the nominee's announced campaign position (whether the nominee is you or someone else) matches your preferences

#### Remember

You need a majority of delegates to win.

You are allowed to offer to make one person your vice president.

You are allowed to offer to make up to two people your cabinet secretaries.

### Student Profile 3    Presidential Nominee Gillespie, Representative from Missouri

Pledged Delegates: 250

Views: Liberal–Moderate

#### Domestic Views

Believes in putting more restrictions on foreign goods imported into the United States. This worries business leaders, who rely on free trade to help sell their products, but sounds good to union leaders who worry that imports are taking away American jobs. Is concerned about American agriculture, and is deeply concerned about the working class throughout the country. Thinks the government has to worry more about helping the working class.

#### Foreign Views

Does not have strong opinions on foreign policy. Is comfortable with traditional American policy and wants to maintain a strong defense, but is not a particularly strong advocate of increasing U.S. military spending.

#### Policy Views

1. Supports new spending on worker training, which means the government cannot afford any tax cuts

2. Wants to increase spending on agriculture, which means there will be no money to increase spending on cities

3. Supports affirmative action

4. Is opposed to school prayer

#### Points Scored

1. 12 points for winning the presidential nomination

2. 5 points for being named vice president by the nominee

3. 3 points for being named to the cabinet by the nominee

4. 1 point for every $10,000 in campaign contributions

5. 1 point for each issue on which the nominee's announced campaign position (whether the nominee is you or someone else) matches your preferences

#### Remember

You need a majority of delegates to win.

You are allowed to offer to make one person your vice president.

You are allowed to offer to make up to two people your cabinet secretaries.

### Student Profile 4   Presidential Nominee Jacobson, Preacher from Illinois

Pledged Delegates: 350

Views: Liberal

#### Domestic Views

Favors a very active national government. Wants government to massively increase programs that help labor, the cities, and minorities. Will pay for this partly by slashing defense spending, and partly by raising taxes on businesses. Sympathetic to farmers, but would rather spend money on the inner cities than on farm country.

#### Foreign Views

Wants to drastically reduce U.S. military presence in the world. Wants to slash defense spending and nuclear arms stockpile, while working harder to negotiate peaceful settlements to the world's crises.

#### Policy Views

1. Supports new spending on worker training, which means the government cannot afford any tax cuts

2. Wants to increase spending on cities, which means there will be no money to increase spending on agriculture

3. Supports affirmative action

4. Wants to cut defense spending

#### Points Scored

1. 12 points for winning the presidential nomination

2. 5 points for being named vice president by the nominee

3. 3 points for being named to the cabinet by the nominee

4. 1 point for every $10,000 in campaign contributions

5. 1 point for each issue on which the nominee's announced campaign position (whether the nominee is you or someone else) matches your preferences

#### Remember

You need a majority of delegates to win.

You are allowed to offer to make one person your vice president.

You are allowed to offer to make up to two people your cabinet secretaries.

### Student Profile 5   Presidential Nominee Harper, Former Senator from Colorado

Pledged Delegates: 225

Views: Moderate

#### Domestic Views

Wants to modernize American government so that it is as efficient as possible with twenty-first-century technology. Wants to redesign farm programs and encourage business to solve its own labor problems. Supports minority and city concerns, but wants to encourage cooperative racial and social solutions at the local level.

#### Foreign Views

Wants to streamline American defense forces in order to produce a more efficient and surgical defense capability. Sees America as an active, peaceful world leader, but one with the will and ability to play hardball when necessary.

#### Policy Views

1. Supports new spending on worker training, which means the government cannot afford any tax cuts

2. Wants to increase spending on cities, which means there will be no money to increase spending on agriculture

3. Wants to get rid of nuclear weapons

4. Wants to increase defense spending

#### Points Scored

1. 12 points for winning the presidential nomination

2. 5 points for being named vice president by the nominee

3. 3 points for being named to the cabinet by the nominee

4. 1 point for every $10,000 in campaign contributions

5. 1 point for each issue on which the nominee's announced campaign position (whether the nominee is you or someone else) matches your preferences

#### Remember

You need a majority of delegates to win.

You are allowed to offer to make one person your vice president.

You are allowed to offer to make up to two people your cabinet secretaries.

## Student Profile 6   California Delegation Chair, Senator Navelson

Delegates: 300

"Dark Horse" Presidential Chances: Good

Vice Presidential Chances: Fair to good

Navelson is a "dark horse" candidate. If none of the current candidates pulls into a clear lead, then your strong state delegate base, California contacts, and flexibility on issues might help you win the nomination. Navelson supports a domestic policy that focuses on economic growth and investing in the future workers of America. Your foreign policy leans toward a strong national defense, but the particulars are not worked out.

### Special Interest Worries

The civil rights and "hawkish" defense interests each command support among at least 15% of your delegates.

### Policy Views

1. Supports new spending on worker training, which means the government cannot afford any tax cuts

2. Wants to reduce defense spending

### Points Scored

1. 10 points for winning the presidential nomination

2. 7 points for being named vice president by the nominee

3. 4 points for being named to the cabinet by the nominee

4. 3 points for voting on the winning nominee on the winning ballot (this requires that you control at least some votes on the last ballot)

5. 2 points for each issue on which the nominee's announced campaign position matches your preferences

6. 1 point for every $10,000 in campaign contributions

## Remember

The winning nominee needs a majority of delegates to win.

The winning nominee is allowed to make one person the vice presidential nominee.

The winning nominee is allowed to name up to two people as cabinet secretaries

*The Unit Rule*: So long as you control 51% of your delegation you can make it vote however you like.

*"Breaking" Your Delegation*: If special interest representatives in your state can agree to vote 51% of your delegates for a candidate, they can force the entire delegation to vote their way. But, each special interest only knows how many votes it has in your delegation—they don't know about anyone else. So find ways to negotiate with the special interest leaders that will protect your control of your delegation.

### Student Profile 7   Texas Delegation Chair, Houston Mayor Alomar

Delegates: 250

"Dark Horse" Presidential Chances: Slim to fair

Vice Presidential Chances: Good

#### Special Interest Worries

The business, agriculture, and "hawkish" defense groups each command support among at least 15% of your delegates.

#### Policy Views

1. Supports school prayer

2. Wants to increase defense spending

#### Points Scored

1. 10 points for winning the presidential nomination

2. 7 points for being named vice president by the nominee

3. 4 points for being named to the cabinet by the nominee

4. 3 points for voting on the winning nominee on the winning ballot (this requires that you control at least some votes on the last ballot)

5. 2 points for each issue on which the nominee's announced campaign position matches your preferences

6. 1 point for every $10,000 in campaign contributions

#### Remember

The winning nominee needs a majority of delegates to win.

The winning nominee is allowed to make one person the vice presidential nominee.

The winning nominee is allowed to name up to two people as cabinet secretaries

*The Unit Rule*: So long as you control 51% of your delegation you can make it vote however you like.

*"Breaking" Your Delegation*: If special interest representatives in your state can agree to vote 51% of your delegates for a candidate, they can force the entire delegation to vote their way. But, each special interest only knows how many votes it has in your delegation—they don't know about anyone else. So find ways to negotiate with the special interest leaders that will protect your control of your delegation.

### Student Profile 8    Florida Delegation Chair, Senator Hernandez

Delegates: 250

"Dark Horse" Presidential Chances: Slim

Vice Presidential Chances: Fair

#### Special Interest Worries

The urban, social conservative, and "hawkish" defense groups each command support among at least 15% of your delegates.

#### Policy Views

1. Opposes school prayer

2. Wants to cut taxes, which means there will be no money to increase spending on worker training or education

#### Points Scored

1. 10 points for winning the presidential nomination

2. 7 points for being named vice president by the nominee

3. 4 points for being named to the cabinet by the nominee

4. 3 points for voting on the winning nominee on the winning ballot (this requires that you control at least some votes on the last ballot)

5. 2 points for each issue on which the nominee's announced campaign position matches your preferences

6. 1 point for every $10,000 in campaign contributions

#### Remember

The winning nominee needs a majority of delegates to win.

The winning nominee is allowed to make one person the vice presidential nominee.

The winning nominee is allowed to name up to two people as cabinet secretaries

*The Unit Rule*: So long as you control 51% of your delegation you can make it vote however you like.

*"Breaking" Your Delegation*: If special interest representatives in your state can agree to vote 51% of your delegates for a candidate, they can force the entire delegation to vote their way. But, each special interest only knows how many votes it has in your delegation—they don't know about anyone else. So find ways to negotiate with the special interest leaders that will protect your control of your delegation.

## Student Profile 9   New York Delegation Chair, Governor Ozio

Delegates: 250

"Dark Horse" Presidential Chances: Good

Vice Presidential Chances: Fair to good

Ozio is a "dark horse" candidate. If none of the current candidates pulls into a clear lead, then your charisma, state delegate base, and New York contacts might help you win the nomination. Ozio supports a domestic policy that focuses on labor and business cooperation. Ozio's foreign policy is undecided, you would leave it to expert advisors while focusing on solving America's domestic problems.

### Special Interest Worries

The "dovish" defense and urban groups each command support among at least 15% of your delegates.

### Policy Views

1. Supports affirmative action
2. Wants to increase spending on cities, which means there will be no money to increase spending on agriculture

### Points Scored

1. 10 points for winning the presidential nomination
2. 7 points for being named vice president by the nominee
3. 4 points for being named to the cabinet by the nominee
4. 3 points for voting on the winning nominee on the winning ballot (this requires that you control at least some votes on the last ballot)
5. 2 points for each issue on which the nominee's announced campaign position matches your preferences
6. 1 point for every $10,000 in campaign contributions

### Remember

The winning nominee needs a majority of delegates to win.

The winning nominee is allowed to make one person the vice presidential nominee.

The winning nominee is allowed to name up to two people as cabinet secretaries

*The Unit Rule*: So long as you control 51% of your delegation you can make it vote however you like.

*"Breaking" Your Delegation*: If special interest representatives in your state can agree to vote 51% of your delegates for a candidate, they can force the entire delegation to vote their way. But, each special interest only knows how many votes it has in your delegation—they don't know about anyone else. So find ways to negotiate with the special interest leaders that will protect your control of your delegation.

### Student Profile 10   Pennsylvania Delegation Chair, Governor Gray

Delegates: 200

"Dark Horse" Presidential Chances: Very slim

Vice Presidential Chances: Fair to good

#### Special Interest Worries

The labor and social conservative groups each command support among at least 15% of your delegates.

#### Policy Views

1. Wants the government to cut taxes, which means it cannot support new spending on worker training or education

2. Supports school prayer

#### Points Scored

1. 10 points for winning the presidential nomination

2. 7 points for being named vice president by the nominee

3. 4 points for being named to the cabinet by the nominee

4. 3 points for voting on the winning nominee on the winning ballot (this requires that you control at least some votes on the last ballot)

5. 2 points for each issue on which the nominee's announced campaign position matches your preferences

6. 1 point for every $10,000 in campaign contributions

#### Remember

The winning nominee needs a majority of delegates to win.

The winning nominee is allowed to make one person the vice presidential nominee.

The winning nominee is allowed to name up to two people as cabinet secretaries

*The Unit Rule*: So long as you control 51% of your delegation you can make it vote however you like.

*"Breaking" Your Delegation*: If special interest representatives in your state can agree to vote 51% of your delegates for a candidate, they can force the entire delegation to vote their way. But, each special interest only knows how many votes it has in your delegation—they don't know about anyone else. So find ways to negotiate with the special interest leaders that will protect your control of your delegation.

**Student Profile 11   Illinois Delegation Chair, Chicago Mayor Sawbuck**

Delegates: 200

"Dark Horse" Presidential Chances: Slim

Vice Presidential Chances: Fair to good

### Special Interest Worries

The labor and urban groups each command support among at least 15% of your delegates.

### Policy Views

1. Supports the elimination of all nuclear weapons

2. Wants to increase spending on cities, which means there will be no money to increase spending on agriculture

### Points Scored

1. 10 points for winning the presidential nomination

2. 7 points for being named vice president by the nominee

3. 4 points for being named to the cabinet by the nominee

4. 3 points for voting on the winning nominee on the winning ballot (this requires that you control at least some votes on the last ballot)

5. 2 points for each issue on which the nominee's announced campaign position matches your preferences

6. 1 point for every $10,000 in campaign contributions

### Remember

The winning nominee needs a majority of delegates to win.

The winning nominee is allowed to make one person the vice presidential nominee.

The winning nominee is allowed to name up to two people as cabinet secretaries

*The Unit Rule*: So long as you control 51% of your delegation you can make it vote however you like.

*"Breaking" Your Delegation*: If special interest representatives in your state can agree to vote 51% of your delegates for a candidate, they can force the entire delegation to vote their way. But, each special interest only knows how many votes it has in your delegation—they don't know about anyone else. So find ways to negotiate with the special interest leaders that will protect your control of your delegation.

### Student Profile 12   Ohio Delegation Chair, Governor Callahan

Delegates: 200

"Dark Horse" Presidential Chances: Very slim

Vice Presidential Chances: Fair

#### Special Interest Worries

The labor, social conservative, and agriculture groups each command support among at least 15% of your delegates.

#### Policy Views

1. Wants to reduce defense spending

2. Supports affirmative action

#### Points Scored

1. 10 points for winning the presidential nomination

2. 7 points for being named vice president by the nominee

3. 4 points for being named to the cabinet by the nominee

4. 3 points for voting on the winning nominee on the winning ballot (this requires that you control at least some votes on the last ballot)

5. 2 points for each issue on which the nominee's announced campaign position matches your preferences

6. 1 point for every $10,000 in campaign contributions

#### Remember

The winning nominee needs a majority of delegates to win.

The winning nominee is allowed to make one person the vice presidential nominee.

The winning nominee is allowed to name up to two people as cabinet secretaries

*The Unit Rule*: So long as you control 51% of your delegation you can make it vote however you like.

*"Breaking" Your Delegation*: If special interest representatives in your state can agree to vote 51% of your delegates for a candidate, they can force the entire delegation to vote their way. But, each special interest only knows how many votes it has in your delegation—they don't know about anyone else. So find ways to negotiate with the special interest leaders that will protect your control of your delegation.

### Student Profile 13  Michigan Delegation Chair, Senator Washington

Delegates: 200

"Dark Horse" Presidential Chances: Very slim

Vice Presidential Chances: Fair

#### Special Interest Worries

The labor, social conservative, and civil rights, and "dovish" defense groups each command support among at least 15% of your delegates.

#### Policy Views

1. Supports affirmative action

2. Wants to increase spending on national defense, both to ensure the safety of the nation and to create jobs in Michigan's giant factories

#### Points Scored

1. 10 points for winning the presidential nomination

2. 7 points for being named vice president by the nominee

3. 4 points for being named to the cabinet by the nominee

4. 3 points for voting on the winning nominee on the winning ballot (this requires that you control at least some votes on the last ballot)

5. 2 points for each issue on which the nominee's announced campaign position matches your preferences

6. 1 point for every $10,000 in campaign contributions

#### Remember

The winning nominee needs a majority of delegates to win.

The winning nominee is allowed to make one person the vice presidential nominee.

The winning nominee is allowed to name up to two people as cabinet secretaries

*The Unit Rule*: So long as you control 51% of your delegation you can make it vote however you like.

*"Breaking" Your Delegation*: If special interest representatives in your state can agree to vote 51% of your delegates for a candidate, they can force the entire delegation to vote their way. But, each special interest only knows how many votes it has in your delegation—they don't know about anyone else. So find ways to negotiate with the special interest leaders that will protect your control of your delegation.

### Student Profile 14   Washington State Delegation Chair, Senator Iuno

Delegates: 150

"Dark Horse" Presidential Chances: Very slim

Vice Presidential Chances: Slim

#### Special Interest Worries

The labor and civil rights groups each command support among at least 15% of your delegates.

#### Policy Views

1. Opposes affirmative action

2. Wants to increase spending on agriculture, which means there will be no money to increase spending on cities

#### Points Scored

1. 10 points for winning the presidential nomination

2. 7 points for being named vice president by the nominee

3. 4 points for being named to the cabinet by the nominee

4. 3 points for voting on the winning nominee on the winning ballot (this requires that you control at least some votes on the last ballot)

5. 2 points for each issue on which the nominee's announced campaign position matches your preferences

6. 1 point for every $10,000 in campaign contributions

#### Remember

The winning nominee needs a majority of delegates to win.

The winning nominee is allowed to make one person the vice presidential nominee.

The winning nominee is allowed to name up to two people as cabinet secretaries

*The Unit Rule*: So long as you control 51% of your delegation you can make it vote however you like.

*"Breaking" Your Delegation*: If special interest representatives in your state can agree to vote 51% of your delegates for a candidate, they can force the entire delegation to vote their way. But, each special interest only knows how many votes it has in your delegation—they don't know about anyone else. So find ways to negotiate with the special interest leaders that will protect your control of your delegation.

### Student Profile 15   Massachusetts Delegation Chair, Boston Mayor O'Finneran

Delegates: 150

"Dark Horse" Presidential Chances: Very slim

Vice Presidential Chances: Slim to fair

#### Special Interest Worries

The "dovish" defense group commands support among at least 15% of your delegates.

#### Policy Views

1. Supports new spending on worker training, which means the government cannot afford any tax cuts

2. Wants to increase spending on cities, which means there will be no money to increase spending on agriculture

#### Points Scored

1. 10 points for winning the presidential nomination

2. 7 points for being named vice president by the nominee

3. 4 points for being named to the cabinet by the nominee

4. 3 points for voting on the winning nominee on the winning ballot (this requires that you control at least some votes on the last ballot)

5. 2 points for each issue on which the nominee's announced campaign position matches your preferences

6. 1 point for every $10,000 in campaign contributions

#### Remember

The winning nominee needs a majority of delegates to win.

The winning nominee is allowed to make one person the vice presidential nominee.

The winning nominee is allowed to name up to two people as cabinet secretaries

*The Unit Rule*: So long as you control 51% of your delegation you can make it vote however you like.

*"Breaking" Your Delegation*: If special interest representatives in your state can agree to vote 51% of your delegates for a candidate, they can force the entire delegation to vote their way. But, each special interest only knows how many votes it has in your delegation—they don't know about anyone else. So find ways to negotiate with the special interest leaders that will protect your control of your delegation.

### Student Profile 16   North Carolina Delegation Chair, Governor Cooper

Delegates: 150

"Dark Horse" Presidential Chances: Very slim

Vice Presidential Chances: Slim

#### Special Interest Worries

The agriculture group commands support among at least 15% of your delegates.

#### Policy Views

1. Wants to increase spending on agriculture, which means there will no money to increase spending on cities

2. Supports school prayer

#### Points Scored

1. 10 points for winning the presidential nomination

2. 7 points for being named vice president by the nominee

3. 4 points for being named to the cabinet by the nominee

4. 3 points for voting on the winning nominee on the winning ballot (this requires that you control at least some votes on the last ballot)

5. 2 points for each issue on which the nominee's announced campaign position matches your preferences

6. 1 point for every $10,000 in campaign contributions

#### Remember

The winning nominee needs a majority of delegates to win.

The winning nominee is allowed to make one person the vice presidential nominee.

The winning nominee is allowed to name up to two people as cabinet secretaries

*The Unit Rule*: So long as you control 51% of your delegation you can make it vote however you like.

*"Breaking" Your Delegation*: If special interest representatives in your state can agree to vote 51% of your delegates for a candidate, they can force the entire delegation to vote their way. But, each special interest only knows how many votes it has in your delegation—they don't know about anyone else. So find ways to negotiate with the special interest leaders that will protect your control of your delegation.

### Student Profile 17   Urban Interest Group, Director Kincaid of the National Conference of Mayors

Delegates: 190

Breakdown of Your Votes Among the Delegations:

California—40
Florida—40
Illinois—30
New York—60
Massachusetts—20

Campaign Funds to Give Away (can be given
away in blocs of $5,000): $25,000

#### Policy Views

1. Wants to increase spending on cities, which means there will be no money to increase spending on agriculture

2. Wants to decrease spending on the military

#### Points Scored

1. 6 points for being named vice president by the nominee

2. 6 points for being named to the cabinet by the nominee

3. 3 points for voting on the winning nominee on the winning ballot (this requires that you control at least some votes on the last ballot)

4. 4 points for each issue on which the nominee's announced campaign position matches your preferences

#### Remember

The winning nominee needs a majority of delegates to win.

The winning nominee is allowed to make one person the vice presidential nominee.

The winning nominee is allowed to name up to two people as cabinet secretaries

Your campaign contributions are worth points to the nominees and the bosses.

*The Unit Rule*: So long as a state boss controls 51% of a delegation, the boss can make the delegation vote however he or she wants. If you, in combination with a boss or with other interest group leaders are able to make 51% of a state's delegation vote for one candidate, then you are able to use the unit rule to vote all the state's votes for that candidate.

*"Breaking" Your Delegation*: If special interest representatives (or even a combination of interest groups and the state chairman) can agree to vote 51% of your delegates for a candidate, they can force the entire delegation to vote their way. Each special interest knows only the votes they control in each state delegation. The bosses know only which interest groups have major blocs of votes in their delegation. It is important to find out who else has votes in delegations so that you can cooperate. It also pays to find out which state chairmen will cooperate with you or will agree to not use the unit rule to control your votes in their delegations.

### Student Profile 18   Agricultural Interest Group, Director Reedy of the United Farmers Alliance

Delegates: 190

Breakdown of Your Votes Among the Delegations:

    California—30
    Texas—50
    Ohio—30
    Washington State—20
    Pennsylvania—20
    North Carolina—40

Campaign Funds to Give Away (can be given
away in blocs of $5,000): $40,000

#### Policy Views

1. Wants to increase spending on agriculture, which means there will be no money to increase spending on cities

2. Opposes affirmative action

#### Points Scored

1. 6 points for being named vice president by the nominee

2. 6 points for being named to the cabinet by the nominee

3. 3 points for voting on the winning nominee on the winning ballot (this requires that you control at least some votes on the last ballot)

4. 4 points for each issue on which the nominee's announced campaign position matches your preferences

#### Remember

The winning nominee needs a majority of delegates to win.

The winning nominee is allowed to make one person the vice presidential nominee.

The winning nominee is allowed to name up to two people as cabinet secretaries

Your campaign contributions are worth points to the nominees and the bosses.

*The Unit Rule*: So long as a state boss controls 51% of a delegation, the boss can make the delegation vote however he or she wants. If you, in combination with a boss or with other interest group leaders are able to make 51% of a state's delegation vote for one candidate, then you are able to use the unit rule to vote all the state's votes for that candidate.

*"Breaking" Your Delegation*: If special interest representatives (or even a combination of interest groups and the state chairman) can agree to vote 51% of your delegates for a candidate, they can force the entire delegation to vote their way. Each special interest knows only the votes they control in each state delegation. The bosses know only which interest groups have major blocs of votes in their delegation. It is important to find out who else has votes in delegations so that you can cooperate. It also pays to find out which state chairmen will cooperate with you or will agree to not use the unit rule to control your votes in their delegations.

### Student Profile 19   Business Interest Group, Director Norman of the U.S. Chamber of Commerce

Delegates: 160

Breakdown of Your Votes Among the Delegations:

Texas—40
Ohio—20
Illinois—20
Florida—30
New York—30
Massachusetts—20

Campaign Funds to Give Away (can be given
away in blocs of $5,000): $45,000

#### Policy Views

1. Want to cut taxes, which means the government cannot afford to spend more money on worker training and education

2. Want to increase spending on cities, which means there will be no money to increase spending on agriculture

#### Points Scored

1. 6 points for being named vice president by the nominee

2. 6 points for being named to the cabinet by the nominee

3. 3 points for voting on the winning nominee on the winning ballot (this requires that you control at least some votes on the last ballot)

4. 4 points for each issue on which the nominee's announced campaign position matches your preferences

#### Remember

The winning nominee needs a majority of delegates to win.

The winning nominee is allowed to make one person the vice presidential nominee.

The winning nominee is allowed to name up to two people as cabinet secretaries

Your campaign contributions are worth points to the nominees and the bosses.

*The Unit Rule*: So long as a state boss controls 51% of a delegation, the boss can make the delegation vote however he or she wants. If you, in combination with a boss or with other interest group leaders are able to make 51% of a state's delegation vote for one candidate, then you are able to use the unit rule to vote all the state's votes for that candidate.

*"Breaking" Your Delegation*: If special interest representatives (or even a combination of interest groups and the state chairman) can agree to vote 51% of your delegates for a candidate, they can force the entire delegation to vote their way. Each special interest knows only the votes they control in each state delegation. The bosses know only which interest groups have major blocs of votes in their delegation. It is important to find out who else has votes in delegations so that you can cooperate. It also pays to find out which state chairmen will cooperate with you or will agree to not use the unit rule to control your votes in their delegations.

### Student Profile 20   Labor Interest Group, Director Coltrain of the AFL-CIO

Delegates: 190

Breakdown of Your Votes Among the Delegations:

Ohio—40
Illinois—40
Washington State—30
Michigan—30
Pennsylvania—50

Campaign Funds to Give Away (can be given
away in blocs of $5,000): $30,000

#### Policy Views

1. Want the government to increase spending on worker education and training, which means taxes cannot be cut

2. Opposed to school prayer

#### Points Scored

1. 6 points for being named vice president by the nominee

2. 6 points for being named to the cabinet by the nominee

3. 3 points for voting on the winning nominee on the winning ballot (this requires that you control at least some votes on the last ballot)

4. 4 points for each issue on which the nominee's announced campaign position matches your preferences

#### Remember

The winning nominee needs a majority of delegates to win.

The winning nominee is allowed to make one person the vice presidential nominee.

The winning nominee is allowed to name up to two people as cabinet secretaries

Your campaign contributions are worth points to the nominees and the bosses.

*The Unit Rule*: So long as a state boss controls 51% of a delegation, the boss can make the delegation vote however he or she wants. If you, in combination with a boss or with other interest group leaders are able to make 51% of a state's delegation vote for one candidate, then you are able to use the unit rule to vote all the state's votes for that candidate.

*"Breaking" Your Delegation*: If special interest representatives (or even a combination of interest groups and the state chairman) can agree to vote 51% of your delegates for a candidate, they can force the entire delegation to vote their way. Each special interest knows only the votes they control in each state delegation. The bosses know only which interest groups have major blocs of votes in their delegation. It is important to find out who else has votes in delegations so that you can cooperate. It also pays to find out which state chairmen will cooperate with you or will agree to not use the unit rule to control your votes in their delegations.

## Student Profile 21  "Hawkish" Defense Group, Director Smithson of Americans for a Safe Nation

Delegates: 210

Breakdown of Your Votes Among the Delegations:

California—50
Texas—60
Florida—50
New York—30
North Carolina—20

Campaign Funds to Give Away (can be given
away in blocs of $5,000): $25,000

### Policy Views

1. Want to increase military spending

2. The government should continue to build and maintain nuclear weapons to deter possible enemies from hostile acts

### Points Scored

1. 6 points for being named vice president by the nominee

2. 6 points for being named to the cabinet by the nominee

3. 3 points for voting on the winning nominee on the winning ballot (this requires that you control at least some votes on the last ballot)

4. 4 points for each issue on which the nominee's announced campaign position matches your preferences

### Remember

The winning nominee needs a majority of delegates to win.

The winning nominee is allowed to make one person the vice presidential nominee.

The winning nominee is allowed to name up to two people as cabinet secretaries

Your campaign contributions are worth points to the nominees and the bosses.

*The Unit Rule*: So long as a state boss controls 51% of a delegation, the boss can make the delegation vote however he or she wants. If you, in combination with a boss or with other interest group leaders are able to make 51% of a state's delegation vote for one candidate, then you are able to use the unit rule to vote all the state's votes for that candidate.

*"Breaking" Your Delegation*: If special interest representatives (or even a combination of interest groups and the state chairman) can agree to vote 51% of your delegates for a candidate, they can force the entire delegation to vote their way. Each special interest knows only the votes they control in each state delegation. The bosses know only which interest groups have major blocs of votes in their delegation. It is important to find out who else has votes in delegations so that you can cooperate. It also pays to find out which state chairmen will cooperate with you or will agree to not use the unit rule to control your votes in their delegations.

### Student Profile 22  "Dovish" Defense Group, Director Martinson of Americans for Peace

Delegates: 190

Breakdown of Your Votes Among the Delegations:

California—40
Illinois—20
New York—40
Pennsylvania—30
Michigan—20
Massachusetts—40

Campaign Funds to Give Away (can be given
away in blocs of $5,000): $30,000

#### Policy Views

1. Military spending should be reduced

2. The government should stop building or developing nuclear weapons, and should get rid of the nuclear weapons the United States currently has

#### Points Scored

1. 6 points for being named vice president by the nominee

2. 6 points for being named to the cabinet by the nominee

3. 3 points for voting on the winning nominee on the winning ballot (this requires that you control at least some votes on the last ballot)

4. 4 points for each issue on which the nominee's announced campaign position matches your preferences

#### Remember

The winning nominee needs a majority of delegates to win.

The winning nominee is allowed to make one person the vice presidential nominee.

The winning nominee is allowed to name up to two people as cabinet secretaries

Your campaign contributions are worth points to the nominees and the bosses.

*The Unit Rule*: So long as a state boss controls 51% of a delegation, the boss can make the delegation vote however he or she wants. If you, in combination with a boss or with other interest group leaders are able to make 51% of a state's delegation vote for one candidate, then you are able to use the unit rule to vote all the state's votes for that candidate.

*"Breaking" Your Delegation*: If special interest representatives (or even a combination of interest groups and the state chairman) can agree to vote 51% of your delegates for a candidate, they can force the entire delegation to vote their way. Each special interest knows only the votes they control in each state delegation. The bosses know only which interest groups have major blocs of votes in their delegation. It is important to find out who else has votes in delegations so that you can cooperate. It also pays to find out which state chairmen will cooperate with you or will agree to not use the unit rule to control your votes in their delegations.

### Student Profile 23 Civil Rights Interest Group, Director Grendlon of the National Association for the Advancement of Colored People (NAACP)

Delegates: 160

Breakdown of Your Votes Among the Delegations:

California—50
New York—20
Washington—30
Michigan—40
North Carolina—20

Campaign Funds to Give Away (can be given away in blocs of $5,000): $30,000

#### Policy Views

1. Support affirmative action

2. Oppose school prayer

#### Points Scored

1. 6 points for being named vice president by the nominee

2. 6 points for being named to the cabinet by the nominee

3. 3 points for voting on the winning nominee on the winning ballot (this requires that you control at least some votes on the last ballot)

4. 4 points for each issue on which the nominee's announced campaign position matches your preferences

#### Remember

The winning nominee needs a majority of delegates to win.

The winning nominee is allowed to make one person the vice presidential nominee.

The winning nominee is allowed to name up to two people as cabinet secretaries

Your campaign contributions are worth points to the nominees and the bosses.

*The Unit Rule*: So long as a state boss controls 51% of a delegation, the boss can make the delegation vote however he or she wants. If you, in combination with a boss or with other interest group leaders are able to make 51% of a state's delegation vote for one candidate, then you are able to use the unit rule to vote all the state's votes for that candidate.

*"Breaking" Your Delegation*: If special interest representatives (or even a combination of interest groups and the state chairman) can agree to vote 51% of your delegates for a candidate, they can force the entire delegation to vote their way. Each special interest knows only the votes they control in each state delegation. The bosses know only which interest groups have major blocs of votes in their delegation. It is important to find out who else has votes in delegations so that you can cooperate. It also pays to find out which state chairmen will cooperate with you or will agree to not use the unit rule to control your votes in their delegations.

## Student Profile 24 Socially Conservative Interest Group, Director Barton of the Americans for a Democratic Majority

Delegates: 200

Breakdown of Your Votes Among the Delegations:

Texas—20
Ohio—40
Illinois—20
Florida—40
Michigan—40
Pennsylvania—40

Campaign Funds to Give Away (can be given
away in blocs of $5,000): $25,000

### Policy Views

1. Opposed to affirmative action

2. Support school prayer

### Points Scored

1. 6 points for being named vice president by the nominee

2. 6 points for being named to the cabinet by the nominee

3. 3 points for voting on the winning nominee on the winning ballot (this requires that you control at least some votes on the last ballot)

4. 4 points for each issue on which the nominee's announced campaign position matches your preferences

### Remember

The winning nominee needs a majority of delegates to win.

The winning nominee is allowed to make one person the vice presidential nominee.

The winning nominee is allowed to name up to two people as cabinet secretaries

Your campaign contributions are worth points to the nominees and the bosses.

*The Unit Rule*: So long as a state boss controls 51% of a delegation, the boss can make the delegation vote however he or she wants. If you, in combination with a boss or with other interest group leaders are able to make 51% of a state's delegation vote for one candidate, then you are able to use the unit rule to vote all the state's votes for that candidate.

*"Breaking" Your Delegation*: If special interest representatives (or even a combination of interest groups and the state chairman) can agree to vote 51% of your delegates for a candidate, they can force the entire delegation to vote their way. Each special interest knows only the votes they control in each state delegation. The bosses know only which interest groups have major blocs of votes in their delegation. It is important to find out who else has votes in delegations so that you can cooperate. It also pays to find out which state chairmen will cooperate with you or will agree to not use the unit rule to control your votes in their delegations.

## The 15 Special Occurrence Slips

---

Announcements about Gillespie's voting record hurt his Southern support, and 80 of his baseline delegates shift to Duke.

---

The New York delegation gets frustrated with the convention and decides to take a day trip to the closest amusement park. They will not vote on the next ballot.

---

A majority of the Florida delegation rebels and refuses to vote according to the unit rule on the next ballot. Interest groups and the Florida boss are free to direct whatever votes they control.

---

The Michigan delegation has a wild party and needs $10,000 to pay the hotel bill, or else it is going to pick up and go home.

---

A big supporter gives the Civil Rights organization a last-minute donation of $10,000.

---

The Iowa delegation, with 70 votes, switches from Duke to Gillespie (changing from the base of one to the other).

---

The North Dakota delegation, with 40 votes, switches from Stiffner to Jacobson (changing from the base of one to the other).

---

The Arkansas delegation, with 60 votes, switches from Gillespie to Harper (changing from the base of one to the other).

---

The Hawaii delegation, with 40 votes, decides to switch from Harper to Stiffner (changing from the base of one to the other).

---

Former President Carter makes a public announcement urging Democrats to rally behind Duke, leading 50 of Stiffner's baseline delegates to switch to Duke.

---

Rebels in the Ohio and Illinois delegations demand that the two delegations vote together on the next ballot. Otherwise, the rebels have enough votes to force both delegations to sit out the next ballot.

---

Embarrassing revelations about Duke's old snowblower cause 70 baseline Duke delegates to switch over to Stiffner.

The Louisiana delegation, with 50 votes, switches from Jacobson to Harper (changing from the base of one to the other).

A major *New York Times* article attacks the chairman of the Chamber of Commerce, causing any Chamber-influenced delegates to go back to the control of the New York boss for the next ballot.

The head of the "Doves" gets thrown in jail during a chaotic party at Democratic headquarters. Needs to spend $5,000 of campaign money on bail, or will be forced to miss the next ballot.

# CHAPTER 7

# A Whirlwind American Tour

*I have always been surprised at how many of my students think of places like New York City, Los Angeles, Boston, or Seattle as far-off and exotic locales. I credit the appeal of this exercise, which was designed to teach students about traveling and U.S. geography, to that curiosity. Students have been willed $4,000 by a distant aunt, but only on the condition that they use the money to travel the United States. While charging around the country, falling into madcap adventures, or solemnly eyeing the Golden Gate Bridge for the first time, students learn the rudiments of budget travel by visiting at least eight American cities in at least four states over a 25-day period.*

*Students must provide a fictional narrative of their travels, a complete itinerary (including modes of transportation and accommodations), and a detailed budget. The budget must cite sources for all figures, in accordance with the requirements on the model form. Students get an opportunity to imagine themselves in new places, to develop budgeting and organizational skills, and to learn geography. Once the exercise is set up, it requires minimal in-class maintenance because the students do the project for homework.*

## TEACHER'S NOTE

*A Whirlwind American Tour* is designed to introduce students to the urban United States and to the practical skills of traveling and budgeting. Students learn a melange of practical skills, useful knowledge, and American geography. Even better (at least from my perspective) is that it really gives the kids a chance to turn their imaginations loose. I remember having Louisiana students who had never left the state just lighting up at the chance to imagine themselves turned loose in Los Angeles, New York, or Chicago.

In its simplest form, the exercise requires students to become their own travel agents, documenting everything they do. Students need to track down airfares, train schedules, rental car prices, hotel locations and prices, restaurants, and leisure-time activities in several of America's premiere cities. The rules (see How the Exercise Proceeds section) explicitly prohibit students from simply renting a car and touring around in that fashion, because that practice drains much of the challenge and many of the useful skills from the game. Travel requirements that students have never thought about or always took for granted become a real and immediate issue. Students learn how to arrange travel and how to squeeze a nickel while doing so.

Additionally, students are required to keep a journal of their 25-day trip and turn in a U.S. map that traces their journey. Some of the enthusiasm demonstrated in these materials has really blown me away. I have received elaborate journals that not only document every meal, activity, and hotel, but that burst with romantic story lines and edge-of-the-law hijinks. Although some students must be squeezed to deliver the required journal entries, I have had other students turn in journals that stretched to 70 or 80 pages of long, creative, and authentic-feeling narrative. The key to making this exercise effective is to be absolutely clear about the minimum requirements for travel, research, and writing. This clarity will force even disinterested students to absorb and practice the desired skills.

This exercise is easy for the teacher to conduct and makes a minimal claim on the teacher's time or on class time. Students are expected to do the vast majority of the work on their own, either in the school library, at home, or by swapping data with friends. The extensive need for research compels students to swap information; this should be strongly encouraged. This interaction teaches cooperation and builds relationships among classmates. Students tend to informally sanction the kids who try to get by without doing any work, while there is a tendency for students to start interacting with those students who do good research. The simple act of assembling the final materials tends to be educational for students, as they learn to map a trip, fill out a budget guide, and write a journal—so even relatively uninterested students take some value away from the exercise.

The lesson is appropriate for a wide range of students. Interested and knowledgeable students often find the exercise an opportunity to imagine doing amazing things, not infrequently turning in fascinating journals. However, even less enthused students often take an interest in certain cities, in the mechanics of travel coordination, or in the practical skills of budgeting a trip. Because urban areas play such a prominent role in the nation's economy, politics, culture, and history, fuller student understanding of cities is crucial to their broader education in American society and geography.

The exercise was originally designed to be the student research project for the U.S. unit in a World Geography course. It has also been used successfully by colleagues in American History and Contemporary Issues classes. In American History courses, colleagues have generally used the exercise as a supplemental assignment at the beginning of the year to develop student research skills and to strengthen their grasp of U.S. geography. The exercise requires roughly one class period in which the teacher explains the parameters of the exercise, and then some occasional in-class time to assist students, answer questions, and foster cooperation.

## BACKGROUND ON LOW-BUDGET TRAVEL

I generated the idea for this particular project while talking with students about the first time I traveled across the United States. Several students were very interested in how I knew where to go, what to do, and how to get around. They found the entire concept to be beyond their scope of experience.

Low-cost travel is as old as humankind. Of course, a traveler's standards and expectations have something to do with how much a person needs to spend. If you expect nice vistas, comfortable beds, good meals, access to high culture, and first-rate transportation, then you spend a fair bit of money. This simulation is designed to introduce students to that other kind of contemporary travel, the kind that traces its roots to low-cost summer treks across Europe. I find that this emphasis helps the exercise appeal to students, because low-cost travel is relevant to their lives and carries the romantic connotations of bohemian travel.

There are a number of ways to inexpensively travel the United States. The emergence of the Internet has revolutionized the ability to access information on these kinds of activities, making it far easier and far cheaper to find information on low-cost travel options. Additionally, the nature of the Internet means that there is much more flux in the source of low-cost information than there once was, so the identities of old standbys are not as significant as they once were. Nowadays, any novice Web-surfer can locate good deals in any American city after 45 minutes of Internet browsing.

Good places to start looking for information on cheap travel ideas and for cheap lodging include the AAA (the American Automobile Association) and IYH (International Youth Hostels). Hostels are much more common and much better known in Europe than in the United States, but the little-known fact is that there are hundreds of youth hostels in the United States. Hostels are scattered across the country and usually charge no more than $20 a night, even in urban areas. Sources of cheap travel include buses, trains, subways, budget airlines, and cheap rental cars.

## USING THIS SIMULATION

### Purpose

Substantively, *A Whirlwind American Tour* allows students to develop their knowledge of American cities. Students learn where cities are located and a great deal about the landscape and nature of individual cities. So much geography is oriented toward the location of countries, states, capitals, and natural features, that students sometimes do not learn much about the flavor or nature of specific locales. The lesson is intended to cultivate student interest in geography.

## Skills Developed

The exercise helps to develop research, creative writing, and math reasoning skills. Students get practice compiling information, locating sources, and keeping careful records—crucial skills in both academic and work settings. Students also exercise their creative writing and communication skills as they maintain their 25-day travel journal tracking their journey. Students develop several practical skills, including knowledge about traveling, arranging travel plans, learning to estimate the length and nature of domestic trips, and devising and tracking a budget. The exercise also fosters collaboration and cooperation among students, because they are encouraged to share their research and their ideas with one another. There is enough work, and generally enough varied interest among students, that students will wind up doing sufficient original work regardless of how extensively they work together.

The nature of the research required helps teach students good research habits. The need for current material discourages the use of encyclopedias and other traditional sources. Students are forced to acquaint themselves with new sources. with which they may be unfamiliar. Not only are students pressed to use new sources, but the disparate sources of information and the lack of predigested analysis force them to integrate material in order to make their own decisions.

## Logistics

This exercise is a project on which students primarily work at home. However, it can be run as an in-class exercise if the teacher desires. Even if it is done primarily as an at-home exercise, it is best to devote some class time to the project. This time is useful, both because students enjoy swapping tips and stories and because it can give the teacher time to address student questions, offer guidance, and steer students along. I found that this interaction helped to sustain student enthusiasm and energy.

Generally, it takes about 20 minutes of class time to explain the exercise to students and get them clear on the materials and the expectations. Once students start gathering the data, more questions will arise. Dealing with these questions makes it useful to set aside another 30 minutes of class time at the end of the first week. At this time, student questions are addressed, student work is checked over, and students are given time to share ideas and information. This can be done in small groups, as a class, or individually. To make this time as useful as possible, it is important that students have started working on the project and encountered the problems they will have. Consequently, students should be required to come in at the end of the first week with the first four days of their trip planned, budgeted, and the journal entries written.

I give students about three to four weeks to complete the project. Longer periods are feasible, but student interest tends to wane as the activity gets longer. I tend to not go shorter than four weeks because I want students to have sufficient time to produce a quality product. At the end of each week, I require that students turn in or show to me certain materials. This is done to ensure that students are not simply leaving the project for a huge all-nighter at the end of the project. After all, it's the extended exposure that develops the key skills and drills them home.

# HOW THE SIMULATION WORKS

## Student Assignments

Students work singly, though I strongly encourage them to collaborate and share research and tips. It is a clear expectation that students will indicate the source of information, giving the credit to classmates when it is appropriate. A teacher could permit students to do this project in pairs or in groups.

---

**BUDGETING A TRIP**

People who have not traveled extensively sometimes are not aware of just how many low-cost options are available to travelers. This is particularly true for folks who haven't taken extended, low-cost trips for a decade or more. The fact is that even the travel guides billed as "budget travel" often overstate the cost of transportation, accommodations, board, and entertainment. The reason is that these budget travel guides strive to hit a broad audience, including families and middle-class travelers. Therefore, the guides tend to mix in a large number of mid-range alternatives. Additionally, on the supposition that most travelers are not willing to risk using facilities that are too cheap or too far off of the beaten path, these guides are not complete.

One of the better guides for this type of travel, *Let's Go: USA*, is known among low-cost travelers as "Let's Get Lost," due to its frequent factual errors and large number of omissions. This book, for instance, is compiled by student travelers sent out by Harvard Student Agencies. These researchers have neither the time nor the resources to provide an exhaustive list of accommodations, transportation, activities, and restaurants, and do not really claim to. The teacher should not heed student gripes that some information is hard to find or that $4,000 is not enough money to travel on. In fact, in 1995 I traveled cross-country for eight weeks on just $1,900. Any student who cannot produce an interesting and fun itinerary for $4,000 is not trying.

---

## Length of Exercise

Students are to plan and detail a trip of 25 days. I normally have the students work on the project for about three to four weeks, with almost all of the work done outside of class. I would recommend that teachers require students to write a minimum of one journal page per travel day.

## How the Exercise Proceeds

***The Rules*** Students are told they have $4,000 to finance their trip. They are to visit 8 cities, in at least 4 different states, over a period of 25 days. Students are required to plan for transportation, food, lodging, entertainment, and other expenses without spending more than their $4,000.

***Record of Trip Activities and Budget*** Students are to track their trips and all expenses incurred on the Student Travel Log Sheet (see Appendix). As part of the process of tracing the activities and expenses of their trip, students are expected to give the source for all information used. This is to teach students about the utilization of sources, how to properly assign credit, and how to conduct careful research.

Students are issued a sample Travel Log sheet. They are expected to use this sheet as a model. The full log is to be tracked in a notebook or on a computer.

Students are expected to identify a particular itinerary for each day. I require students to include three meals, their evening's lodging, a general statement of transportation for the day, and at least one daytime and one evening activity for each day.

Students are required to include a budgetary line, and an information source, for each activity. I tell students that they can occasionally include a guesstimate (and source it as such) for an item—because this keeps students from getting hung up on hard-to-find individual items. However, such guesstimates are to account for no more than 20% of all budgetary sources.

Identifying sources for each expenditure is really nothing more than footnoting. Although it does not necessarily help matters to explain it to students in these terms, the teacher should understand that the student is really being taught how to research and to document data. One of the reasons for documenting the various sources—whether it be Internet sites, travel guides, parents, phone calls, airlines, or anyone else—is to help students understand that research is nothing more than collecting useful data from a number of sources. It also helps students to make the connection between "research" in school and its possible applicability to real-life situations.

***Travel Journal*** While planning the actual events of their trip, students are to write a Travel Journal that narrates the story of their trip. The journal is to be a work of fiction, discussing what the student did and saw in each locale. Students are expected to make up some kind of narrative theme for their journal (whether it is romantic, adventurous, heroic, comedic, suspenseful, or whatever is up to them) and to use the journal to convey the sense that they have achieved some understanding of the culture and nature of the cities they choose to visit. Students should show that they have made an effort to weave the color of each city into their narrative.

The journal should not just repeat what students track on their budget sheets, but should embellish it, bring it to life, and really show that the student has gotten some sense of the locale. The key is for the student to demonstrate that he or she has established a comfort level with the geography, culture, and makeup of the city.

---

**ENTRIES IN THE TRAVEL JOURNAL**

The key to the journal is for students to strive for authenticity. It should be obvious that they have gained some familiarity with the city they are writing about. For instance, an ideal student journal entry for a day in Boston once read, ". . . And then we caught the Red Sox afternoon game at Fenway Park. It was a perfect Saturday for a ballgame, with a brilliant blue sky and a temperature in the high 70s. The Sox beat the Rangers 5 to 3 on a ninth-inning home run that cleared the Green Monster in left field. After the game we caught the T and took the green line over to Faneuil Hall.

We walked around the Quincy Market area, headed over to the wharf to look at the ships in the harbor, and then ate a late lunch of clam chowder and burgers at the Durgin Park restaurant. While we were eating, we started chatting with a couple of college kids at the next table. They were juniors at Boston College, and said they think that Durgin Park has the best clam chowder in the city. We then walked down Boylston Street back toward our suite at the Copley Marriott. Along the way we stopped into FAO Schwartz to look for a gift for Sarah and Jill . . ."

---

***Map*** The teacher will distribute a copy of the U.S. map (see Appendix) to each student at the beginning of the exercise. Students will create a map of their journey, either by using the map distributed to them in class, by tracing their trip on a mass-produced U.S. map, or by creating their own map.

***At the Start*** Each student should be given a copy of the Student Guidelines Sheet and the U.S. map included in the Appendix. The teacher should go over the simple rules and be sure to emphasize the expectations for the journal, for the citation of research sources, and for the nature of activities and budgeting accuracy.

I normally give the students the first day of class to get themselves started and to chat with each other about possible travel plans. I try to make some materials available to help students ease into the project. A classroom equipped with Internet access provides more material than students will ever need. Alternatively, a trip might be scheduled to the library or resources might be brought to the classroom. Giving students this time on the first day allows them to start sketching out their trip and gives the teacher a chance to handle any obvious points of confusion.

## COMMENTS FROM EXPERIENCE

It is important to help students get a real feel for the exercise and get engaged in it during the first week. If the students become interested early, they tend to view the whole exercise as a fun activity and do the work willingly and good-naturedly. If the exercise gets well along before students start to pay attention to it, they are much less likely to invest

**SUMMARY TEACHER INSTRUCTIONS**

*The day the simulation begins*
- Objective is to teach students about U.S. and urban geography, and to develop their research and travel skills.
- Explain to students the purpose and nature of the exercise.
- Pass out Guidelines sheet and map. Explain the exercise parameters to the students, emphasizing that: they have up to $4,000 to spend, they must visit at least 8 cities in at least 4 states, and they must travel for at least 25 days and nights.
- Students cannot simply drive around in a car they already own and that a rental car can only be used for a portion of their travel.
- Students must track three meals, transportation, lodging, and at least two activities for each day.
- Students must cite a price for each activity, and must cite the source for each price. Some omissions or fudging are acceptable here, especially for items that are really difficult to track down, but it is expected that at least 80% of the prices will be documented.
- Pass out Student Guidelines sheet and Student Travel Log to each student.

*After the simulation*
- Along with the project, students are required to turn in completed Travel Log sheets with budget figures and sources, a travel journal, a map of their trip (either homemade or traced on a road map), and any miscellaneous or additional materials that enhance the project.
- Administer a brief quiz.

themselves in the research or to have their interest fired by the creative opportunities. I have found that the students who particularly enjoyed the exercise either really pictured themselves doing all the things that they had never thought about or else were able to think of at least part of the trip as a dry run for something they might be able to do in the next few years (either during college or before they start work).

Every student, of course, is not going to buy into the activity. However, talking up the creative aspects and helping students to understand that this is something they could do one day *if they choose to* will make it much easier for teachers to get students interested in the project. This is an exercise that can really snowball if a critical mass of the class gets excited. The activity lends itself to lunch table, hallway, and school bus banter, as goofing around in L.A. or New York is just the kind of thing students of many abilities and interests will shoot the breeze about if enough of them are invested in the material.

I remember walking across the courtyard one morning and seeing a half-dozen of my scruffier boys in an intense argument about whether, while in Chicago, one of them should see the Bears play at Soldier's Field or Michael Jordan and the Bulls play, because he didn't have enough money left to do both. I have found that boys tend to place a lot of emphasis on seeing sports teams and sports arenas, but that is fine. Remember, the substance of the leisure activities is not particularly crucial to the exercise. The goals are to develop travel skills, budgeting skills, information collecting skills, and knowledge of urban geography, none of which particularly depend on any one kind of leisure-time activity.

The first time I used this exercise I instructed students to select their cities before tackling any of the other elements of the project. The problem with this linear approach was that some students felt stifled. I decided that the advantages of consistency were minimal, so I allow students to arrange their trip in as orderly or as hectic a fashion as they like. Naturally, even with this more relaxed approach, some students will tire of the project before it is finished. There's always the trade-off between ensuring that students receive adequate exposure to the material, and not having them tire of the exercise. Some teachers might want to shorten the exercise to require fewer cities or less information in order to adjust the balance I have struck here.

Another problem I encountered in the first iteration of the exercise was that several students stipulated that they were just going to buy a cheap used car and drive it across the country. This prevented the students from learning about travel arrangements, sucked out much of the research emphasis, and made for a generally shoddy project. As a result, I strongly suggest that students not be permitted to travel by automobile (or that they be allowed to do so only infrequently).

Teachers can expect students to have questions regarding minimum expectations and where they can find certain types of data. For this reason, the teacher should be clear from the beginning about the following:

- The minimum number of cities students will visit
- The minimum number of meals and activities students are expected to track each day
- The minimum number of pages students are to include in the travel journal
- The minimum amount of sourcing for data that will be acceptable

## POSSIBLE MODIFICATIONS

This exercise lends itself to easy modification in several dimensions. The most basic is to adjust the amount of time that students are required to travel. If 25 days makes too much of a demand on the students, a 14-day or 21-day trip can be used instead. Teachers should adjust the projected budget and the required number of cities accordingly.

Teachers can also dramatically change the nature of the trip by making it into a millionaire's holiday. I chose not to go this route for reasons already addressed, but the teacher might find it fun to give students $100,000 or so to spend on their 25-day vacation. Although it obviously is less applicable to student lives and potentially less useful, this type of exercise can have compensating advantages and certainly offers students the chance to tap into their creative urges.

The travel theme is obviously compatible with a number of types of travel. Two of the more attractive alternatives, both of which have been used successfully by teaching colleagues, are suggested here. One approach is to shift away from the urban orientation of this exercise. Some teachers may feel that their students will gain more by having the target locales be other kinds of places, such as national parks, or a mixture of urban areas and national parks.

The problem with relying more heavily on parks and other more natural venues is that there are fewer activities to write about, there are fewer expenses for students to budget and track, and I have found that most students find it easier to write a good narrative about urban activity. Additionally, the teacher might want to expand the choice of venues from the United States to include Canada and Mexico. This has the advantage of requiring students to address questions of exchange rates and currency and will offer students some exposure to places with which they may be very unfamiliar.

A second approach to broadening the exercise is to use a region other than North America. By far, the most promising way to do this is by having the students travel Europe by train. For those teachers unfamiliar with the tradition of "packing" (backpacking) across Europe, it is sufficient to note that it is an annual rite engaged in by tens of thousands of young adults from the United States, Canada, Australia, and other nations. Youths under 26 are able to buy a discounted train ticket that will allow them to travel as much as they like through roughly a dozen nations in Europe. A 25-day pass runs in the ballpark of $500. In Europe, the trains run to every urban center. European train stations are universally well-maintained, are centrally located, and are efficiently connected to the entire city.

There are a slew of major travel guides that offer advice on budget travel in Europe, and students can easily find a plethora of suggestions for cultural activities, hotels, restaurants, transportation, and nightlife. Because this exercise can really help to bring far-off cities to life, this variation may prove useful in a European History or World Geography class.

Teachers may want to take into account the effects of inflation. Inflation causes the value of money to decrease over time. Consequently, $4,000 in 1999 will not be the same as $4,000 in 2007. For that reason, it may be useful for teachers to adjust the budgetary limits as they see fit.

## Advanced Students

The more thoroughly students are encouraged to wade through their target cities, the more they will learn. Consequently, teachers may want to increase the level of detail demanded of students. For instance, students might be asked to turn in maps that trace the routes they travel while visiting their target cities, to describe buildings they visit, or to discuss the alternative modes of transport available in the cities they visit.

## Junior High or Less Advanced Students

The exercise can be easily simplified and lightened by reducing the expectations for research and documentation. Teachers can allow students to simply make up some (or all) of their activities, can do away with the requirement that students research costs, and can allow students to discuss fewer activities and visit fewer places. The teacher may also want to consider having younger students conduct this activity in small groups. This will lighten the workload for each student. I would suggest that the teacher still require each student to keep a personal travel journal during the group's trip. However, the fundamental logic of the exercise works as well with groups as it does for individuals.

## ASSESSMENT

This exercise is less complex to evaluate than are some of the other simulations. Evaluation is almost entirely based on the student's final product. Students should demonstrate increased geographic familiarity, effective budgeting and travel research, and some effort to produce an interesting and personal project. The final project consists primarily of three components, each of which should be taken into account. The components are the completed Travel Log sheets, a map of the student's travels, and a travel journal. The teacher should also consider any additional creative material or supporting documentation students may wish to turn in.

The map and the supporting materials are relatively straightforward, but any initiative shown by students should be recognized and rewarded. The journal should represent a combination of research, creativity, and thoroughness. Students should have made a real effort to interact with the travel environment, and to show that they have become aware of what exists in the locales they have visited. Students should also strive to weave a narrative story line into their travels.

The budget documentation should be complete, accurate, mathematically correct, and should particularly show student attention to documenting the source of their information. While some filler and the occasional "McDonald's, $3.99" is acceptable, students should have made an effort to engage with the cities they visit and to discover new restaurants and alternative accommodations and activities. Particularly because students are encouraged to collaborate, there is little justification for too much filler.

In addition to the project, I like to administer a simple factual quiz on U.S. geography at the completion of the project. Students are asked to identify the proper state for 20 major cities. I announce this quiz at the beginning of the project so that students are encouraged to pay attention to the location of their cities and to check with their fellow students for the location of those they do not know. I generally also include a few questions that ask students to identify the city in which certain landmarks, such as the Empire State Building or the Jefferson Memorial, are located. This quiz is simple, but it helps make sure that all students come away with some basic factual knowledge.

# APPENDIX—MATERIALS

## List of Materials

- Student Guidelines (copy for each student)
- U.S. Map (copy for each student)
- Student Travel Logs (copy for each student)
- Access to Internet, travel books, or similar guides on traveling and visiting U.S. cities

---

## Student Guidelines

1. You have up to $4,000 to spend.

2. You must visit at least 8 cities in at least 4 states during your trip.

3. You must travel for at least 25 days and nights.

4. You cannot simply drive around in a car that you already own, and you can only use a rental car for portions of your travel.

5. You must track three meals, transportation, lodging, and at least two activities for each day.

6. You must cite a price for each activity, and must cite source for each price. Some omissions or fudging are acceptable here, especially for stuff that is really difficult to track down, but it is expected that at least 80% of the prices and sources will be authentic.

7. Along with the project, you are required to turn in:
   - Completed Travel Log sheets with budget figures and sources
   - A travel journal
   - A map of your trip (either homemade or traced on a road map)
   - Any miscellaneous or additional materials that enhance the project

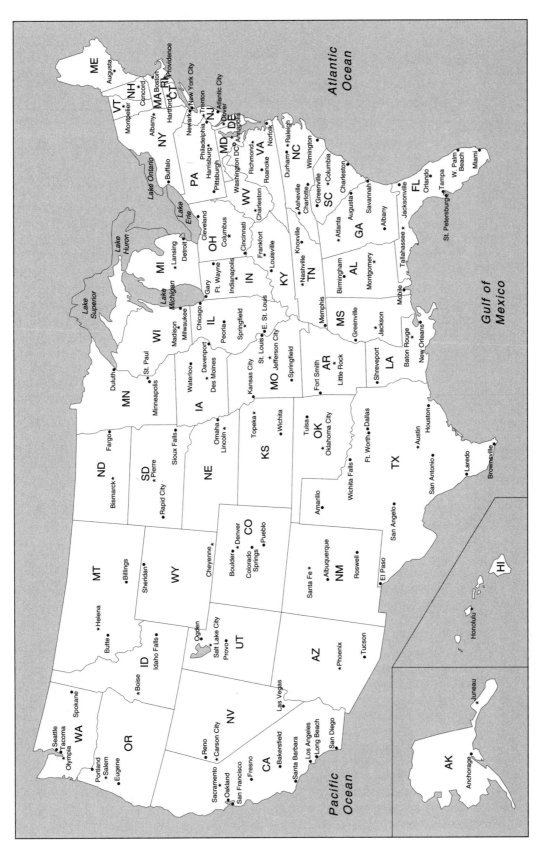

**FIGURE 7.1  U.S. Map**

## Student Travel Log

| Day | Category | Item | Source of data | Price |
|---|---|---|---|---|
| | Travel | | | |
| | Lodging | | | |
| | Meals    –breakfast | | | |
| | –lunch | | | |
| | –dinner | | | |
| | Activities –day | | | |
| | –night | | | |
| | –other | | | |
| | Miscellaneous | | | |
| | **Total Spent** | | | |
| | Travel | | | |
| | Lodging | | | |
| | Meals    –breakfast | | | |
| | –lunch | | | |
| | –dinner | | | |
| | Activities –day | | | |
| | –night | | | |
| | –other | | | |
| | Miscellaneous | | | |
| | **Total Spent** | | | |
| | Travel | | | |
| | Lodging | | | |
| | Meals    –breakfast | | | |
| | –lunch | | | |
| | –dinner | | | |
| | Activities –day | | | |
| | –night | | | |
| | –other | | | |
| | Miscellaneous | | | |
| | **Total Spent** | | | |

# CHAPTER 8

# Passing a Crime Bill

*The classroom becomes the U.S. Congress, with the students getting the opportunity to serve as powerful legislators, lobbyists, and executive branch figures. Charged with writing a new crime bill, students are forced to wrestle with position-specific electoral and professional incentives. This glut of deal-making, negotiating, and power politics begins with committee-level meetings of students in both the House and Senate, before moving on to the full chambers and then to conference committees. Along the way, congressional members are continually pressured by lobbyists, executive branch figures, and the congressional leadership, all of whom have their own inducements to offer and their own positional incentives. Students are forced to wrestle with such contemporary issues as drug prevention, gun control, midnight basketball, and curfews.*

## TEACHER'S NOTE

This exercise is designed to give students a taste of life on Capitol Hill. Students encounter committees, House–Senate conferences, the President's veto authority, lobbyists, and the substance of legislative negotiation. As they wend their way through a streamlined version of the legislative process, students experience the legislative labyrinth which shapes national policy in the United States. The class, playing the roles of Senators, Representatives, the President, and lobbyists, must find a way to draft and pass a comprehensive crime bill. The characters have all been created without any gender identification, permitting the teacher maximum flexibility and minimal worries when assigning roles.

Originally designed for a tenth-grade American Civics class, this exercise works equally well for a political science or American government class. Additionally, a teacher in an American history or current affairs class who wants to teach the law-making process may also find this a useful exercise. The exercise is designed as a two- or three-class affair, although teachers will find the simulation to run more smoothly and to be more productive if students have already been made familiar with the workings of Congress and the nature of the legislative process.

The simulation is relatively complex because it seeks to force students to sort through the multiple incentives that motivate lawmakers and lobbyists. At the same time, the process has been stripped down so that students are able to focus on the business of negotiation, compromise, deal-making, and influence-wielding. The exercise has been designed so that students are not distracted by arcane issues of parliamentary procedure.

Although the game itself is largely about deal-making and arm-twisting, the subtext that students should acknowledge is that governing in the United States is an intrinsically messy and conflictual task. Taking account of the needs, desires, and beliefs of the residents of a large and diverse nation requires lawmakers to seek compromises when they can, and to fight to make sure they do the best they can when compromise is not possible.

## BACKGROUND ON THE LEGISLATIVE PROCESS

One of the central principles of the U.S. Constitution is the distinction between the legislative and executive powers. Within the legislative branch itself, the Constitution outlines a bicameral (two-house) legislature that is intended both to reflect the will of the voters and to frustrate the passions of temporary majorities. The separation of powers between the President and Congress and the bicameral design of Congress make it difficult for advocates of one particular policy to enact the desired changes. It is almost impossible to enact legislation without substantial compromise.

The U.S. Congress has grown substantially beyond the initial body described in the Constitution. The first Congress that met in 1789 had a House of Representatives of 65 members and a Senate of 24. (The Constitution granted each state two senators and Rhode Island had not yet joined the new nation.) That Congress did not have standing committees, had few staff, and was largely isolated from organized interests or executive influence. On the other hand, the contemporary Congress has a House of 435 members, a Senate of 100, hundreds of standing committees and subcommittees, thousands of permanent institutional and individual staff, and is ceaselessly buffeted by interest-group and executive demands.

In theory, it is simple for a bill to become a law. A measure must pass the House and the Senate, and then be signed by the President. In reality, the process is nowhere near that simple. The number of issues with which Congress deals, the size of the membership, and various institutional needs have produced a model that accords very significant powers to subcommittees and committees to shape legislation and make policy.

The legislative process is initiated when a bill is introduced in at least one house, where it is sent to the appropriate committee. That committee then sends the bill down to a subcommittee, where hearings are held and the bill is buried or eventually voted on. If the bill makes it out of subcommittee, the process is repeated at the committee level. If the bill makes it out of committee and is scheduled for a floor vote, it is then debated and voted on by the full body of that house. The bill must go through this same procedure in the other body as well.

If the bill makes it through all three levels in both houses, unless it emerges in precisely the same form in both cases, it must go to a House–Senate conference committee where a compromise version of the bill is worked out. That conference bill must then win the approval of both the House and Senate. At this point, the President can either sign or veto the bill. If the bill is vetoed, then the House and Senate must each override the veto by a two-thirds majority. Finally, this entire process must take place within one two-year session of Congress. If a new election is held before a bill has made it all the way through this process, then the bill starts all over at square one in the next Congress.

This general description is only a sketchy outline of the process and ignores several complexities of the legislative process. A couple of particularly significant problems loom for the eager legislator. One is the House Rules committee, which determines when legislation will come up for a vote, what amendments can be offered, and how the voting process on a bill will be structured. A second problem is the Senate filibuster. The Senate's culture resists hasty decisions. To bring an end to Senate debate and force a vote, 60 of the 100 Senators must vote for "cloture." Consequently, just 41 out of the 100 senators are able to kill a piece of legislation. While no allowance is made for the Rules committee in this simulation, the filibuster is taken into account.

One of the great frustrations for legislators and interested actors in this complex and multi-tiered legislative process is that a victory at one level does not necessarily translate into a final or lasting victory. Securing the passage of a provision in a bill at the subcommittee level is irrelevant if the decision is reversed by the committee, the full body, or the conference committee. The result is that there is no such thing as a final victory on a piece of legislation until the bill is actually signed into law by the President.

## Parties in Congress

The U.S. Congress is primarily organized around political parties. Except for incredibly rare cases, Representatives and Senators are all members of either the Democratic or the Republican party. Each party begins each two-year session of Congress with a "caucus" at which it selects its leaders. In each House of Congress, it is the leaders of the two parties who oversee the management of legislation and related business. The majority party in each house selects the chamber's top official (the Speaker in the House and the Majority Leader in the Senate), gives itself a majority on each of the chamber's committees, and is generally able to dominate the tenor of legislation and debate.

Between the 1940s and 1994, the Democratic party controlled Congress the vast majority of the time. Democratic dominance in the House and Senate came to an abrupt end when the Republicans took control of both chambers in 1994.

Most legislative conflict takes place across party lines. Of course, there have been significant groups of legislators who consistently crossed their party's leaders. Some of the better-known party-crossers in recent political history were the *boll weevils* (Southern Democrats who strongly supported President Ronald Reagan in the 1980s) and the *gypsy moths* (Northern Republicans who consistently voted against Reagan in the 1980s). It is the interplay of party, region, and personal circumstance and beliefs that shape the actual behavior of any given congressman.

# USING THIS SIMULATION

## Purpose of the Simulation

Substantively, this lesson was designed to develop student understanding of the legislative process. Students learn about interactions within the legislature; about relationships between legislators, executives, and special interests; and about the nitty-gritty of the legislative process. The very means by which students score points in the exercise forces them to pay attention to each of the steps of a stylized legislative process and makes them aware of such considerations as the Senate filibuster, the presidential veto, the role of lobbyist campaign contributions, and the uncertain significance of committee decisions. Additionally, students learn a little bit about some of the fundamental disputes in criminal justice while they try to forge a crime bill.

## Skills Developed

The exercise helps to develop negotiating, public speaking, analytic writing, and their interpersonal skills. As students attempt to construct a workable compromise document, the exercise cultivates analytic skills in the practice of negotiation and coordination. Each student must strive to fulfill certain role-determined objectives, and the assessment instruments require each student to recall and analyze what took place at the conclusion of the exercise.

The exercise also cultivates analytic writing skills. Students are forced to keep track of their points and then explain and justify their score to the teacher. Additionally, students must write an essay that documents, explains, and analyzes what transpired in the course of the game. During the simulation, students need to keep track of the preferences and commitments of their classmates. Successful negotiation requires awareness of the needs and resources of other players.

## Logistics

The exercise generally requires about two 40-minute class periods. Preparation on the teacher's part, after reading these materials, should require less than an hour. Because students need to prepare a brief on their state (for Representatives and Senators), their pet issues (for lobbyists), or the President's responsibility (for the President), the teacher should assign roles and describe the briefing assignment about a week before the exercise is to take place.

If possible, it helps to have multiple classrooms available, because I like to at least have the House and Senate groups meet in different rooms. If students are responsible enough and the space is available, I imagine it would be even more effective to have the two House and two Senate committees meet in different rooms. However, this would require having up to four available classrooms.

The game was optimally designed for a class of 30, but it can comfortably accommodate a class ranging in size from 20 to 38. In a class of 30, the students play the roles of 16 Representatives, 6 Senators, 7 lobbyists, and the President. For a smaller class, the teacher should simply reduce the number of Representatives and lobbyists as suggested in the box that follows. For classes larger than 30, the teacher should assign two students to the presidency (one will act as the White House lobbyist) and to the various lobbyist positions. Dual lobbyists work fine, permitting one student to concentrate on the House and one on the Senate.

---

**SMALLER CLASSES**

For classes with fewer than 30 students, the teacher should make the following modifications. The demands, balance, and nuances of the game were taken into account in designing these changes. No additional adjustments need to be made.

- class of 29 students—don't use lobbyist Jennings
- class of 28 students—also don't use Representative Cliffson
- class of 27 students—also don't use lobbyist Johnson
- class of 26 students—also don't use Representative Henderson
- class of 25 students—also don't use Representative Claycut
- class of 24 students—also don't use Representative McIntyre
- class of 23 students—also don't use Representative Paterson
- class of 22 students—also don't use Representative Washington
- class of 21 students—also don't use lobbyist Naamans
- class of 20 students—also don't use lobbyist Arkanian

---

## HOW THE SIMULATION WORKS

Students are asked to hammer out a crime bill that addresses six specific issues. Students must write a piece of legislation that can pass both houses of Congress and be signed by the President.

Students begin the simulation by separating into House and Senate contingents. The House and the Senate each convenes in two committees dealing with the first draft of the bill. Each committee will draft legislation addressing three of the six issues to be resolved.

Once the two committees have passed preliminary measures, the House and Senate each convene as a full body to hammer out an overall crime bill. The two committee bills are used as the basis for assembling the full chamber bill. In each chamber, it takes a majority vote of members to amend a provision of the committee bill. Unless the House and Senate bills are identical, those two bills then need to be reconciled by a conference committee. If the conference committee's compromise is then passed by a majority vote of both the House and Senate, it goes to the President for his or her signature (or veto). If the bill is vetoed, Congress can try to override the veto.

Lobbyists and legislators have incentives to get the bills to look the way they want them to at every stage of the process. However, the incentives encourage all players to worry most about the shape of the final bill. The President and the leaders in the House and in the Senate have other incentives that also encourage them to worry about getting a bill—any bill—passed and to respect the substance of committee bills.

### Student Roles

Students are assigned specific roles. Roles are all designated by last name only and do not use gender identifiers, so it is simple for a boy or a girl to play any role. Students represent Senators and Representatives, lobbyists, and one student plays the President. The distribution of power and action is such that the student playing the President or Senate

Majority Leader has only moderately more responsibility than the lobbyists or House backbenchers. Each student is to prepare a two-page brief appropriate to his or her role prior to the beginning of the exercise.

## Object

First, students seek to forge a bill that gets passed—students have very strong incentives to get a bill through the legislative hoops. Second, students (whether Congressmen, lobbyists, or the President) attempt to shape the bill so that it comes out consistent with their assigned preferences. Students score points in various ways, depending on the role they play.

Students are responsible for tracking their own score, and for turning in the score and explaining it as part of their assessment paper. At each stage of the exercise, after both of the committees in the House and both of the committees in the Senate have written their bills, after each of the chambers has written bills, and after a final piece of legislation is enacted, the teacher should write the explicit pieces of the legislation on the board so that students can track how they fared on each of their issue preferences. The teacher should also keep track of the same information on paper for reference purposes.

Congressmen can score points for lobbyist donations. Teachers should be careful to minimize confusion over their funds. See Donation Transaction Sheet (p. 102) and discussion of Campaign Funds (p. 96) in Chapter 6.

***How Congressmen Score Points***   House members and Senators score points by getting their preferences into the legislation and by collecting campaign funds from lobbyists. For each preference that is written into a committee bill in the player's chamber (either the House or the Senate), a player gets 1 point. For each preference written into the chamber's final bill, a player gets 1 more point. For each preference written into legislation that is enacted into law (either with the President's signature or over a veto), a player gets 2 more points. Players have four issue preferences, which means a player could theoretically score up to 16 points from issues (each of four issue preferences can produce up to 4 points).

Additionally, Congressmen get 1 extra point for each $5,000 in campaign funds that they receive from lobbyists.

***House and Senate Leaders***   The committee leaders, the Senate Majority Leader, and the House Majority Leader have a slightly different role from other players. As in real life, these figures are worried about their prestige and about their chamber's influence. Consequently, committee chairs receive 5 points if the full chamber bill matches their committee's bill on the three issues that come out of their committee. Majority leaders receive 5 points if their chamber produces a piece of legislation and 4 more points if the final enacted legislation matches their chamber's bill on at least four of the six issues. To keep the scoring equitable, committee leaders have only three issue preferences for which they can score, and majority leaders have only two issue preferences for which they can score. Consequently, Congressional leaders can theoretically score up to 17 points based on issue preferences and the fate of the legislation. Like their colleagues, congressional leaders get 1 extra point for each $5,000 in campaign funds that they receive from lobbyists.

***Lobbyists***   Lobbyists seek to have their preferences enacted into law. To do this they use their powers of persuasion and campaign donations. Lobbyists each have two issues they are concerned about. Lobbyists receive 1 point for each issue preference that is written into the committee bill in the House, and 1 for each written into the committee bill in the Senate. They receive 2 points for each written into the full House bill, and 2 for each written into the full Senate bill. Plus, they receive 4 points for each preference written into the legislation that is enacted into law. Since lobbyists have two issue preferences, they can theoretically score up to 20 points.

***The President***   The President wants final legislation to pass and wants his or her preferences reflected in the legislation. The President gets 5 points if a piece of legislation passes with his or her signature, 2 points for each issue preference in the final legislation, and 5 points for keeping the budget under control by not having the bill spend more than $5 billion in total. The President can theoretically score up to 20 points.

## Length of the Game

The exercise is played until students have worked the bill through all the stages of the legislative process. The teacher will find it useful to apply time limits to each stage, so as to fit the game within the intended time frame (I suggest two 40-minute classes as a reasonable time frame). The suggested time limits here total a maximum of 75 minutes (although it is rare for every stage to bump into the time caps). These time limits permit the teacher to squeeze the exercise into 80 minutes of class time.

The stages of the game consist of the following:

1. Senators and Representatives each draft bills in committees (cap at 20 minutes). There are four groups meeting, because two committees in each of the two chambers meet separately, either on opposite sides of the classroom or in two rooms. Each chamber has two committees that are meeting simultaneously. Each committee is to address three of the six issues the chamber must address (the three issues each committee addresses are predetermined).
2. Senators and Representatives each meet as a full body to forge a full bill from the two committee bills that are reported to each chamber (cap at 25 minutes). The two chambers should continue to meet in two rooms or on opposite sides of the room.
3. Senators and Representatives meet in conference to hammer out any differences (cap at 5 minutes). The conference, consisting of the two majority leaders and the four committee chairs, should be held outside of the classroom. If that is not possible, it needs to be held in a corner of the room that is sheltered from all the eager and prying lobbyists and assorted congressmen.
4. The Senate and House each decide whether to vote the conference bill up or down (cap at 5 minutes). If the conference bill is voted down, the teacher may permit the class to reconvene the conference to try again.
5. The President signs or vetoes the final bill (cap at 5 minutes).
6. If the President vetoes the bill, the House and Senate can either attempt to overturn the veto or seek to pass compromise legislation (15-minute time limit).

## How the Simulation Proceeds

About a week prior to the exercise, the teacher should outline the simulation and assign each student his or her role. The students are to prepare a two-page brief that will help them play their role effectively. Senators and Representatives are to briefly describe the political nature of their state, the nature of their chamber, and one of the issues that they are concerned about. The President is to briefly discuss the nature of the presidency, including the powers and weaknesses of the office, and two of the issues that the President cares about. The lobbyists are to prepare a brief that will help them argue the two policies that they are to advocate. Each student will use his or her brief as a reference during the exercise. Briefs will be evaluated based on the quality and usefulness of information and clarity of organization.

On the day of the exercise, the teacher should explain the purpose and nature of the simulation. At that point, Senators should go to one side of the classroom (or to a second room) and the Representatives should move to the other side of the room. The lobbyists and the President are free to mill about. Affairs in the House and Senate will be transpiring simultaneously at all times.

The Senators and Representatives should get seated and organize themselves. At that point, each body is to break into the assigned committees. Both bodies will break into two committees. Each committee needs to forge compromises over three provisions that will be in the crime bill (the three for each committee have been determined in the accompanying materials). While the committees meet, committee members will negotiate and debate, but they are also free to mill about and talk to lobbyists.

Once each of the committees has reached a decision on the three issues it is to address, the full House should meet in one place and the full Senate in another. The full bodies then need to merge the provisions of the two bills into one overall bill. Provisions of the committee bills can be amended by a majority vote.

Once the House has assembled a bill that addresses all six issues, it needs to pass the full bill by a majority vote. In the Senate, because just 41 Senators are enough to filibuster a decision, three-fifths (60%) of all Senators must vote for the full bill.

If the House and Senate bills are not identical, the two bills are sent to a joint conference. The leader of each chamber and the chairs of the two committees in each body must forge a compromise bill that irons out differences in the House and Senate bills. The brief joint session takes place in another room or an isolated corner of the room. No other students may enter the conference, although conference members can come out to talk to others.

The conference bill then goes back to the full House and Senate for votes. The conference bill requires a majority vote in the House and a three-fifths majority vote in the Senate in order to pass. If the conference bill does not pass, the class may, at the teacher's discretion, convene another conference to write an acceptable bill.

Once both Houses of Congress have passed an identical bill, it goes to the President for his or her signature. The President can sign the bill, in which case the class has passed legislation, or can veto it. If the President vetoes the bill, there are two options. The first is that the President can rapidly work out an amended alternative with the House and Senate leadership. This bill must pass both houses and then be signed before the end of the session. The second option is that two-thirds of each house can vote to override the veto, in which case the law takes effect despite the veto.

---

**SUMMARY TEACHER INSTRUCTIONS**

*Prior to the beginning of the simulation*
- About a week prior to the exercise, the general exercise is explained and students are assigned their roles for the purpose of preparing their briefing papers.

*The day of the simulation*
- Objective is for students to construct a bill that gets passed and is consistent with their assigned preferences.
- Explain the background on the legislative process.
- Explain the rules of the exercise and the issues to be addressed in the Crime bill.
- Explain how points are earned based on getting their preferences into the legislation and for receiving campaign fund donations.

*During the simulation*
- Students meet in their committees to draft preliminary bills.
- Full House and full Senate meet to finalize committee bills.
- The House and Senate bills must be identical or there is a joint conference to iron out the differences.
- The President must sign or veto the bill, and a veto will lead to a congressional attempt at an override.

*After the simulation*
- Require students to write an analytic essay which tallies and explains the number of points they received, and explains why they were effective representatives in compiling the score that they did.
- Assess simulation using Student Assessment Sheet (see Chapter 12), classroom observations of participation, written analysis of simulation, and a quiz.

## COMMENTS FROM EXPERIENCE

It is important that the teacher use the scoring system to influence students. Given the delicate interplay of forces that shape legislation, leaving students to their own devices is a recipe for either chaos or popularity-driven action. I recall one fellow teacher who attempted to do the exercise without incentives. She naturally wound up with students debating about what they wanted the laws to be. While there is a certain value to having students discuss these issues, that is not the purpose of the lesson and this lesson is probably not the most effective way to structure that debate. Fundamentally, it is important for the teacher to get comfortable with the point system and then make the class comfortable with the system if the exercise is to prove as effective as possible.

The point system encourages the leadership figures to be less concerned with personal preferences than with the product of their chamber, which helps the game run smoothly and replicates the cross-cutting issue- and prestige-based conflicts that shape legislation in Washington.

It is important that the teacher seek to put mature and interested students into the key leadership roles. These players are in a position to shepherd the game along, and having quality leadership can enhance the experience for everyone.

## POSSIBLE MODIFICATIONS

### Advanced Students

As it is, the game is really rich enough for students of a relatively high level. Colleagues have used the game very successfully with advanced seniors in government class. These students tended to take the negotiating and influence-wielding to high levels of sophistication. For extremely advanced students, the teacher may want to add subcommittees to the existing committee structure or may want to increase the role of partisanship by giving more sway to the majority party leaders.

### Junior High and Less Advanced Student

Two elements of this exercise provide most of the complications. One is the point system, which requires students to understand the process of how a bill moves through the legislative process and forces them to keep track of the bill at each point. The second is the very complexity of the multi-ring, multi-hoop process. For junior high or less advanced students, these elements may be more trouble than they are worth. For younger students, the teacher should probably do away with the scoring altogether, even though this will have the effect of making issue positions nothing more than suggestions. Second, the teacher may want to streamline the exercise. For instance, a teacher may want to do away with committees, and simply have the students start off by meeting as the full House and full Senate.

## ASSESSMENT

Four kinds of assessment are suggested for this exercise. Each of the assessments offers feedback on different elements of student performance in the activity. Students should be informed of all assessments when they are first told that the simulation will be played, *before* the simulation begins. By requiring students to pay attention throughout the exercise, the assessment devices make the exercise more productive and maximize student participation.

First, each student is asked to compose a two-page briefing paper in preparation for the exercise. Senators and Representatives are to briefly describe the political nature of their state, the nature of their chamber, and one of the issues they are concerned about. The President is to briefly discuss the nature of the presidency, including the powers and weaknesses of the office, and two of the issues the President cares about. The lobbyists are to prepare some materials that will help them argue the two policies they are to advocate. Briefs will be turned in at the conclusion of the exercise. Briefs are to be evaluated based on the quality and usefulness of information and the clarity of organization.

Second, I evaluate students based on my observations of their participation in the exercise. In particular, I look for students who take guidance from their characters' incentives and then use their ingenuity and skills to pursue those incentives in an effective manner. At the end of the exercise, I also have each student fill out the standard Student Assessment Sheet for Group Exercises feedback form (see Chapter 12, Final Thoughts), which asks them to assess the contributions of their classmates. Using my observations and the evaluations, I assess students based on their efforts and contributions to the exercise. The feedback form takes about five minutes to fill out, so this assessment can be completed by the day after the exercise.

Third, students are asked to write a two-page first-person essay that analyzes the simulation. First and foremost, they are asked to total the number of points they scored and to explain how that total was achieved. The intention is that students take their incentives seriously, and the essay should discuss the scoring to demonstrate that they did so and that they played the character as effectively as was possible. This essay forces students to discuss the multiple checkpoints of the legislative process, their roles as leaders, and/or the role of campaign finance.

Students are also asked to recount what actually happened and to explain why the final bill looked like it did. In addition, students should explain how they would act differently if the exercise were conducted again and discuss any particulars they found interesting or significant. Foreknowledge of this assignment helps motivate students to pay closer attention throughout the exercise, increasing students' interest and attentiveness. Students are to write the paper the night after the exercise; the teacher collects it the next day.

Fourth, students are quizzed on rules of the game, the substance of the bill, and major events that took place during negotiations. This short quiz should take no more than 30 minutes. The purpose is to ensure that students paid attention to what transpired around them during the game and to encourage students to make themselves familiar with the rules of the exercise.

All the assessments are finished by the end of the day after the simulation. The approaches offer a well-rounded view of student participation and performance, while cultivating useful skills. By informing students of the multiple assessments *before* the simulation, the teacher encourages students to pay attention to the substance and the dynamic of the exercise.

# APPENDIX—MATERIALS

## List of Materials

- The Issues Addressed in the Crime Bill sheet, which also specifies the committee in which each issue originates (for each student)
- Student Profile Sheets for each student (Senators, Representatives, President, and lobbyists)

---

**THE ISSUES ADDRESSED IN THE CRIME BILL**

*First Addressed in the Judiciary Committee*

1. Whether to legalize marijuana

2. Whether to impose the death penalty for drug dealers who traffic in large amounts of heroin, cocaine, or related drugs

3. Whether to pass gun control legislation (and, if so, whether to restrict just handguns, or rifles as well)

*First Addressed in the Urban Affairs Committee*

4. Whether to fund new spending on drug abuse treatment and rehabilitation (and, if so, how many billions of dollars to spend)

5. Whether to spend money to build additional prisons (and, if so, how many billions of dollars to spend)

6. Whether to require urban areas to impose curfews (and, if so, what the specified time should be and what age group the curfew should apply to)

---

### Student Profile Sheet 1   Senator Stearns (Republican-NJ), Chairman of Senate Judiciary Committee

A third-term senior Senator from New Jersey, Stearns is secure back home. Stearns won 78% of the vote in last reelection bid. New Jersey is a fairly conservative state, which is tough on crime and worried about urban violence. However, it is also an urban area with more relaxed views about some social issues, such as marijuana.

#### *Stearns's Positions*

1. Death penalty for trafficking large amounts of heroin, cocaine, or related drugs
2. Build more prisons (spend at least $3 billion more per year)
3. Legalize marijuana

#### *Scoring*

1 point for each position that is in Senate committee bills

1 point for each position that is in full Senate bill

2 points for each position that is in final bill enacted into law

1 point for each $5,000 in lobbyist campaign contributions

Also, as Chair, Stearns wants the full Senate bill to be the same as the committee bill in order to bolster a reputation as an effective chairman. If the full Senate bill matches the three provisions in the committee bill, that is worth 5 points.

### Student Profile Sheet 2   Senator Oxsfeld (Democrat-WA), member Senate Urban Affairs Committee

A first-term junior Senator from Washington, Oxsfeld won big in first statewide election. Oxsfeld upset a famous three-term Republican Senator who had forgotten about the people back home. Washington is an outdoorsy state with low crime rates where people do a lot of hunting.

#### *Oxsfeld's Positions*

1. Gun control for handguns, but no restrictions on rifles
2. Urban areas should not be permitted to impose curfews, because curfews violate personal freedom
3. Spend more money on drug abuse treatment and prevention (at least $4 billion per year)
4. Spend more money to build prisons (at least $2 billion per year)

#### *Scoring*

1 point for each position that is in Senate committee bills

1 point for each position that is in full Senate bill

2 points for each position that is in final bill enacted into law

1 point for each $5,000 in lobbyist campaign contributions

## Student Profile Sheet 3   Senator Dowden (Democrat-TX), member Senate Judiciary Committee

A fourth-term senior Senator from Texas, Dowden is one of the senior Democrats in the Senate. Dowden ran for President once a few years ago, and didn't run too poorly. Dowden now has a large national reputation and winds up a frequent guest of the Sunday morning TV news shows. However, Texas is an increasingly conservative state, so Dowden has to be worried about upsetting constituents. Texans tend to oppose gun control and to support tough penalties for criminals.

### Dowden's Positions

1. Spend more on prison construction (at least $2 billion per year)
2. Death penalty for trafficking large amounts of heroin, cocaine, or related drugs
3. Opposed to the legalization of marijuana
4. No control or regulation of guns, owning guns is a constitutional right that should not be restricted

### Scoring

1 point for each position that is in Senate committee bills

1 point for each position that is in full Senate bill

2 points for each position that is in final bill enacted into law

1 point for each $5,000 in lobbyist campaign contributions

## Student Profile Sheet 4   Senator Walton (Republican-NM), Senate Majority Leader and member of Senate Judiciary Committee

A senior and highly respected fifth-term Senator from New Mexico, Walton is one of the longest-serving members of the Senate. Walton is a fixture in New Mexico—no one even ran against the Senator in the last election, so the Senator doesn't worry too much about what the voters back home want. In fact, as leader of the Senate's majority party (the Republicans), Walton may be more concerned that the Senate functions smoothly and has a big voice in legislation. Walton's primary concern is keeping taxes low by not having the government spend more money.

### Walton's Positions

1. Spend no new money for prisons—wants to see zero money spent for prisons
2. Spend no new money for drug abuse treatment and prevention—wants to see zero money spent for these programs

### Scoring

1 point for each position that is in Senate committee bills

1 point for each position that is in full Senate bill

2 points for each position that is in final bill enacted into law

1 point for each $5,000 in lobbyist campaign contributions

Also, as Senate Majority Leader, Walton is most concerned with having the Senate work smoothly and take a lead role in policy. Walton wants to see a Senate bill voted out and wants a final bill that is close to the Senate version. If a piece of legislation is enacted, either with the President's signature or over the President's veto, Walton receives 5 points. If the final law matches the final Senate bill on at least four of the six elements, Walton receives 4 more points.

## Student Profile Sheet 5    Senator Richards (Republican-AL), Chairman of Senate Urban Affairs Committee

A third-term senior Senator from Alabama, Richards is a famous "Old South" folk hero who served two terms as governor before becoming a Senator. This old-fashioned superconservative is tough on crime and opposed to taxes or government spending.

### Richards's Positions

1. Urban areas should be required to have a curfew that starts no later than 12 P.M. and includes at least all youths under 16
2. Spend more on prison construction (at least $4 billion per year)
3. Spend no new money for drug abuse treatment and prevention—wants to see zero money spent for these programs

### Scoring

1 point for each position that is in Senate committee bills

1 point for each position that is in full Senate bill

2 points for each position that is in final bill enacted into law

1 point for each $5,000 in lobbyist campaign contributions

Also, as Chair, Richards wants the full Senate bill to be the same as the committee bill in order to bolster a reputation as an effective chairman. If the full Senate bill matches the three provisions in the committee bill, that is worth 5 points.

## Student Profile Sheet 6    Senator Leffingwell (Republican-CA), member Senate Urban Affairs Committee

A first-term junior Senator from California, Leffingwell is a former mayor of San Diego. Leffingwell became well-known for success in working with community groups and the police to dramatically reduce crime rates. California, the nation's largest state, encompasses a wide range of political views. To win reelection in a state that has large numbers of extremely conservative and extremely liberal voters, Leffingwell has to be careful to walk a middle course.

### Leffingwell's Positions

1. Spend more on building prisons (at least $3 billion a year)
2. Spend more money on drug abuse treatment and prevention (at least $4 billion per year)
3. Urban areas should be required to have a curfew that starts no later than 11 P.M. and includes at least all youths under 17
4. Outlaw the death penalty

### Scoring

1 point for each position that is in Senate committee bills

1 point for each position that is in full Senate bill

2 points for each position that is in final bill enacted into law

1 point for each $5,000 in lobbyist campaign contributions

## Student Profile Sheet 7   Representative Hamill (Republican-FL), Chairman of House Judiciary Committee

A fourteenth-term representative from Tampa Bay, Florida, Hamill has served on the Judiciary Committee for over 20 years. Hamill used to be a district attorney before being elected to Congress and has strong feelings about law and order. Hamill's district is subject to a great deal of crime caused by the drug trade, pressuring Hamill to see that efforts are made to combat drug-related crime.

### Hamill's Positions

1. Death penalty for trafficking large amounts of heroin, cocaine, or related drugs
2. Spend money to build more prisons (spend at least $4 billion more per year)
3. Do not legalize marijuana

### Scoring

1 point for each position that is in House committee bills

1 point for each position that is in full House bill

2 points for each position that is in final bill enacted into law

1 point for each $5,000 in lobbyist campaign contributions

Also, as Chair, Hamill wants the full House bill to be the same as the committee bill in order to bolster a reputation as an effective chairman. If the full House bill matches the three provisions in the committee bill, that is worth 5 points.

## Student Profile Sheet 8   Representative Ellery (Republican-TX), Chairman of House Urban Affairs Committee

A seventh-term representative from Houston, Texas, Ellery got the chairmanship when the committee revolted against an obnoxious predecessor. Ellery's power base is this committee, so it is important that the committee work efficiently to produce a useful bill. Ellery is a moderate Houston Republican who supports getting tougher on crime but who opposes the death penalty.

### Ellery's Positions

1. Urban areas should be required to have a curfew that starts no later than 12 P.M. and includes youths under 15, but definitely not those over 16
2. Spend more money on building prisons (at least $3 billion per year)
3. No death penalty regardless of the crime

### Scoring

1 point for each position that is in House committee bills

1 point for each position that is in full House bill

2 points for each position that is in final bill enacted into law

1 point for each $5,000 in lobbyist campaign contributions

Also, as Chair, Ellery wants the full House bill to be the same as the committee bill in order to bolster a reputation as an effective chairman. If the full House bill matches the three provisions in the committee bill, that is worth 5 points.

### Student Profile Sheet 9   Representative Sturbridge (Republican-CA), House Majority Leader and member of House Judiciary Committee

A fifteenth-term representative from Santa Cruz, California, Sturbridge is the number two person in the House (after the Speaker, who gets less involved in the day-to-day business of legislation). Sturbridge has been a powerhouse in California politics for decades, and is known for convincing others to support some very conservative views. Sturbridge is most concerned that the House write a good, useful crime bill, and not as much about the particulars of the bill.

#### Sturbridge's Positions

1. Death penalty for trafficking large amounts of heroin, cocaine, or related drugs
2. Opposed to the legalization of marijuana

*Scoring*

1 point for each position that is in House committee bills

1 point for each position that is in full House bill

2 points for each position that is in final bill enacted into law

1 point for each $5,000 in lobbyist campaign contributions

Also, as House Majority Leader, Sturbridge is most concerned with having the House work smoothly and take a lead role in policy. Sturbridge wants to see a House bill voted out and wants a final bill that is close to the House version. If a piece of legislation is enacted, either with the President's signature or over the President's veto, Sturbridge receives 5 points. If the final law matches the final House bill on at least four of the six elements, Sturbridge receives 4 more points.

### Student Profile Sheet 10   Representative Bromfeld (Democrat-NY), member House Judiciary Committee

A second-term representative from New York City, Bromfeld is a former preacher who went into politics after several racial incidents inflamed the community. Bromfeld is a liberal who thinks that the problems of central cities make it very difficult for urban youths to get their lives headed in the right direction. Bromfeld wants the government to work harder to help troubled urban youths get their lives together.

#### Bromfeld's Positions

1. Spend more on drug abuse treatment and rehabilitation (at least $5 billion per year)
2. No death penalty for drug trafficking
3. Marijuana should be legalized so that people who want to smoke it are no longer forced to get acquainted with the culture of drug dealing
4. No one except military personnel and police should be permitted to carry handguns, and rifles should be highly restricted as well

*Scoring*

1 point for each position that is in House committee bills

1 point for each position that is in full House bill

2 points for each position that is in final bill enacted into law

1 point for each $5,000 in lobbyist campaign contributions

### Student Profile Sheet 11    Representative Delangelo (Democrat-NJ), member House Judiciary Committee

A fifth-term representative from outside Trenton, New Jersey, Delangelo represents a heavily Italian, "blue-collar" area. The district is dominated by traditional families who worry about the effects that drugs and violence are having on the schools. Delangelo is an old-style Democrat, who started out as a labor union official before running for Congress, and has no use for "bleeding hearts" who get carried away with concern for criminals or their rights.

#### Delangelo's Positions

1. Spend more on prisons (at least $3 billion per year)
2. No death penalty
3. Marijuana should not be legalized, since that would just encourage drug abuse
4. There should be strict gun controls on both handguns and rifles

#### Scoring

1 point for each position that is in House committee bills

1 point for each position that is in full House bill

2 points for each position that is in final bill enacted into law

1 point for each $5,000 in lobbyist campaign contributions

### Student Profile Sheet 12    Representative Martinez (Republican-GA), member House Judiciary Committee

A first-term representative from Atlanta, Georgia, Martinez is from a district where the races are often very close. In the last election Martinez just barely edged out the Democratic incumbent, who had only been in office for four years after beating a previous Republican. Martinez ran a small business before moving into Congress, and takes a practical, businesslike view of issues.

#### Martinez's Positions

1. Spend more to build new prisons (at least $2 billion per year)
2. Death penalty for trafficking large amounts of heroin, cocaine, or related drugs
3. Marijuana should not be legalized
4. There should be no controls on handguns, since the Second Amendment guarantees the rights to bear arms and because guns deter criminals

#### Scoring

1 point for each position that is in House committee bills

1 point for each position that is in full House bill

2 points for each position that is in final bill enacted into law

1 point for each $5,000 in lobbyist campaign contributions

### Student Profile Sheet 13   Representative Paterson (Democrat-IA), member House Judiciary Committee

A third-term representative from Des Moines, Iowa, Paterson likes to be referred to as a middle-American Democrat, representing commonsense liberal values. Paterson won 91% of the vote in the last election, so isn't real worried about being reelected. Paterson comes from a relatively peaceful community and is less concerned about urban troubles than are many colleagues in the House.

#### Paterson's Positions

1. No death penalty for drug trafficking
2. Marijuana should not be legalized
3. Spend more on drug abuse treatment and rehabilitation (at least $2 billion per year, but no more than $5 billion)
4. The government should control handguns, but it should not regulate owners of rifles

#### Scoring

1 point for each position that is in House committee bills

1 point for each position that is in full House bill

2 points for each position that is in final bill enacted into law

1 point for each $5,000 in lobbyist campaign contributions

### Student Profile Sheet 14   Representative Henderson (Republican-SD), member House Judiciary Committee

A nineteenth-term congressman from South Dakota, Henderson is the powerful long-term chairman of the House Armed Services Committee. Henderson has sat on the Judiciary Committee since the 1960s. Henderson, a crusty old member who hasn't had a real opponent in an election since the 1970s, feels pretty free to vote without regard to the district's views.

#### Henderson's Positions

1. Spend more on prison construction (at least $2 billion per year)
2. Death penalty for trafficking large amounts of heroin, cocaine, or related drugs
3. Opposed to the legalization of marijuana
4. No control or regulation of guns, since owning guns is a constitutional right that should not be restricted

#### Scoring

1 point for each position that is in House committee bills

1 point for each position that is in full House bill

2 points for each position that is in final bill enacted into law

1 point for each $5,000 in lobbyist campaign contributions

### Student Profile Sheet 15   Representative Blutarsky (Democrat-PA), member House Urban Affairs Committee

A twelfth-term representative from Pittsburgh, Pennsylvania, Blutarsky grew up in a coal mining town. Blutarsky went to Penn State, and had never lived outside of Pennsylvania until getting elected to Congress. Blutarsky became famous for challenging the mayor of Philadelphia to an arm-wrestling contest when the mayor had said, before a Steelers–Eagles football game, that Philadelphia was the toughest town in the state. Pittsburgh is a middle-American town and Blutarsky supports traditional conservative values.

#### *Blutarsky's Positions*

1. The government needs to impose controls on handguns and on rifles
2. Urban areas should not be permitted to impose curfews, because curfews violate the freedom of youths
3. Spend more money on drug abuse treatment and prevention (at least $1 billion per year, but no more than $3 billion per year)
4. Spend more money to build prisons (at least $3 billion per year)

#### *Scoring*

1 point for each position that is in House committee bills

1 point for each position that is in full House bill

2 points for each position that is in final bill enacted into law

1 point for each $5,000 in lobbyist campaign contributions

### Student Profile Sheet 16   Representative Mickelson (Republican-AK), member House Urban Affairs Committee

A third-term representative from Juneau, Alaska, Mickelson is a superconservative who thinks criminals need to take full responsibility for their actions. Mickelson is a big believer in complete personal freedom. After getting out of the army during the Vietnam War, Mickelson picked up, moved to Alaska, and made a fortune in the oil business. In the last election Mickelson won 80% of the vote.

#### *Mickelson's Positions*

1. Supports the death penalty even for dealers who deal a small amount of hard drugs
2. Spend more money to build prisons (at least $4 billion a year)
3. Spend no more money on drug abuse treatment or rehabilitation—that will just produce a need for more taxes
4. Opposes any kind of urban curfew, Mickelson is one of the few Republicans to oppose curfews (because he believes they are a violation of personal freedom)

#### *Scoring*

1 point for each position that is in House committee bills

1 point for each position that is in full House bill

2 points for each position that is in final bill enacted into law

1 point for each $5,000 in lobbyist campaign contributions

### Student Profile Sheet 17　Representative Bartington (Republican-CA), member House Urban Affairs Committee

A second-term representative from northern California, Bartington is very conservative. Bartington thinks America is far too soft on criminals, and represents a district that feels strongly about the issue. Barely won reelection last time, with 52% of the vote, largely because voters thought Bartington might not be tough enough. Now, Bartington needs to demonstrate toughness.

#### *Bartington's Positions*

1. Supports the death penalty for dealers who deal large amounts of hard drugs
2. Spend more money to build prisons (at least $3 billion a year)
3. Spend more money on drug abuse treatment and rehabilitation (at least $2 billion, but no more than $4 billion a year)
4. Opposes any kind of gun control because a lot of district residents are hunters who travel up to Oregon for hunting season

#### *Scoring*

1 point for each position that is in House committee bills

1 point for each position that is in full House bill

2 points for each position that is in final bill enacted into law

1 point for each $5,000 in lobbyist campaign contributions

### Student Profile Sheet 18　Representative Chase (Democrat-VA), member House Urban Affairs Committee

A third-term representative from Richmond, Virginia, Chase is young and moderate. Started as a high-ranking aid to the governor who decided to seek office. Got law degree at the University of Virginia and practiced criminal law for two years before running for Congress. Very popular back home, in a heavily Republican district, largely because of easygoing manner.

#### *Chase's Positions*

1. Marijuana should be legalized
2. Urban areas should have a curfew of 11 P.M. or earlier for youths under the age of 16
3. Spend more money on drug abuse treatment and prevention (at least $3 billion per year)
4. Spend a little more money to build new prisons (at least $1 billion per year, but no more than $2 billion per year)

#### *Scoring*

1 point for each position that is in House committee bills

1 point for each position that is in full House bill

2 points for each position that is in final bill enacted into law

1 point for each $5,000 in lobbyist campaign contributions

### Student Profile Sheet 19   Representative McIntyre (Republican-OK), member House Urban Affairs Committee

A sixth-term representative from Tulsa, Oklahoma, McIntyre is a maverick Republican who is known for strong principles and doing what the representative thinks is right. McIntyre served four years as governor and is well-liked back home, so can get away with some stuff. Oklahoma, being open and on the edge of the Great Plains, only has one major demand, and that is a desire that McIntyre fight gun control.

#### McIntyre's Positions

1. Wants a nationwide curfew of no later than 10 P.M. for youths under the age of 16
2. Spend more money to build prisons (at least $3 billion a year)
3. Spend no more money on drug abuse treatment and rehabilitation—the government already spends enough
4. Opposes any kind of gun control

#### Scoring

1 point for each position that is in House committee bills

1 point for each position that is in full House bill

2 points for each position that is in final bill enacted into law

1 point for each $5,000 in lobbyist campaign contributions

### Student Profile Sheet 20   Representative Claycut (Democrat-OH), member House Urban Affairs Committee

A ninth-term representative from Cleveland, Ohio, Claycut has only recently joined the Urban Affairs Committee. Claycut had been a teacher back in Ohio before deciding to run for Congress. The Cleveland teaching experience has made Claycut very concerned about the needs and problems of teenagers. Claycut's district is relatively Democratic, and tends to support liberal positions on spending and drug policy.

#### Claycut's Positions

1. The government needs to impose strict controls on handguns and on rifles
2. Urban areas should not be permitted to impose curfews, because curfews violate the freedom of youths
3. The government needs to spend more money on drug abuse treatment and prevention (at least $3 billion per year)
4. More money needs to be spent building prisons (at least $2 billion per year)

#### Scoring

1 point for each position that is in House committee bills

1 point for each position that is in full House bill

2 points for each position that is in final bill enacted into law

1 point for each $5,000 in lobbyist campaign contributions

### Student Profile Sheet 21   Representative Cliffson (Republican-NH), member House Urban Affairs Committee

A fourth-term representative from Manchester, New Hampshire, Cliffson is an old-school Republican who is known for strong principles. Cliffson grew up in a dangerous part of Manchester before joining the Navy. In the Navy, Cliffson learned a strong respect for discipline, and those beliefs help shape Cliffson's views today. New Hampshire is a very conservative state, which takes great pride in its low taxes and respect for freedom.

#### Cliffson's Positions

1. Wants a nationwide curfew of no later than 12 P.M. for youths under the age of 14
2. Spend more money to build prisons (at least $4 billion a year)
3. Spend no more money on drug abuse treatment and rehabilitation—the government already spends enough
4. Opposes legalization of marijuana

*Scoring*

1 point for each position that is in House committee bills

1 point for each position that is in full House bill

2 points for each position that is in final bill enacted into law

1 point for each $5,000 in lobbyist campaign contributions

### Student Profile Sheet 22   Representative Washington (Republican-MI), member House Judiciary Committee

A tenth-termer from Detroit, Michigan, Washington is a respected moderate voice on urban issues. Washington has a medical degree from the University of Michigan and was a family practice doctor for years before eventually running for the House. As a result of this medical background, Washington is considered something of an expert on the medical needs of urban communities.

#### Washington's Positions

1. Spend more on drug abuse prevention and treatment (at least $4 billion per year)
2. Death penalty for trafficking large amounts of heroin, cocaine, or related drugs
3. Supports the legalization of marijuana, at least for medical purposes
4. Wants to control handguns in order to reduce urban crime, doesn't care about rifles

*Scoring*

1 point for each position that is in House committee bills

1 point for each position that is in full House bill

2 points for each position that is in final bill enacted into law

1 point for each $5,000 in lobbyist campaign contributions

## Student Profile Sheet 23   President Jenkins (Democrat-NC)

Jenkins is a first-term President from North Carolina. Jenkins is a moderate who ran on a platform of pulling the country together. As a Democratic President facing a Republican majority in the House and in the Senate, Jenkins is used to hard bargaining. Jenkins wants the crime bill to toughen up the nation's policies on drugs, but also wants the bill to help control crime by limiting handguns and spending more money to help fight drug abuse.

The President's key negotiating tool is the ability to veto the crime bill if not satisfied. If Jenkins vetoes the bill, it requires two-thirds of the House and two-thirds of the Senate to override the President's decision. Therefore, Jenkins should be able to carefully wield this power in order to guarantee an acceptable bill.

### Jenkins's Positions

1. Keep marijuana illegal
2. Approve the death penalty for drug dealers trafficking in large amounts of heroin and cocaine
3. Opposed to any kind of curfew for youth
4. For gun control of handguns, doesn't care whether rifles are restricted
5. Supports spending more money on drug abuse prevention and treatment (at least $2 billion per year)

### Scoring

5 points if a crime bill is enacted into law with the President's signature (not if it's enacted over a veto)

2 points for each position that is in the enacted legislation

5 points if the new bill calls for no more than $5 billion in total new spending (counting both prison construction and drug abuse prevention and treatment money)

## Student Profile Sheet 24   Lobbyist Jennings, Alliance for More Prisons and Punishment (AMPP)

Jennings represents a coalition of builders, architects, and people who believe America is too soft on criminals. Your lobby wants to see new prisons built and they want to see the death penalty used more widely. Your job is to make sure that Congress spends its money on building new prisons and supports wider use of the death penalty. Do as much research as you can to find data to support this point of view.

The AFMPP has $30,000 that you can contribute to Senators or Representatives for their next reelection campaign. They get 1 point for each $5,000 in contributions they receive. Use the money wisely and be sure that you can rely on them to vote as they have promised. Keep careful track of who you give campaign donations to, and turn in those records as part of the final assignment. You can give the money away in $1,000 chunks.

### Jennings's/AMPP's Positions

1. Spend more money on building prisons (at least $2.5 billion per year)
2. Supports the death penalty for drug dealers trafficking in heroin or cocaine

### Scoring

2 points for each position that is in a committee bill in the House or Senate

2 points for each position that is in full House or full Senate bill

4 points for each position that is in final bill enacted into law

### Student Profile Sheet 25    Lobbyist Johnson, Organization for Helping Society (OHS)

Johnson represents an organization of church, civil rights, pro-poor, and humanitarian groups that want Americans to spend more helping the poor develop their options and less on punishing crime. Your job is to make sure that Congress spends money on social programs and crime prevention, not on building new prisons. Do as much research as you can to find data to support this point of view.

The OHS has $25,000 that you can contribute to Senators or Representatives for their next reelection campaign. They get 1 point for each $5,000 in contributions they receive. Use the money wisely and be sure that you can rely on them to vote as they have promised. Keep careful track of who you give campaign donations to, and turn in those records as part of the final assignment. You can give the money away in $1,000 chunks.

#### Johnson's/OHS's Positions

   **1.** Spend no more money on building prisons
   **2.** Spend more money on drug abuse treatment and prevention (at least $2.5 billion a year)

#### Scoring

2 points for each position that is in a committee bill in the House or Senate

2 points for each position that is in full House or full Senate bill

4 points for each position that is in final bill enacted into law

### Student Profile Sheet 26    Lobbyist Williamson, The Association for the Right to Bear Arms (ARBA)

Williamson represents a group that includes millions of gun owners nationwide. The ARBA is opposed to any limitation on gun ownership or use. Your job is to make sure Congress doesn't pass any restrictions. At the same time, the ARBA is worried that criminals and drug dealers are causing people to oppose gun ownership. Therefore, ARBA wants to see stricter punishments for drug dealers. Do as much research as you can to find data to support this point of view.

The ARBA has $30,000 that you can contribute to Senators or Representatives for their next reelection campaign. They get 1 point for each $5,000 in contributions they receive. Use the money wisely and be sure that you can rely on them to vote as they have promised. Keep careful track of who you give campaign donations to, and turn in those records as part of the final assignment. You can give the money away in $1,000 chunks.

#### Williamson's/ARBA's Positions

   **1.** No controls on buying or using handguns or rifles
   **2.** Supports the death penalty for drug dealers trafficking in heroin or cocaine

#### Scoring

2 points for each position that is in a committee bill in the House or Senate

2 points for each position that is in full House or full Senate bill

4 points for each position that is in final bill enacted into law

## Student Profile Sheet 27    Lobbyist Arkanian, Citizens for a Safer America (CFSA)

Arkanian represents a group of police forces, big city leaders, and antigun citizens who think the government needs to work harder at fighting urban violence. The organization wants the government to control the sale and use of handguns and rifles and they want a curfew for youths to be imposed in urban areas. Your job is to see that Congress passes these restrictions. Do as much research as you can to find data to support this point of view.

The CFSA has $25,000 that you can contribute to Senators or Representatives for their next reelection campaign. They get 1 point for each $5,000 in contributions they receive. Use the money wisely and be sure that you can rely on them to vote as they have promised. Keep careful track of who you give campaign donations to, and turn in those records as part of the final assignment. You can give the money away in $1,000 chunks.

### *Arkanian's/CFSA's Positions*

1. Controls on buying and using handguns, though the alliance isn't as concerned about rifles (because they are a lot harder to carry around in a city)

2. Supports a curfew in urban areas of no later than 11 P.M., at least for youths younger than 16

### *Scoring*

2 points for each position that is in a committee bill in the House or Senate

2 points for each position that is in full House or full Senate bill

4 points for each position that is in final bill enacted into law

## Student Profile Sheet 28    Lobbyist Naamans, Get Our Nation Clean (GON CLEAN)

Naamans represents churches, schools, citizens, and communities that are trying to increase the penalties for drug use and drug dealing. The organization is led by teachers and ministers who are worried that children are too vulnerable to the drug trade. Your job is to get Congress to support these tougher penalties and to keep drugs illegal. Do as much research as you can to find data to support this point of view.

GON CLEAN has $25,000 that you can contribute to Senators or Representatives for their next re-election campaign. They get 1 point for each $5,000 in contributions they receive. Use the money wisely and be sure that you can rely on them to vote as they have promised. Keep careful track of who you give campaign donations to, and turn in those records as part of the final assignment. You can give the money away in $1,000 chunks.

### *Naamans's/GON CLEAN's Positions*

1. Support death penalty for drug dealers who traffic in cocaine or heroin

2. Oppose the legalization of marijuana on any grounds

### *Scoring*

2 points for each position that is in a committee bill in the House or Senate

2 points for each position that is in full House or full Senate bill

4 points for each position that is in final bill enacted into law

## Student Profile Sheet 29   Lobbyist Curtano, Americans for Personal Freedom (APF)

Curtano represents people who think that the decision to use drugs should be a person's private choice, so long as the person does it safely and in a way that doesn't bother others. The organization is also opposed to curfews, because they see them as a violation of the freedoms of young people. The group's strongest support is from liberal Democrats and from people on the East and West coasts. Your job is to convince Congress to legalize marijuana and to oppose curfews. Do as much research as you can to find data to support this point of view.

The APF has $25,000 that you can contribute to Senators or Representatives for their next reelection campaign. They get 1 point for each $5,000 in contributions they receive. Use the money wisely and be sure that you can rely on them to vote as they have promised. Keep careful track of who you give campaign donations to, and turn in those records as part of the final assignment. You can give the money away in $1,000 chunks.

### *Curtano's APF's Positions*

 **1.** Oppose any kind of curfew

 **2.** Support the legalization of marijuana

### *Scoring*

2 points for each position that is in a committee bill in the House or Senate

2 points for each position that is in full House or full Senate bill

4 points for each position that is in final bill enacted into law

## Student Profile Sheet 30   Lobbyist Verheoven, United Against Legal Murder (UALM)

Verheoven represents a collection of churches, liberal activists, and humanitarian groups that believe the death penalty is wrong. They also believe it is a mistake to punish criminals who are addicted to drugs before they are given a chance for treatment and to get straight. Your job is to ensure that Congress doesn't encourage any more use of the death penalty and to push for more spending on rehabilitation for drug abusers. Do as much research as you can to find data to support this point of view.

The UALM has $35,000 that you can contribute to Senators or Representatives for their next reelection campaign. They get 1 point for each $5,000 in contributions they receive. Use the money wisely and be sure that you can rely on them to vote as they have promised. Keep careful track of who you give campaign donations to, and turn in those records as part of the final assignment. You can give the money away in $1,000 chunks.

### *Verheoven's/UALM's Positions*

 **1.** Increase government spending on drug abuse treatment and rehabilitation (spend at least $2.5 billion a year)

 **2.** Oppose the use of the death penalty

### *Scoring*

2 points for each position that is in a committee bill in the House or Senate

2 points for each position that is in full House or full Senate bill

4 points for each position that is in final bill enacted into law

# CHAPTER 9
# *Living on a Paycheck*

*This straightforward exercise is one of my favorite lessons in this collection. Designed for my many tenth-graders who were fascinated with the idea of dropping out and working full-time, this exercise teaches students how to think about what it takes to support oneself. Students are given roughly three weeks to use the want ads and other local listings to find a job, an apartment, a car, and furniture. Students use a budgetary framework to design a monthly budget that includes both necessities and luxuries.*

*Students are permitted to share data and contacts, but they are required to document all their research with specific ads or with the source of the data. (It's amazing how many parents have told me that their children engage in respectful conversation when charged with finding out the cost of auto tags or electric heat.) Students are also required to take the data collection one step further, and are taught to make polite calls to ascertain informational details.*

## TEACHER'S NOTE

High school students are fascinated by money. Yet there is little room for financial or budgetary issues in the high school curriculum. Students receive grades, take tests, try to make teams, apply for admission to colleges—all in a moneyless environment, where the rewards are much less immediate than are the earnings that students take home from after-school jobs. Failing to teach students about the realities of paychecks and spending can only serve to accentuate, to the detriment of our classrooms, the distinction between the "real" rewards of working and the long-term benefits of schooling. This exercise seeks to harness student interest in money, in paychecks, and in visceral issues of working and living in order to teach critical budgeting skills and to demonstrate just how useful academic skills can be in the real world.

Budgeting is generally thought to be boring. Just thinking about the subject is enough to cause the eyes of some teachers and most students to glaze over. That impulse, while understandable, is a major mistake. Budgeting is a vital, practical, and challenging skill. In fact, in a classroom setting, it is really rather fun. If taught as a rite of passage and a test of self-reliance (and budgeting really is both) then it is not that hard to turn budgeting into a stimulating and enjoyable topic for teen-agers. As dull as this topic may sound to some teachers at first, I cannot emphasize sufficiently enough how important I think this subject is and how willing students are to buy into this exercise.

If one teaches in a college environment, one gets used to hard-luck stories about undergraduates who are generally broke. Every fall one can count on seeing newspaper stories about the problems new college students have with money management. These stories are about relatively privileged children who are able to continue their education. Anecdotal evidence suggests that youths who move straight from high school to the workforce encounter even more severe credit and budgeting problems.

These problems can be reduced or avoided if students have some understanding of money management before they are tempted by their newfound freedoms. Teaching students how to responsibly budget while they are young is one crucial piece of this job. This exercise gives students a "dry run" at managing household income, before they are put in a position to make mistakes.

It is not only recent graduates who have problems with money management. A large segment of the adult population has problems with cash flow. Only a fragment of the adult population saves at the recommended 10% annual rate. The *national savings rate* (the amount of disposal income workers save) is generally closer to 3% or 4%. Defaults on credit card balances now run at an annual rate of about 5%. More than one million individuals now declare bankruptcy each year. In this environment, it is important for students to be schooled in financial discipline because it is very possible that they are not receiving this training at home.

This exercise is intended to serve several purposes. Fundamentally, it is designed to introduce students to the ideas of budgeting and money management. It also helps to give students a more realistic sense of what it costs to live in the adult world, and how much their parents pay for the things students so often take for granted. The exercise gives students an opportunity to develop applied research skills and to put their basic math skills to good use. Students seem to have a surprisingly good time with this simple exercise. Finally, I happily recall several students who—driven to ask their parents for necessary budgeting data—have expressed amazement at their parents' wealth of useful knowledge.

For me, one of the most enjoyable parts of the exercise is seeing students start to take an interest in so many things they take for granted. Watching students argue about grocery or clothing budgets can soften even an economics teacher's stony heart. And having a couple of students arrange to spend a Saturday afternoon pricing furniture is a natural way to integrate the classroom into their broader lives.

Initially, I designed this exercise for a tenth-grade Free Enterprise class. I have also had colleagues use it successfully in Contemporary Issues and Economics classes. The exercise only requires one class period to set up, but it will prove more successful if the teacher makes some class time available during the course of the project for students to ask questions, share information, and receive advice about locating research resources.

## BACKGROUND ON BUDGETING

There are no hard-and-fast rules on how someone should budget. The nature of one's budgeting needs to take into account one's lifestyle, interests, income, and behavior. However, there are general guidelines that professional advisors generally recommend.

The first point that needs to be understood in budgeting is the difference between gross and net income. *Gross* income is the total amount of money that a worker earns. *Net* income is the amount of money earned *after* subtracting taxes. Because taxes (including entitlement contributions) often consume a quarter or more of a worker's paycheck, there is a significant difference between gross income and the smaller net income.

The most important lesson that personal finance managers try to drill into their clients is the importance of consistent saving. Workers should try to save at least 10% of their net income. This goal is not always possible, and its significance can depend on the types of debt an individual accumulates, but it should be the guiding principle of financial planning.

After contributing to saving, general guidelines can help individuals apportion their spending. For instance, it is suggested that rent consume no more than 25% of one's net income. However, these guidelines are not hard and fast, and must reflect individual preferences and local price variation. Someone who loves to travel and lives in a city will need to squeeze spending much more than someone who lives in an inexpensive area and spends a great deal of time at home.

Once these basic rules have been learned, budgeting requires only common sense and a willingness to prioritize. Students should realize that they will simply *have* to live within the confines of their earnings. This is not that hard if students are willing to choose what they really need to have and what they can do without (at least in the short term). Developing this ability to say "I can wait for that" is all you really need to do to be an effective budgeter.

Restraint is made somewhat easier if students realize the costs of impatience and the rewards for self-discipline. Consumers who cannot prioritize and cannot wait generally wind up in debt. Most Americans carry consumer debt on their credit cards—a situation that slowly sucks the debtor dry. If a student carries an average debt of $5,000 for one year, they will have paid roughly $900 in *interest* alone during that year if the credit card has an 18% interest rate. That is the after-tax pay for about *two weeks*—or 80 hours—of work at a $30,000 per year job. On the other hand, students can expect each dollar they save to work for them by generating interest. For instance, $10,000 saved and invested in stocks can be expected to generate about $1,000 per year in interest over the long-term. That $1,000 (somewhat reduced by taxes) is essentially *free* money—earned simply because the investor let other people temporarily use his or her savings.

# USING THIS SIMULATION

## Purpose of the Simulation

The simulation is designed to introduce students to the real-world complexities of money management, to teach them about saving and good fiscal habits, and to help give them a sense of what salaries and expenses look like in the post-high school world. Students are required to find a local job for which they are currently qualified. This process helps students to become more realistic about the earning potential of a high school graduate. One of the benefits of this exercise is that students get a much clearer picture of what they can expect to earn if they do not attend college and of what their desired lifestyle will actually cost. This sometimes causes students to reconsider their educational choices.

## Skills Developed

The exercise helps to develop research, math reasoning, and analytic writing skills. The need to collect information, to develop and track budget expenditures, and to perform the required calculations gives students a chance to exercise these skills in an applied context. Because most data are collected from available sources, such as parents, newspaper advertisements, and utility bills, students are forced to extend their classroom research skills into new venues and apply them in new ways. The practical dimension of this helps students comprehend both the value of the research skills they have learned and become more proficient at collecting and analyzing information.

## Logistics

This exercise can run for almost any period of time. I generally give students about three weeks, while colleagues have used time periods ranging from two to five weeks. From all reports, the period of time used has little impact on the value of the exercise. The exercise requires 20 or 30 minutes of class time on the first day. Aside from that first day, the exercise requires no further class time, although it may benefit from a few additional minutes of class consideration at various points. The exercise works equally well for a class of 4 or 40.

Students collect the information necessary to construct their budget from a variety of sources, all of which should be readily attainable. Household utilities, auto expenses, and related outlays can be collected from parents. Prices for appliances, cars, and furniture can be collected from ads in newspapers, magazines, or circulars, or they can be located on the Internet. Apartment prices and available jobs can be obtained from newspapers, community tabloids, or other sources. Because a student does not need daily access to these materials, few logistical problems are presented. Students do not require class time, so the project can be run while the class progresses with other affairs.

# HOW THE SIMULATION WORKS

## Student Groups

Students are placed in small groups. Part of the fun of the exercise is for students to imagine sharing a place with friends. Each group member formulates his or her budget on the assumption that the group members are sharing a house or apartment. To keep this dimension relatively realistic, and to require that each student does a substantial amount of investigation, I recommend keeping groups to a size of no more than two or three people. Because there is no competitive dimension to this exercise, the teacher need not worry about balancing group skill levels. Consequently, I permit students to choose their own groups, which tends to make students more enthusiastic about the exercise.

## Length of the Exercise

After the introduction, the exercise requires only as much class time as the teacher wishes to devote to it. I generally let the project run for about three weeks. The trick is to run the project long enough that concerns about cost, budgets, price tags, and savings start to sink in. However, if the exercise stretches out too long, you risk having students put the work off or simply lose interest. I would suggest running the exercise for at least a week and a half or two weeks, and for no longer than four weeks.

## Rules of the Exercise

Once students have organized themselves into groups, they are given a Student Tax Worksheet and a Budget Worksheet (both can be found in the Appendix—*Materials*). At the end of the project, each group member will be required to turn in a personal household budget. The budget cover sheet dictates the ten major categories that students must budget, as well as the numerous subcategories that comprise the major budget categories. The summary figures for the major budget categories and subcategories will be entered on the budget sheet, while all the detail on specific expenditures will be collected within the body of the budget beneath that summary cover.

Students are expected to break down the expenses involved in their annual budget and to document each of the projections. They are also expected to write a short supplementary piece that explains how they went about finding a job, a place to live, a car, and other essentials, and how they went about collecting the data they used to compile the report. Some of the subcategories (such as movies) are straightforward and really only include one item. Other subcategories (such as furniture) can potentially include a dozen or more items. Students are to work in groups to come up with lists of necessary expenditures. Students then begin working to track down the costs of fixed expenses and to decide what other costs they will incur. Students are *to finance or to lease* major purchases, including autos and furniture, and therefore need to find out about the terms and costs of available financing and leasing plans.

***Citing Sources and Sharing Information***   Students are perfectly free to share information, both within groups and across groups. In fact, I encourage this kind of sharing because it fosters communication, builds cooperation, and encourages students to respect peers who are good at research and analysis. It is expected that students, when citing the source for each piece of information, will be sure to indicate the contributions of classmates when appropriate.

***Finding a Job***   Students begin by finding a job. They should use want ads in the newspaper, in a community circular, or some other kind of posting that they can physically include in their project. The job should be a position the student is currently qualified to hold. This keeps students reasonable, makes the exercise more useful, and has shocked more than one student into reevaluating a decision to forego any post-high school education or training. The student should provide a description of the job that includes a discussion of job qualifications, and explain how he or she is qualified for the job. The student also needs to provide the annual salary.

***Taxes***   As we all know, gross earnings only have a vague relationship to after-tax take-home pay. The money left after taxes is known as *net* earnings. I would recommend using the simple Student Tax Worksheet included in the Appendix. The worksheet should be photocopied and distributed to students, who should include the completed sheet as part of their final project.

Students are to pay a flat 15% of their gross pay in federal taxes, 5% in state taxes, and 7% for social security and medicare. This total 27% rate is a reasonable approximation of the actual tax rate for lower-paying jobs. The simple worksheet has several advantages. It teaches students to explicitly calculate tax burdens, forces them to think about where their money goes, and it does so without generating much additional confusion.

***Savings*** One of the key goals is to teach good financial management habits. Therefore, students are required to save 10% of their net earnings. After calculating taxes, this should be the very first budget line plugged in. Quite simply, teachers should drum into students the notion that saving 10% of one's salary is a given.

***Sharing Costs with Teammates*** Students are permitted to share costs with teammates. In fact, given the low salaries they can expect to earn, they will most likely need to share expenses such as rent, utilities, and furniture payments. Students are not permitted to plead poverty and skip over basic utility or furniture costs. The ability to share these expenses is one of the reasons for having students perform this exercise in teams. It is necessary, however, for students to indicate in their report the full cost of the expenses and then how they and their roommates are sharing the costs.

***Sharing Costs When There Are No Teams*** If the teacher chooses to do the exercise without teams, I would still recommend allowing students to live together and to split the costs of rent, utilities, and furniture. Just require students to indicate with whom they are living, the nature of cost sharing, and the appropriate source for this information.

***Furniture*** Students are expected to procure a reasonable amount of furniture for their house or apartment. Simply buying beds, a couch, and a television is not adequate. This expectation should be clearly explained at the beginning of the exercise. It is not acceptable for students to plead that they cannot afford to purchase a reasonable amount of furniture. Nor are students permitted to simply claim that their family will set them up with adequate furniture. Students are permitted to claim a piece or two this way, but they are expected to purchase the bulk of their furnishings. They may buy new or used furniture; and they may buy new furniture on installment plans, in which case all the costs are not paid for during the first year.

---

**SUMMARY TEACHER INSTRUCTIONS**

*The day the simulation begins*
- Objective is to introduce students to money management, and to give them a sense of what salaries look like.
- Explain net and gross income and the fundamentals of money management.
- Discuss requirements: Completed tax and budget worksheets, job description, salary and how the student meets the requirements, sources of information, two-page discussion of what the student has learned about budgeting.
- Either assign students to groups or allow them to group themselves according to desired living arrangements (roommates or independent living).
- Pass out project sheets, tax and budget worksheets.

*During the simulation*
- Students find a job, a place to live, an automobile, and other essential items (students may finance or lease major purchases).
- After finding a job, students project annual earnings by using the tax worksheet.
- Students research their projected annual budgets, documenting and summarizing projections.

*After the simulation*
- Students turn in their completed budget project.
- Assess simulation using classroom observations of participation, class evaluations, and a quiz.

---

## COMMENTS FROM EXPERIENCE

Perhaps surprisingly, large numbers of students get quite enthusiastic about this exercise. In fact, I find that students from low-income families tend to be among the most interested in this exercise, both because of its practicality and because these students often expect to be coping with real-world budgeting and spending decisions before long. Students who are looking forward to entering the working world can use this exercise as a chance to daydream about the life they are anticipating. Some of these students have wanted to expand the budgeting exercise into a broader discussion of their expected finances, living arrangements, and lifestyle. This enthusiasm is wonderful to see, and I have generally encouraged it, so long as the students understand that supplementary work and additional materials will not be accepted in place of the required assignment. I give extra credit for additional work, but clearly remind students that the primary purpose of this exercise is to learn about budgeting.

Students tend to enjoy planning to live with friends, the opportunity to think about finding and equipping their first apartment, and the chance to imagine what their life will be like when they are on their own. Teachers will find it rewarding to emphasize these themes, by tying them into class discussions and by prompting students to think about budgeting and expenses as *lifestyle* choices—not just questions of boring math.

Students can learn a great deal of practical value by going into a furniture store and asking questions of the salesperson or by visiting an apartment building and asking the manager to show them a sample unit. Although it is vital for you to stress that students need to be courteous, undemanding, and unobtrusive when calling about an advertisement or visiting a place of business, it is my experience that students generally are on excellent behavior. In fact, the students seem to enjoy this chance to interact with real people doing real things, and I have never had any complaints about student behavior as a result of this exercise. Even the most troublesome students seem to view this real-world interaction as cause for behaving responsibly.

I strongly recommend that teachers be explicit at the beginning about just what students are expected to turn in. Ambiguity encourages students who do not get invested in the project to assemble a shoddy report and then claim that it met the vague requirements outlined by the teacher. Enthusiastic students can also get frustrated by unclear requirements, because they may have trouble deciding which parts of a vaguely designed budget to concentrate on. Specifying what students are to budget for, where they should turn for information, and what kind of documentation they need to provide regarding the source of their information helps make the exercise more valuable.

## POSSIBLE MODIFICATIONS

Depending on the age and ability of students, teachers may demand more or less detail in the construction of projects.

### More Advanced Students

These students may be asked to present charts and figures tracing their spending and earnings or to prepare monthly breakdowns that take into account seasonal variations (e.g., Christmas expenses, summer air conditioning, a week-long vacation). Similarly, a teacher might want to teach more advanced classes about taxes in more depth. Teachers can have the students actually fill out an IRS 1040 form using their projected salary, and can even use it as an opportunity to teach students about deductions and graduated tax rates.

### Junior High and Less Advanced Students

A teacher can simplify this exercise by reducing its specificity. Teachers can drop the Tax Worksheet component, the need to identify sources for all expenditures, and/or many of the subcategory expenses. At the most basic level, the teacher might find it useful to just have students construct a simple budget based on a discussion with their parents. This sacrifices many of the strong points of the exercise, but does bring budgeting to the students' attention and does introduce students to the principles that should guide their spending.

# ASSESSMENT

Three kinds of assessment are recommended for this simulation. The assessments are intended to ensure that students have had a chance to absorb the nature and purpose of budgeting, have learned the basic rules, and have thought about applying the lessons they have learned.

The primary assessment tool is the budget itself. Students should be evaluated on the comprehensiveness and specificity of their project. A good finished project should look like something students could actually use as a budgeting blueprint were they to move straight into the workforce on graduation. Both depth and breadth are desirable. Students should be as explicit and detailed as possible about each line item, and they should strive to include as complete a summary of likely expenditures as they possibly can. A carefully constructed project will force students to learn where to gather useful information, expose them to the range of goods available, give them a sense of prices, and make them wedge all their demands into a realistic set of budget guidelines. Ingenuity ought to be rewarded, and the time-intensive efforts of students who visit auto dealers, inspect apartments for rent, check out appliance sales at the mall, or compare the prices of local fitness clubs should be rewarded when assessing projects.

Second, as part of the project, students are required to write a two-page essay. They are to discuss what they learned that they had not realized before and what advice they would offer to a younger sibling who wants to move out on his or her own but knows nothing about budgeting. Students should be encouraged to discuss their own misconceptions and how their understanding has changed. The essay is an opportunity for students to show that they have not simply collected and processed information, but that they have thought about the implications of the exercise.

The third assessment tool is a short written quiz on budgeting guidelines. Students are told before the exercise begins that they will be given this quiz at the end of the unit. The quiz is quite simple, asking students to demonstrate knowledge of the projected budget guidelines indicated on the Budget Worksheet (in the Appendix), of the kinds of taxes employees pay, and of similarly practical questions that arise during the project. The quiz should be administered in class on the day students turn in their projects. It should be a mix of short factual inquiries and a handful of slightly more thought-provoking questions. The entire quiz need not contain more than 20 or 25 questions, and probably should take no more than a half hour.

# APPENDIX—MATERIALS

## List of Materials

- Student Tax Worksheet
- Student Project Sheet
- Budget Worksheet
- Students will need access to local newspapers, advertising circulars, community weeklies, and similar materials.

## Student Tax Worksheet

| | *Tax rate* | *Amount* |
|---|---|---|
| 1. Total annual earnings (gross) | | |
| 2a. Federal taxes | 15% × total earnings = | |
| 2b. State taxes | 5% × total earnings = | |
| 2c. Social security and medicare | 7% × total earnings = | |
| 3. Total taxes (2a + 2b + 2c) | | |

Subtract total taxes (3) from total annual earnings (1).
Enter this new total as after-tax annual earnings (4).

| | | |
|---|---|---|
| 4. After-tax annual earnings (net) | | |

---

**STUDENT PROJECT SHEET**

The completed student project is to include the following items:

1. The completed Student Tax Worksheet

2. The completed Budget Worksheet

3. A description of the job the student has found, including a discussion of qualifications, what the job entails, how the student is qualified for the job, and the salary

4. A detailed discussion of the specific items within budget category, including the source of data for each purchase (materials, such as sample bills or advertisements, should be attached or glued in, when appropriate, as data sources)

5. Any supplementary materials that would enhance the finished project

6. A two-page discussion of what the student has learned about budgeting, and what advice he or she would now give about money to a younger sibling who wanted to move out on his or her own at the age of 18.

---

**Budget Worksheet**

| After-tax annual earnings | —— | —— | $ | —— |
|---|---|---|---|---|
| Spending categories and subcategories | 1997 U.S. average | Experts[1] suggested target % | Amount actually spent | % of actual amount spent |
| Housing | 19% | 25% | | |
| renter's insurance | | | | |
| Savings and/or investments | 5% | 10% | | |
| Food | 14% | 13% | | |
| groceries | | | | |
| restaurants | | | | |
| lunch/snacks at work | | | | |
| Transportation | 18% | 16% | | |
| car insurance | | | | |
| gas | | | | |
| car maintenance/repair | | | | |
| other travel | | | | |
| Household expenses/utilities | 15% | 11% | | |
| furniture | | | | |
| cleaning (supplies) | | | | |
| wall stuff/decorations | | | | |
| cable | | | | |
| electricity | | | | |
| phone (local) | | | | |
| phone (long distance) | | | | |
| Entertainment/vacations | 9% | 5% | | |
| movies/video rentals | | | | |
| ballgames/culture | | | | |
| nightlife/clubs | | | | |
| vacations/trips | | | | |
| Health care | 5% | 5% | | |
| doctor | | | | |
| dentist | | | | |
| medication | | | | |
| glasses/contacts/eye exams | | | | |

*continued*

## Budget Worksheet *(Continued)*

| After-tax annual earnings | ——— | ——— | $ | ——— |
|---|---|---|---|---|
| *Spending categories and subcategories* | *1997 U.S. average* | *Experts[1] suggested target %* | *Amount actually spent* | *% of actual amount spent* |
| Miscellaneous | 9% | 6% | | |
|    books | | | | |
|    makeup/personal items | | | | |
|    computer | | | | |
|    charity | | | | |
|    gifts | | | | |
|    music | | | | |
|    magazines/newspapers | | | | |
|    membership fees | | | | |
|    athletic equipment | | | | |
|    other | | | | |
| Clothing | 5% | 5% | | |
|    leisure clothing | | | | |
|    work clothing | | | | |
|    laundry/dry cleaning | | | | |
|    shoes | | | | |
| Education/child care | 2% | 5% | | |
|    college tuition | | | | |
|    day care | | | | |

[1]Recommended and 1997 U.S. average percentages are taken from *Money* magazine (October 1997: 218).

# CHAPTER *10*

# *The Delicate Balance of Power*

*Students use diplomacy and deterrence to fend off war while wielding alliances and nurturing economic growth in an attempt to gain continental preeminence. This exercise has proved to be one of the most popular in this book; students even used to implore me to schedule an after-school rematch so that they might have another shot at continental glory.*

*Students serve as diplomats, as six groups govern nations representing the dominant European powers in the years preceding the Great War. Simulating the 1870 to 1914 period, the game requires groups of students to exercise nonstop diplomacy and balance geopolitical, economic, and national security concerns. The lesson illustrates the fragility of peace in prewar Europe, the tenuous nature of alliances in a multipower world, and the various dimensions of high-level diplomacy.*

## TEACHER'S NOTE

*The Delicate Balance of Power* is designed to simulate the conditions in Europe prior to the out-break of World War I. The simulation requires students to manage the political fates of six intertwined countries. Students must keep an eye on the economic and military condition of their nation, as well as the condition of their rivals and allies. I initially developed this lesson for use in an American History class, with the purpose of helping students to understand the causes behind the outbreak of the Great War. However, the lesson has also been used as part of a late nineteenth-century unit in a European History class and as part of a unit on international conflict in a Social Studies class. The simulation itself generally takes one or two classes to conduct, although teachers will find the exercise more valuable if students have already learned something about the historic context that shaped the 1870 to 1914 period in Europe.

One of the particularly attractive features of this lesson is that it lets students experience first-hand the concepts of balance of power, brinkmanship, and appeasement—concepts that repeatedly take center stage in international politics when studying the 1945 to 1989 period. Students govern the nations of Faux Europa, balancing resources between national defense and the economy while seeking to manage foreign policy.

The six countries of Faux Europa are fictional representations of Great Britain, France, Russia, Germany, Austria–Hungary, and Italy. These nations were at the center of the web of interlocking alliances and deceptive diplomacy that commenced with the conclusion of the Franco–Prussian War in 1871 and finally exploded into war with the assassination of Archduke Francis Ferdinand in 1914. The simulation allows students to experience the competition and constant suspicion that characterized an era when so many significant powers coexisted on a single continent. I have found that helping students to understand this *multipolar* environment (characterized by three or more significant powers) also makes it easier to later explain the nature of the *bipolar* Cold War.

The exercise's central premise is that the structure of power in Europe during 1870 to 1914 made a continental war very likely. The structure was one of entangling alliances in which any one standoff could have exploded into an all-out war. Further, the ambition and growing strength of some nations (such as Germany) and the sliding status and strength of others (such as Britain and Austria–Hungary) meant that the temptation to initiate preemptive war was present for some countries throughout the period.

The simulation reduces statesmanship to concerns about relative economic standing, maintaining national defense, and conducting negotiations. This simplicity helps to keep the emphasis on understanding how delicate the balance of power is in a world of equals, and on the basic "guns-versus-butter" trade-off that political leaders have always faced. Keeping this lesson simple highlights the two secondary themes I want to convey: the importance of geopolitics and the need for leaders to carefully weigh economic and military priorities.

The simplicity of the design makes the exercise appropriate for a wide range of students. Interested and knowledgeable students are able to interpret the game on a sophisticated level, while students with less background tend to be interested in the strategy of the exercise itself. In terms of its more sophisticated appeal, I have had ninth- and tenth-grade students finish the simulation and ask me to teach them about international relations theory, about the nature of arms races, or about the compatibility of religious beliefs and statesmanship. In terms of mass appeal, this exercise drummed up so much enthusiasm that students have requested an after-school class so that they could replay the game.

The key to making the game interesting is the tension that existed between France and Germany (in the simulation, between the nations of Bordeaux and Munich) during the 1870 to 1945 era. The bitter rivalry between the two nations drove many of the developments in Europe in that period, and the rules of the simulation account for that by specifying that those two nations may not both be part of a game-winning alliance. This proviso helps to give the simulation its zip. After all, no matter how harsh the realization might be, the shape of international affairs in the 1870 to 1914 time period meant that some nations would be losers. I think that this is a valuable understanding for students to have.

Although the behavior of the six nations is shaped by the possibility of conflict, it is important to realize that the game itself is about diplomacy. Conflict in the game is infrequent, rarely successful, and determined by a simple numerical calculation. Over time, I have found that this approach produces the desired classroom dynamic, while not engendering concern that students are participating in "militaristic" lessons.

# BACKGROUND ON EUROPE BEFORE WORLD WAR I

World War I was the culmination of more than four decades of interlocking alliances among the dominant European powers. The period preceding the war was shaped by the efforts of powerful nations to maintain their stature, and by the efforts of weaker nations to claim a greater role within Europe. After the defeat of Napoleon's France, the balance of power in Europe gradually began to change. By the latter half of the nineteenth century, the once-major nations of The Netherlands, Portugal, and Spain had entered a period of marked decline. Meanwhile, Germany and Italy, united in 1861 and 1871 respectively, clamored for recognition as powerful new nations in central Europe.

The emergence of Germany as the dominant power of central Europe reshaped the balance of power in Europe after 1871. The brilliant Prussian statesman Otto van Bismarck was largely responsible for uniting Germany. Bismarck's early machinations culminated in the Austro–Prussian War of 1866. Ending with the 1866 Treaty of Prague, the Austro–Prussian War produced the North German Confederation (dominated by Bismarck's Prussia) and reduced the stature of the sprawling Austrian Empire. The diminished Austrian Empire was renamed Austria–Hungary, acknowledging the new parity of Austria and Hungary.

Bismarck next took advantage of delicate French–Prussian negotiations, produced by a revolution in Spain, to strengthen Germany's western front. Bismarck doctored a private communication during negotiations, aggravating war sentiment in both countries and prompting France to declare war on Germany in 1870. As the aggressor nation, and in accord with Bismarck's designs, France stood alone. Bismarck, via various threats and inducements, kept Britain, Russia, Italy, and Austria from entering the conflict. Within six weeks of the outbreak of the war, the French army surrendered.

In January 1871, at the palace of the French kings at Versailles, King William was proclaimed the German emperor. In May 1871, France and Germany made peace in Frankfurt with a treaty that created long-standing animosities between France and the new German nation. The treaty imposed an enormous indemnity on France and gave Germany the French provinces of Alsace and (part of) Lorraine, producing tensions between Germany and France that would fester for 40 years. By the 1880s, Germany had initiated an effort to attain military superiority in Europe (and, hence, the world). This buildup was not fully recognized until about 1900, at which time it prompted France and Britain to respond in kind, producing an arms race that culminated in 1914 with the onset of World War I.

After its defeat by the newly unified Germany, France was significantly weakened. Entering the 1870s, France had already endured an unstable century. Since the chaos of the French Revolution in 1789, France had been through two republics, several monarchs, and at least one incipient communist revolt. Between 1871 and 1875, the Third Republic slowly emerged, and France remained a dominant nation in Europe. However, political instability (highlighted by the infamous Dreyfus case, involving trumped-up espionage charges and anti-Semitism) was rampant within the centralized state apparatus, leaving France enmeshed in religious and social conflict.

The Austrian Empire entered a period of marked decline after its 1866 defeat by Prussia. Once the dominant power of central Europe, Austria–Hungary became the junior partner in its relationship with an ascendant Germany. Ruled by a dual monarchy, Austria–Hungary was plagued by quarrels among its multiple ethnic groups. The country's slow decline lent an air of desperation to Austria–Hungarian diplomacy, and helps explain the nation's willingness to fan the flames of Balkan conflict into war in the years immediately preceding 1914. Quite simply, Austria–Hungary felt compelled to reassert its influence before it slipped into the status of second-class power. One of the ironies of World War I may be that Austria–Hungary waited too long, thus ensuring its demise.

Like the Germans, the Italians were a culturally distinct people who had been fragmented for centuries by external invasion and internal division. In 1861, the Kingdom of Italy was proclaimed, although Venice was still in Austrian hands and the Pope still reigned in Rome. By 1870, both Rome and Venice had been brought into the Kingdom, and in late 1870 Rome became the capital of Italy. The relatively late unification of Italy, in 1871, and the new nation's reliance on other countries in claiming its full territory, fostered an inferiority complex that shaped the erratic Italian diplomacy throughout the 1870 to 1914 period.

Unlike newly ascendant Italy or Germany, Britain entered the 1870 to 1914 period with unquestioned might and a rich heritage. Ruler of a sprawling empire, Britain had a highly developed industrial economy, the most developed and stable democratic government in Europe, and the world's dominant navy. In fact, Britain undertook a major series of democratizing reforms during the 1867 to 1885 era. In those years, Britain enfranchised workingmen, instituted the secret ballot, created nearly universal male suffrage, and dramatically reworked parliamentary representation.

The sprawling Russian nation, ruled by incompetent monarchs and reactionary counselors after the assassination of Czar Alexander II in 1881, remained a potentially powerful but unstable force throughout the 1870 to 1914 period. Defeated by Japan in the Russo–Japanese War of 1904, and imperiled by an abortive revolution in 1905, Russia staggered into World War I. With its vast peasantry frustrated with war and continued privation, Russia fell to revolution in 1917—and promptly surrendered to the Germans.

The wars of mid-century and the great success of the German military in the late 1800s caused statesmen and generals to reevaluate the nature of warfare. The increasing adoption of universal military service was coupled with new theories of warfare and increased efforts to apply scientific advances to war. The 1870 to 1914 period saw the creation of the mine, the torpedo, and the submarine, as well as new ideas for military engineering and logistics. Particular attention was given to the potential of steel-plated warships. Because the ability to maintain sea lines was essential to the economic health of the colonial European powers, major warships were very important. Around the turn of the century, Germany sought to complement its fearsome army by building a navy that would rival Britain's. The result was an unprecedented arms race that entailed the buildup of both land and sea forces and that did not end until the outbreak of war in 1914.

## The Alliances

Entering the 1870 to 1914 period, Britain and France had enjoyed a long-standing, on-again, off-again, affinity. Bismarck had plotted carefully to keep Britain from aiding France in the Franco–Prussian War, but he was not confident he could continue to rely on clever diplomacy to fend off Britain. To protect Germany's ascendant position, Bismarck allied Germany with Austria–Hungary in 1879. In 1882, Italy joined these two nations to form the Triple Alliance. The Italian addition was less significant than it appeared, however, because the Italian treaty was not a full-fledged military pact. (Instead, Italy merely promised not to intercede in an Austro–Russian conflict, and Germany promised to help Italy in the event of a French–Italian conflict.)

In 1881, Bismarck secretly revived an agreement with Russia and, in 1887, Germany agreed to a bilateral Reinsurance Treaty with Russia. During the period that Germany was allied with both Austria–Hungary and Russia, its real sympathies were unclear because ethnic divisions in southeast Europe produced Austro–Russian tensions. When Bismarck fell from power in 1890, his successors refused to renew the unpopular German–Russian pact, finally ensuring Austria–Hungary that it could confidently rely on German support.

In 1882, Britain invaded and occupied Egypt, alienating France. This left France isolated in the face of the Austro–German alliance. Consequently, when German–Russian relations collapsed in 1890, France quickly made overtures to Russia. The result was the Franco–Russian alliance of 1893, an alliance that embraced the continent and confronted Germany with potential foes on both its eastern and western borders. As part of this alliance, France sought to invest heavily in its new ally in order to foster Russian stability and economic development.

Isolated from the continent, Britain turned increasingly to its Commonwealth of self-governing colonies and to potential allies across the ocean. Britain entered into an alliance with Japan in 1902, and began to cultivate an extraordinarily important tacit alliance with the growing and industrializing United States. As the arms race with Germany began to spiral out of control, Britain also gingerly began to renew its involvement in European alliances. Between 1904 and 1907, Britain entered into new agreements with France and Russia, forming the Triple Entente. However, the secretive and informal agreements that characterized the Triple Entente made it appear weaker than it actually was to the Triple Alliance.

By the dawn of 1914, Europe was split into two camps. The Triple Alliance (Central Powers) of Italy, Germany, and Austria–Hungary dominated central Europe and included the most aggressive and powerful country on the continent. The Triple Entente of Russia, Britain, and France embraced the continent from both sides, but relied heavily on Russia's shaky monarchy. The Central Powers enjoyed certain military advantages in a short conflict, with Germany's highly regarded army the backbone of their strength. In a long war, however, Russia's vast manpower reserves and the British navy's control of sea routes would likely tilt the scales toward the Triple Entente.

## The War

Ethnic conflict suffused the Balkan region in the years between 1900 and 1914. Discord among the various ethnic groups that populated the region led to a series of incidents and potential conflicts. Austria–Hungary and Russia, the dominant powers in southeastern Europe, were frequently confronted with diplomatic tensions fueled by ethnic group fragmentation across the nations in that region. On June 28, 1914, Archduke Francis Ferdinand, heir to the Austro–Hungarian throne, was assassinated in Sarajevo by a member of a secret society of Serbian nationalists.

Austria–Hungary, with German support, used the opportunity to impose a list of stringent demands on Serbia. Although the Serbians replied with almost complete surrender, Austria–Hungary proclaimed that it was not satisfied and declared war. Russia, a Serbian ally, responded with a partial mobilization. This quickly triggered a countermobilization by Germany, coupled with a German request that France promise to remain neutral in the event of a Russo–German conflict. When France refused to promise neutrality, Germany declared war on France, and the Great War had begun.

Of the six powers, only Italy chose not to enter the war. Having always maintained weak ties with the Central Powers, Italy remained neutral until 1915, when it responded to the Triple Entente's lucrative promises by entering the war on the side of Britain and France. The balance of power that had so effectively kept the peace for most of 40 years had proven equally adept at speeding Europe into a continental war.

## USING THIS SIMULATION

### Purpose

Substantively, the lesson was designed to serve as an introduction to the causes of World War I. Thematically, the simulation includes material on international relations and European history. The lesson provides an accessible introduction to international relations concerns which I find to be invaluable in explaining much twentieth-century history. The exercise introduces and makes concrete the concept of *multipolarity*—a situation in which there are multiple actors of roughly equal power. In doing so, the exercise demonstrates the danger inherent in a peace that rests on evenly matched alliances.

Related concepts, such as appeasement, brinkmanship, and deterrence, are also clarified. *Appeasement* is the attempt to forestall an aggressor by satisfying a country's demands. *Deterrence* is the opposite strategy, it is the attempt to prevent aggression by remaining so powerful that potential aggressors are scared off. *Brinkmanship* is an extreme case of deterrence, in which the defending nation goes to the brink of war to deter an aggressor. These concepts are crucial to understanding post-World War II history. Students also absorb the rudiments of the 1870 to 1914 European situation in a way that helps make clear the seismic forces that pushed Europe into World War I.

### Skills Developed

*The Delicate Balance of Power* offers a chance to develop teamwork, negotiating, math reasoning, and analytic writing skills. Students cooperate in groups to represent the government of each of the six nations. The need to conduct negotiations while keeping track of their changing military and economic standing increases the challenge, as does the need of each group to determine how best to invest its economic growth from one turn to the next. A country's performance depends on students keeping track of their resources, of the resources of other nations, and of the balance of power among the competing alliances.

The exercise cultivates analytic skills both during play and in the assessment activities, when students must attempt to "unpack" what took place. Students are forced to recount and then explain the reasons why the simulation unfolded as it did, developing their ability to explain political behavior.

### Logistics

*The Delicate Balance of Power* is a convenient lesson to use. The exercise usually runs about 60 minutes. However, I once had a class that finished a game in about 15 minutes, when five countries quickly formed a massive alliance, preemptively attacked the other country, and then maintained an unshakable coalition through the end of the game (Below, I offer some suggestions for minimizing the likelihood of this eventuality or for managing it if it occurs.)

Students generally want to play this game a second time in order to attempt to remedy their mistakes and apply what they learned the first time. Depending on how long the first game took, I have been inclined to run the simulation a second time. I have found, and I have had this sense seconded by colleagues, that playing again can really help to concretize the lessons learned.

Because each of the six countries is played by a group, the exercise can effectively accommodate a class of 18 to 36. I have found that classes of 24 to 30 students, where each country is played by four or five students, work best.

All the materials necessary for the simulation are included in the Appendix in this chapter. Once a teacher has read this chapter and is comfortable with the exercise, preparation for the simulation should take no more than 25 minutes. Once a teacher is familiar with the rules and has photocopied the necessary materials, the only real preparation necessary is to organize groups, prepare explanatory remarks, and arrange the classroom. The rules are laid out in the Summary of Rules Sheet and prepared for distribution to the class (see the Appendix).

## HOW THE SIMULATION WORKS

### Student Groups

The students are grouped into six nations which make up the continent of Faux Europa (see map of the continent in the Appendix). The six nations are named after a city in each of the simulated nations (permitting the observant student to gain some additional insight)—Newcastle (a proxy for Britain), Bourdeaux (France), Munich (Germany), Budapest (Austria–Hungary), Sicily (Italy), and Yalta (Russia).

The class should be distributed evenly among the countries, with each group of desks clustered so that the students ruling each country have as much privacy as possible. The idea is to maximize deal-making and quiet negotiation, both of which benefit from negotiators being able to operate with privacy. I find it advisable to permit each group to send out no more than two or three ambassadors at one time, with the rest of the group at home receiving ambassadors, analyzing data, and coordinating strategy. This restriction forces groups to coordinate their activities and helps to maintain order.

### Object

Groups win by being part of the dominant economic coalition in 1920, when the game ends. For purposes of assessing the dominant economy, countries may either compete singly or as part of an *entente* (coalition of countries). If countries elect to compete as part of an entente, their economic strength is combined, and that combined figure is used to determine the strongest coalition. The one restriction on the ability of countries to form ententes and to win the game economically is that Bordeaux and Munich can never be part of a joint economic entente. This means that one of those two powerful countries must always lose in a peaceful game, and it is this dynamic that drives the alliances and conflict.

If one country has eliminated all other nations, it is victorious. However, the design of the game makes that eventuality almost impossible. If one entente has militarily eliminated all opponents, the members of that entente can simply maintain their entente until 1920 and claim victory. To increase the unpredictability of the international situation, I make the reward for winning as part of an entente proportionately smaller than for winning alone. This helps to avoid the paralysis that can set in when a dominant coalition eliminates its opposition.

### Length of Game

The game is composed of ten turns, each representing a five-year period. The first five-year period begins in 1870. The last period ends in 1920 with the comparison of economic strength among surviving countries and/or ententes. The game can be played at least once in two 40-minute classes, but because the length depends on how the simulation unfolds, no precise time estimate is possible. The time required for each turn depends on the teacher and the class, but I have found five to eight minutes per turn is a reasonable amount of time.

## Key Elements of the Game

Alliances can take many forms, with the only crucial distinction being between alliances and ententes. *Alliances* can be formal or informal, based on written or oral agreements, and address issues of national defense and international conflict. *Ententes* are agreements that two or more nations will closely bind their fate together, and have agreed to combine their gross national product (GNP) for purposes of determining the winner at the simulation's end. An entente has to be formally presented in writing to the teacher, and dissolving an entente requires that a request be formally presented to the teacher by one of the parties.

***Economic Strength***   This is measured by a single figure that represents GNP. At the start of the simulation, each country possesses a specific GNP. During the course of the next 50 years, that figure increases by varying amounts at the beginning of each turn. Victory at game's end is determined by comparing the game-ending 1920 GNP for each surviving country and/or entente.

***Military Strength***   This is measured by a single figure that represents the number of men under arms. To keep the game simple, this approach does away with the distinction between naval and land-based strength (notice that pseudo-Britain is no longer an island in the simulation). This single measure also helps to clarify the guns-versus-butter distinction that political leaders must make. If the students desire to form some kind of disarmament agreement and sacrifice part or all of their defense, that is permitted.

***Military Conflict***   This is easy to manage. Countries can only declare war on a country they border. If one country is involved in conflict, its allies can also take part, whether or not they border the opponent. If a country is conquered during the game, countries that bordered on the defeated nation are now regarded as sharing a border.

The attacking nation, and whatever allies are joining them in the endeavor, must declare their intention to attack. Once the full complement of aggressors is exposed, then any allies of the attacked country announce whether they are assisting in the victim's defense. This means that aggressors always operate with less knowledge than the victim and the victim's allies. The attacking country's and/or alliance's aggregate number of men under arms is compared to that of the defender and the defender's allies. The attackers must have twice the number of men in order to win. The teacher should count and calculate these numbers in secret so as not to expose the strength of countries that have carefully shielded their strength. To ensure that conflicts are resolved correctly, the teacher needs to keep the master sheets updated.

If the attackers do not have twice the number of men of the defending country or alliance, the attackers are defeated and have their number of men under arms reduced by one-third (round down). The defenders, who are dug in, emerge unscathed.

If the attackers' win, they still lose one-third of their men (casualties of war), but the vanquished country is occupied and two-thirds of its GNP (round down) is accorded in equal shares to the victors. (One-third of the vanquished nation's GNP is destroyed in the conflict.) Aggressor nations, whether they win or lose, always emerge from a war with their military one-third weaker than when they entered.

***Defeated Countries***   As their economies are absorbed by the victors, defeated countries cease to exist. Nations that bordered on the defeated nation are now presumed to border one another. Members of the defeated nation can either be added to the government of the victors or asked to begin working on the assessment instruments (see Chapter 12, Final Thoughts).

The continental map of Faux Europa is included in the Appendix. The geopolitics are fairly reflective of the prewar situation. For instance, Budapest is in a very vulnerable location, while Newcastle cannot be assailed so long as it is on friendly terms with Bourdeaux.

***Economic Growth***   As noted before, economic growth takes place at the beginning of each five-year turn. The amount of growth accorded to each country in each turn is indicated on the Teacher's Master Sheet (see Appendix). The varying rates of growth mean that countries gain and lose strength in a vague approximation of 1870 to 1914 Europe. At the beginning of each turn, the teacher should have all diplomats rejoin their groups and all students resume their seats. The teacher should then rapidly read out the growth for each nation. This moment tends to become ritualistic and quite exciting, as students become highly invested in the figures for their group, their enemies, and their allies.

After each group's growth rate for that turn has been announced by the teacher, students must make the perennial guns-versus-butter decision, and decide how they should allocate their resources between GNP and military strength. Each $10 million of economic growth can either be added to the nation's GNP or converted into an additional 10,000 men under arms. Each group should give the teacher their decision on a piece of notebook paper, veiling its decision. The teacher should secretly record the changes to each country's GNP and defense on the Men Under Arms and GNP Summary Sheets provided in the Appendix.

## How the Simulation Proceeds

***At the Start***   After explaining the simulation, the teacher should break the students into six groups, and arrange the groups so that each has some degree of privacy. Each group is then assigned a nation and given copies of their nation's Country Profile Sheet, the simulation Summary of Rules, and the continental map (see Appendix). Meanwhile, the teacher should have copies of the Teacher's Master Sheet, as well as the rules and the continental map for himself or herself. Students begin the simulation with minimal information about any country besides their own. This early lack of information and the initial alliances between Bourdeaux–Yalta and Munich–Budapest tend to ensure some early stability while the simulation takes shape.

Students are initially occupied by efforts to learn about other nations and judge their relative strength. Meanwhile, Sicily, Newcastle, and the alliances usually enter into a frantic immediate round of musical-chair negotiations. Students quickly learn to play their cards close to the vest, and those who foolishly gave away too much information too quickly tend to invite trouble.

---

**HOW A TURN MIGHT WORK**

I know this can seem a little abstract, so let me try to concretize it. Say it is the beginning of the second turn of the game. There is an alliance between Sicily, Bourdeaux, and Yalta. Newcastle and Budapest have a secret alliance, which they have not made public, as do Newcastle and Bourdeaux. Munich is alone. The teacher calls out the GNP growth figures and each country decides how to allocate its growth. Budapest and Newcastle then spring the announcement that they are mounting an invasion of Munich. No other nation joins the assault, and no one comes to Munich's defense. It is strictly between Munich the Newcastle–Budapest duo. Having put much of their GNP into building up their armed forces, by mutual agreement, Newcastle now has 350,000 men under arms while Budapest has 460,000. Together, they attack with 810,000 troops. Munich, which grows at a very slow rate early in the game, has put all its GNP into building up its military. The rulers of Munich are fortunate, because adding 90,000 troops to their initial 340,000 gives them 430,000 men under arms. Since the Newcastle–Budapest force of 810,000 is not twice Munich's 430,000, the attack is repulsed. Newcastle loses one-third of its forces (rounding down), so it loses 120,000 men and is left with 230,000. Budapest loses 150,000, and is left with 310,000. Munich's men, dug safely into their foxholes, emerge unscathed. After the conflict is resolved, it is likely that a new round of frantic negotiating on the part of a weakened Newcastle and Budapest will take place before the next turn begins.

At the beginning of the game, by design, no single nation is capable of conquering any other nation. Additionally, the strength of the Munich–Budapest and Yalta–Bourdeaux alliances ensures a standoff. Finally, Newcastle and Sicily have sufficient strength that, if they ally together, they cannot be defeated by either of the two initial alliances.

***The First Turn***     Once the students have sorted through their information and engaged in some preliminary negotiations, the teacher should announce the first turn. All students must return to their groups, and the teacher then announces the economic growth of each country. This is the only publicly available data on the condition of other countries, so savvy students will take note of the growth rate of all the other nations. After the round of announcements, which should take about 30 seconds, each group submits a piece of paper to the teacher that tells how that group is allocating the new resources between GNP and defense. The teacher should mark these changes down on the Summary Sheets, updating each nation's initial figures.

The five-year interim begins, and students are free to negotiate, consult, and analyze (i.e., be diplomats). This period should generally run between five and eight minutes. Students should then be required to resume their seats so that a second round of economic growth figures can be released. This pattern should be repeated for each of the game's ten turns.

***Conflict***     Students can initiate a conflict at any time. Because of the massive disadvantages associated with being the aggressor, declarations of war are relatively infrequent. Conflicts tend to be few in number and spaced out.

***At Game's End***     At the conclusion of the last turn, the surviving nations compete to see which has emerged as economically dominant. To simulate the power of economic blocs in international affairs, nations are allowed to win either individually or as part of an economic entente. Any final changes in economic ententes must be filed in writing with the teacher before the end of the last turn. Because all ententes must be formally registered, there should be no confusion as to the status of economic ententes. The teacher should put up the final GNP for each country, using the Master Sheet to ensure that proper figures are used in all cases. The GNP for nations in an economic entente are then

---

**SUMMARY TEACHER INSTRUCTIONS**

*The day the simulation begins*
- Objective is to dominate Faux Europa through carefully managed growth and diplomacy.
- Group students into the six nations of Faux Europa.
- Review key elements of game: Economic strength, military strength, military conflict, results of conflict, alliances, ententes.
- Pass a Country Profile Sheet and a Summary of Rules sheet out to the students in each group.
- Allow students to sort through information and engage in preliminary negotiations.

*During the simulation*
- Students negotiate, have the option of initiating conflict, and then regroup.
- The teacher announces economic growth of each country.
- Groups submit to the teacher, on paper, how much of their growth they are allotting to GNP and to defense.
- Teacher marks changes and updates each nation's status on the GNP Summary and Men Under Arms sheets.
- This pattern is repeated for each of the ten turns.
- At the conclusion of the last turn, the surviving nations compare alliance structures to determine economic dominance of the continent.

*After the simulation*
- Assess activity using observed participation, analytic essay, and quiz.

combined. The highest total among ententes and individual countries is declared the dominant power of Faux Europa.

Notice that up to five countries can win (a winning entente could conceivably include Newcastle, Yalta, Sicily, Budapest, and either Munich or Bourdeaux). Also, if either Bourdeaux or Munich has been conquered, it is possible that a continent-wide entente can ease into victory.

## COMMENTS FROM EXPERIENCE

It is useful to encourage students to treat their economic and defense figures as crucial, secretive information. The uncertainty generated by not knowing one's relative strength shapes early diplomacy, makes groups reticent to initiate conflict, and provides a strong appreciation for the value of diplomatic intelligence. Savvy groups will make a concerted effort to obtain information and will take meticulous notes on the growth rates of all six nations. This uncertainty, and the stable status quo produced by the Munich–Budapest and Yalta–Bourdeaux alliances, helps the simulation get off to a rollicking start (and helps to ensure that almost all countries survive well into the game). Additionally, the penalties for aggression, including the stacked odds and the automatic loss of armed forces, help to ensure an uneasy peace. I always like to see the initial uneasy peace stretch as long as possible, because it keeps all the students involved and helps raise the tension to a high pitch.

The rules have been designed to make war an unattractive option. This helps to keep all countries (and therefore all students) involved in the game. Because conquering countries lose military strength and must divvy up the conquered country's GNP, it is always more profitable to form an entente with a country than to conquer it. Additionally, nations that wage war always emerge militarily weaker, while nations that forge alliances are able to pool their defensive strength. This balance helps to produce the desired effect of unstable and uneasy peace.

Some countries, especially the geographically central ones, quickly become engaged in a frantic arms race. These countries often try to form ententes and encourage their allies to pursue economic growth. This is a valuable lesson for students, because the rulers of economically vibrant countries soon realize that they have become attractive and vulnerable targets.

The initial levels of economic and military strength have been calibrated to ensure a standoff between the two initial alliances that somewhat mirrors the situation in Europe in 1870. Growth rates have been designed and refined to produce tensions and uneven fates for the six nations.

Unless Bordeaux is conquered, Newcastle can only be attacked by an alliance that includes Bourdeaux. Therefore, although Newcastle begins with a relatively small military, it is much stronger than it appears. This dynamic tends to reproduce the traditional British–French alliance. Budapest starts off as the most powerful nation in the game, and then proceeds to spend the entire simulation losing ground. Meanwhile, Yalta begins with a strong military and a weak economy and then proceeds to grow mightily, although unevenly, during the simulation.

Students will find, and the teacher should emphasize the message, that good diplomacy requires skillful negotiation, good information, and careful coordination. Students will learn during the exercise that the people performing each of these roles are crucial. Depending on the nature of the classroom situation, I have found that permitting pairs and small groups of students to use the nearby hallway for secretive negotiations can add to the intricacy of the diplomacy.

Although infrequent, a quick five-on-one war or a quickly congealing alliance framework sometimes occurs and can make for a boring simulation. Although still effective at demonstrating the relevant concepts, neither of these scenarios is as exciting or instructive as a less stable exercise. Desirable instability can be encouraged in several ways.

First, make an effort to distribute students so that cliques of friends are not in control of a powerful bloc of countries. Some classes will have influential friends who may be predisposed to form alliances. This is not a problem, so long as the teacher takes patterns of friendship into account. For instance, it is not a problem if good friends dominate both Bordeaux and Newcastle, because the exercise may actually work better if those two countries are in a tight alliance. However, the teacher should be careful to see that a group of close, popular, and influential friends (who may be able to dominate their countrymates) are not in a position to control, say, Munich, Newcastle, and Yalta.

Second, Sicily and Newcastle should be given talented leaders. Because both of these nations are initially vulnerable, it is important that they have leaders who are able to sell their countries as attractive allies rather than possible targets of invasion. The longer these countries survive, the more interesting the exercise is. The group sheets have been written so as to subtly encourage all countries to view these two as desirable allies.

Third, the teacher should take pains to subtly alert students that early aggression or all-embracing alliances can be dangerous to a nation's health. Either course can lead to too simple and too placid a game. The teacher can use hints and suggestions to help steer the class along a middle course. Remind students that aggression hurts even victorious countries, leaving them more vulnerable to other surviving nations. Point out that the larger an alliance, the more difficult it can be to sustain bonds of trust. Nations sometimes use all-encompassing alliances to lure other countries into a false sense of security, causing the seemingly safe allies to underinvest in defense and become lucrative targets for attack.

Fourth, students should be subtly steered away from thinking *about* conflict and into thinking about the preparation *for* and avoidance *of* conflict (i.e., arms races and disarmament). I fondly recall that a teaching colleague once told me how the dominant economic power in her class had convinced the class to enter a continental disarmament conference, which required all six nations to expose their actual defense strength and to sacrifice a portion of it each turn. This may indeed lead to a variation of the all-encompassing alliance, which siphons some of the excitement out of the game, but makes up for that loss by teaching other valuable lessons.

Finally, a teacher may want to prepare a second set of initial GNP and defense rankings to permit a rapid replay of the game. Often, the dynamic of a second simulation is very different from the first. The teacher can simply issue each group its new starting figures in secret, then make up and jot down economic growth data during the course of the replay. Teachers who intend to play the game with a class more than once should take care to alter the initial GNP, defense levels, and growth rates to maintain desirable uncertainty.

## POSSIBLE MODIFICATIONS

This game has worked relatively well with a variety of grade levels. More advanced students tend to complicate the exercise themselves by pursuing more sophisticated strategies, such as disarmament conferences and convoluted nonaggression pacts, while I have been told that junior high school students get caught up in the total size of their alliance and in trying to spy on one another.

### More Advanced Students

With older students, the teacher can complicate affairs by visiting random disasters on the countries or by altering the GNP growth rates included in the teacher's materials. With a class of advanced students who seem to have affairs well in hand, this kind of shock may help to reestablish fragility. One approach that I have considered but never used is to have students play the game outside of the classroom over the course of two weeks. National growth and any student activity would be announced at the beginning of class, and then the teacher would teach a normal day's lesson. With a sufficiently enthusiastic group, where students would plot and negotiate outside of class, I've thought that this might be a lot of fun.

## Junior High and Less Advanced Students

Extra care should be taken when explaining the procedures to younger students, particularly in emphasizing that they need to be secretive and that there are real costs for aggression. For classes in which the teacher is concerned about possible inequities due to the varying strength of the nations in the game, he or she may want to equalize strength and rates of growth. Additionally, a teacher of lower-level students may want to do away with any alliance restrictions and simply allow students to negotiate at will.

The exercise can also be dramatically simplified by doing away with uneven rates of growth. Instead, have the GNP of each nation grow by a fixed amount (say, $60 or $80 million a year). This approach obviously locks in the inequities that exist at the start of the exercise, so the teacher may want to equalize initial economic and military conditions.

## ASSESSMENT

Three kinds of assessment are recommended for *The Delicate Balance of Power*. Each is designed to evaluate and offer feedback on a different set of skills. By requiring the students to pay attention to what is taking place throughout the exercise, the assessments help to increase student attentiveness and cooperation. The assessments take into account student participation, student knowledge, and the student's ability to analyze the exercise.

First, the teacher should observe and take note of student interaction throughout the simulation. I particularly look for students who are acting constructively and contributing concrete value to their group. Students can contribute by negotiating, coordinating negotiations, collecting or tracking data, analyzing affairs, floating ideas, or managing their nation's strategy. At the end of the simulation, I have each student fill out the standard Student Assessment Sheet feedback form (see Chapter 12, Final Thoughts), which asks them to assess the contribution of their teammates. Using their group evaluations and my observations, I assess students on their contribution to the group product and their personal interactions. The feedback form takes each student about five minutes to fill out.

Second (and students are told *before* the exercise commences that this will be coming), the students are given a short written quiz on the rules of the game and on the simulation's major events. The quiz, which should take no more than 25 to 30 minutes, encourages students to pay attention to the rules and to the course of events during the exercise. The heightened attention makes it easier to point out the historic parallels the game illustrates. This quiz measures how much actual information the student absorbed from the simulation. The short quiz is given the day after the simulation, so this assessment is also completed the following day.

Third, students write a two-page first-person essay analyzing the simulation and explaining and evaluating their group's strategy. They explain how they would change their strategy if they were to do the exercise again and compare the course of the game to what they have learned about prewar European history. They are also asked to use the simulation to illustrate specific concepts such as brinkmanship, balance of power, interlocking alliances, and détente. Students are informed of this assignment when the simulation is introduced so that they are more likely to take notes during the conduct of the exercise. This helps students remain busy all the time and makes sure they are plugged into the substance of the lesson. Students write the paper the night after the exercise, and it is collected the next day.

All the assessments are completed by the end of the day after the simulation ends. Informing students about the assessment devices *before* the simulation encourages them to pay attention to what is going on within the groups and across the class. The result is that students are much less likely to tune out or to shirk responsibilities, because that kind of behavior usually hurts their group evaluation, their knowledge for the quiz, *and* their ability to write the essay.

# APPENDIX—MATERIALS

## List of Materials

- Economic Growth for Each Turn (the Teacher's Master Sheet)
- Summary of Rules sheet (for each student)
- GNP Summary Sheet (for teacher)
- Men Under Arms Summary Sheet (for teacher)
- Continental Map (for each of the six nations and the teacher)
- Country Profile Sheets (for each of the six nations)

### Economic Growth for Each Turn—Teacher's Master Sheet

| Year | Newcastle | Bourdeaux | Budapest | Munich | Yalta | Sicily |
|------|-----------|-----------|----------|--------|-------|--------|
| 1875 | + $ 70 mil | + $ 80 mil | + $100 mil | + $ 40 mil | + $ 70 mil | + $ 90 mil |
| 1880 | + $100 mil | + $ 100 mil | + $110 mil | + $ 50 mil | + $ 90 mil | + $ 110 mil |
| 1885 | + $110 mil | + $ 120 mil | + $ 80 mil | + $ 110 mil | + $130 mil | + $ 60 mil |
| 1890 | + $ 40 mil | + $ 140 mil | + $ 60 mil | + $ 130 mil | + $160 mil | + $ 100 mil |
| 1895 | + $ 50 mil | + $ 70 mil | + $ 90 mil | + $ 150 mil | + $200 mil | + $ 130 mil |
| 1900 | + $150 mil | + $ 150 mil | + $ 90 mil | + $ 50 mil | + $220 mil | + $ 130 mil |
| 1905 | + $180 mil | + $ 170 mil | + $120 mil | + $ 150 mil | + $ 40 mil | + $ 140 mil |
| 1910 | + $100 mil | + $ 110 mil | + $ 90 mil | + $ 170 mil | + $ 90 mil | + $ 150 mil |
| 1915 | + $100 mil | + $ 100 mil | + $100 mil | + $ 200 mil | + $120 mil | + $ 160 mil |
| 1920 | | | simulation | finished | | |
| Total | + $900 mil | + $1,040 mil | + $840 mil | + $1,050 mil | + $1,120 mil | + $1,070 mil |

**Note:** For the teacher's eyes only.

**SUMMARY OF RULES**

*The Setting:* Six countries share the continent of Faux Europa. The year is 1870. Through carefully managed growth and skillful diplomacy, the trick is to dominate or be part of the entente that dominates Faux Europa by 1920.

*Object:* Win by having highest GNP, or be part of the economic entente with highest combined GNP.

*Condition:* Due to long-standing tensions, Munich and Bourdeaux can never be part of the same economic entente.

*Length of Game:* Ten turns (each turn represents five years).

*GNP:* Gross national product measures a nation's economic productivity. Each country's figure at the beginning of the game is known only to that country's rulers.

*Military Defense:* The number of men in the armed forces measures the strength of a nation's defense. Each country's figure at the beginning of the game is known only to that country's rulers. If a country wishes to, for any reason, it is allowed to give up part of its military.

*Economic Growth:* This is announced at the beginning of each turn. Each $10 million in economic growth can either be added to GNP or used to add 10,000 men to the size of the nation's defense.

*Military Conflict:* Countries can only attack nations they border, or that border an ally who is also involved in the conflict. The invading country, and all allies involved in the attack, begin an invasion by announcing their intended aggression. After that, any allies coming to the victim's aid must announce their intention. If the aggressors have at least two times the manpower of the defender(s) then the defender(s) are conquered. If the aggressors don't have twice the manpower, the aggressors are defeated.

*Results of Military Conflict:* If the attacking countries are defeated, each loses one-third of its military to wartime casualties. The victorious defenders lose nothing. If the defenders are conquered, then the invaders still lose one-third of their military to wartime casualties, but the invaders also get to divvy up in even shares two-thirds of the defender(s) GNP (one-third of the defender(s) GNP was destroyed in the war). Countries that used to border on the defeated nation(s) now border on one another.

*Alliances and Ententes:* Alliances are military agreements. They can be formal or informal, and as complicated or simple as nations' desire. Ententes are agreements which state that two or more countries will try to jointly dominate Faux Europa. At the end of the game, the country or entente with the largest GNP is the dominant power of Faux Europa.

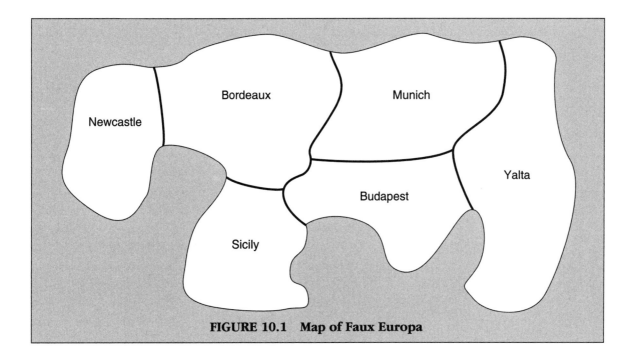

**FIGURE 10.1   Map of Faux Europa**

**GNP Summary Sheet**

| Year | Newcastle | Bourdeaux | Budapest | Munich | Yalta | Sicily |
|------|-----------|-----------|----------|--------|-------|--------|
| 1870 | $420 mil | $330 mil | $480 mil | $240 mil | $110 mil | $280 mil |
| 1875 | | | | | | |
| 1880 | | | | | | |
| 1885 | | | | | | |
| 1890 | | | | | | |
| 1895 | | | | | | |
| 1900 | | | | | | |
| 1905 | | | | | | |
| 1910 | | | | | | |
| 1915 | | | | | | |
| 1920 | | | | | | |

**Men Under Arms Summary Sheet** (in 10,000s)

| Year | Newcastle | Bourdeaux | Budapest | Munich | Yalta | Sicily |
|------|-----------|-----------|----------|--------|-------|--------|
| 1870 | 21 | 26 | 31 | 34 | 35 | 20 |
| 1875 | | | | | | |
| 1880 | | | | | | |
| 1885 | | | | | | |
| 1890 | | | | | | |
| 1895 | | | | | | |
| 1900 | | | | | | |
| 1905 | | | | | | |
| 1910 | | | | | | |
| 1915 | | | | | | |
| 1920 | | | | | | |

## Country Profile Sheet A   NEWCASTLE

NEWCASTLE is a rocky country with many beaches and a number of major cities. You have a very large industrial economy that produces most of the continent's steel and coal. You trade much of this factory output to YALTA, the "breadbasket" of Faux Europa, in order to import needed food. You are one of the two democracies in Faux Europa, BORDEAUX is the other. NEWCASTLE occupies an isolated position, because the only country it borders on is BORDEAUX. This means NEWCASTLE cannot be invaded as long as you are on good terms with BORDEAUX and BORDEAUX is unconquered.

### GNP

NEWCASTLE is one of the leading economies on the continent, so you're in good shape, even though the long-term outlook suggests that other countries will be gaining on you over time. BUDAPEST is the other dominant economy on the continent, but you don't know how things may change over time. Historically, due to your isolated position, you have worried less about defense and added more to GNP than other countries.

### Defense

Due to your protected geographic position, NEWCASTLE has traditionally kept a relatively small military. For now, BORDEAUX is not strong enough to conquer you by itself, but you don't know what their alliance situation is. If it attacked with allies, BORDEAUX might be able to conquer NEWCASTLE, so you want to make sure you are on good terms with them. However, it is important that you explore all your options, particularly a possible alliance with a military power like MUNICH or YALTA.

### Allies

NEWCASTLE is naturally friendly with BORDEAUX because of your location. You and YALTA can bookend the continent, and your large GNP might be very attractive to YALTA. An alliance with powerful BUDAPEST or MUNICH could be useful, but an alliance with MUNICH is also likely to anger BORDEAUX. Don't forget SICILY, because if BORDEAUX falls, you'll need all the help you can get.

### Newcastle's Economic and Military Strength

| Year | GNP | Men under arms |
|------|-----|----------------|
| 1870 | $420 million | 210,000 |
| 1880 | | |
| 1885 | | |
| 1890 | | |
| 1895 | | |
| 1900 | | |
| 1905 | | |
| 1910 | | |
| 1915 | | |
| 1920 | | |

*Data on Other Nations' Economic and Military Strength (track it as you collect it)*

| | | |
|------|-----|----------------|
| Bordeaux | | |
| Budapest | | |
| Munich | | |
| Yalta | | |
| Sicily | | |

## Country Profile Sheet B   BORDEAUX

BORDEAUX is an agricultural country that depends largely on its farms and its wine industry. You have just ended a fierce war with MUNICH. That war, and a bitter history between your two countries, has made the possibility of an economic entente between you two impossible. BORDEAUX's central position and historic role at the center of Faux Europa make your country both strategically important and highly vulnerable. BORDEAUX is the only country that borders on isolated NEWCASTLE, a position that makes you very important to the defense of that economic power. You are one of the two democracies in Faux Europa—NEWCASTLE is the other.

### GNP

The economy of agricultural BORDEAUX is solid, if not fantastic. In addition, you expect to have the economy grow at a good rate in coming years. NEWCASTLE is one of the leading economies on the continent, so that could be a fruitful alliance. BUDAPEST, a MUNICH ally, is the other dominant economy on the continent.

### Defense

The just-finished war with MUNICH has left your forces weaker than you would like. Currently, MUNICH is somewhat stronger than you, and it is allied with powerful BUDAPEST. The good news is that you have completed a defense treaty with YALTA which says that your two nations will defend each other if MUNICH attacks either of you. Since NEWCASTLE can only be attacked by an alliance that includes you, or if you are defeated, there is a natural opportunity there to form an alliance.

### Allies

You have your defense treaty with YALTA, but you have serious troubles with powerful MUNICH. Also, things aren't very friendly with BUDAPEST, which has very good relations with MUNICH. SICILY isn't very strong, but they only border on you and BUDAPEST. For that reason, if no other, they are probably willing to form some kind of agreement and may be able to give you the extra strength you need.

### Bordeaux's Economic and Military Strength

| Year | GNP | Men under arms |
|------|-----|----------------|
| 1870 | $330 million | 260,000 |
| 1880 | | |
| 1885 | | |
| 1890 | | |
| 1895 | | |
| 1900 | | |
| 1905 | | |
| 1910 | | |
| 1915 | | |
| 1920 | | |

*Data on Other Nations' Economic and Military Strength (track it as you collect it)*

| | | |
|------|-----|----------------|
| Newcastle | | |
| Budapest | | |
| Munich | | |
| Yalta | | |
| Sicily | | |

## Country Profile Sheet C   BUDAPEST

BUDAPEST is a large, rocky country with scenic rivers and beautiful mountains. Your country is also known for its skilled tailors and carpenters. BUDAPEST is currently the richest country in Faux Europa, but you have been on a downward slide since an ill-fated war with MUNICH several years ago. Since that time you have become allies with MUNICH. Your nation is a "dual monarchy" ruled by two sets of royal families. Your powerful present position, combined with what looks to be a coming slide, means that you need to think carefully about how to protect yourself. Your problems are also complicated because you sit smack in the center of the continent, bordering on every country except NEWCASTLE.

### GNP

You have one of the continent's highest GNPs. NEWCASTLE is the other dominant economic power. MUNICH is not as economically powerful as you, but they have a stronger defense. Maintaining your strong GNP in the coming years will be crucial.

### Defense

BUDAPEST has a solid army, though your central position means that it had better be. You are squeezed between MUNICH and YALTA, both of which have powerful armies. Your lack of expected growth in coming years means that it may be difficult for you to afford to keep a large army, although no one knows this but you.

### Allies

You have an alliance with powerful MUNICH which states that your two countries will defend each other if either is attacked by YALTA. Because of your exposed position, you had better start looking for new allies if you don't trust MUNICH. You could ally with BORDEAUX, although that would probably anger MUNICH. SICILY, on your southern border, might be a good potential ally, especially since they only border on you and BORDEAUX. An alliance with NEWCASTLE would allow you to sandwich BORDEAUX.

### Budapest's Economic and Military Strength

| Year | GNP | Men under arms |
|------|-----|----------------|
| 1870 | $480 million | 310,000 |
| 1880 | | |
| 1885 | | |
| 1890 | | |
| 1895 | | |
| 1900 | | |
| 1905 | | |
| 1910 | | |
| 1915 | | |
| 1920 | | |

*Data on Other Nations' Economic and Military Strength (track it as you collect it)*

| | | |
|------|-----|----------------|
| Newcastle | | |
| Bordeaux | | |
| Munich | | |
| Yalta | | |
| Sicily | | |

## Country Profile Sheet D   MUNICH

MUNICH is a military powerhouse. You have a large and disciplined army, and have fought several successful wars in recent years. Because your country has only been unified recently, your economy is not yet fully developed. Ruled by a monarch, MUNICH is a rapidly growing country that sits in the middle of Faux Europa. You have just completed a successful war with BORDEAUX and are regarded as one of the continent's dominant powers. That war, and a bitter history between your two countries, has made the possibility of an economic entente between you two impossible.

### GNP

Your economy is not very developed, but the conditions are in place for it to grow rapidly in the years to come. Particularly with territory you have just captured in your war with BORDEAUX, you can look forward to a high rate of growth.

### Defense

MUNICH has one of the continent's most powerful armed forces. This, combined with skillful diplomacy, has lifted you to your present position. Nonetheless, your arms was not strong enough to capture your ancient enemy BORDEAUX, and BORDEAUX has recently formed a mutual defense treaty with powerful YALTA. Fortunately, you and BUDAPEST have formed a defense treaty in which you promise to defend each other in case one of you is attacked by YALTA.

### Allies

You have an alliance with powerful BUDAPEST which states that your two countries will defend each other if either is attacked by YALTA. Because of your central position, you had better start looking for new allies if you don't trust BUDAPEST. You could ally with SICILY or NEWCASTLE, either of which would help you to isolate BORDEAUX. Especially because of your central position, it is important that you not be isolated and left without allies.

### Munich's Economic and Military Strength

| Year | GNP | Men under arms |
|------|-----|----------------|
| 1870 | $240 million | 340,000 |
| 1880 |     |     |
| 1885 |     |     |
| 1890 |     |     |
| 1895 |     |     |
| 1900 |     |     |
| 1905 |     |     |
| 1910 |     |     |
| 1915 |     |     |
| 1920 |     |     |

*Data on Other Nations' Economic and Military Strength (track it as you collect it)*

| Newcastle |     |     |
|-----------|-----|-----|
| Bordeaux  |     |     |
| Budapest  |     |     |
| Yalta     |     |     |
| Sicily    |     |     |

## Country Profile Sheet E   YALTA

YALTA is a huge country with sprawling farms, a massive population, and a vast natural resources. Your massive population has permitted you to assemble one of the strongest armies on the entire continent even though your country is quite poor. Known as the "breadbasket" of Faux Europa, YALTA is an agricultural country without a heavy industrial base. However, a recent treaty with BORDEAUX has started to bring investment into YALTA, and your rich natural deposits of iron, coal, and oil should start to be developed in coming years. Your government is a monarchy, ruled by a czar.

### GNP

Your economy is not very developed, but the conditions are in place for it to grow rapidly in the years to come. Particularly with the new investment that's coming from BORDEAUX, you can look forward to a high rate of growth in coming years.

### Defense

YALTA has one of the continent's most powerful armed forces. Nonetheless, you border on BUDAPEST and MUNICH, two strong and aggressive countries. Fortunately, you have a defense alliance with BORDEAUX, a country that is on very bad terms with MUNICH. Of course, if you were on good terms with MUNICH and BUDAPEST, you would be safe from attack. But that would require you to break your treaty with BORDEAUX, and would expose you to a MUNICH–BUDAPEST double-cross.

### Allies

You have completed a defense treaty with BORDEAUX which says that your two nations will defend each other if MUNICH attacks either of you. You should probably also look toward SICILY or NEWCASTLE. Neither is as militarily powerful as you, and they might welcome the chance to ally with a country as strong as YALTA.

### Yalta's Economic and Military Strength

| Year | GNP | Men under arms |
|------|-----|----------------|
| 1870 | $110 million | 350,000 |
| 1880 | | |
| 1885 | | |
| 1890 | | |
| 1895 | | |
| 1900 | | |
| 1905 | | |
| 1910 | | |
| 1915 | | |
| 1920 | | |

*Data on Other Nations' Economic and Military Strength (track it as you collect it)*

| | | |
|------|-----|----------------|
| Newcastle | | |
| Bordeaux | | |
| Budapest | | |
| Munich | | |
| Sicily | | |

## Country Profile Sheet F   SICILY

First the bad news. SICILY has a relatively small army and your economy is solid but unspectacular. Because SICILY just became a unified nation in recent decades, you are not yet as developed or powerful as many other countries on the continent. The good news, however, is that you expect to grow quickly and steadily in coming years. Additionally, you have great weather, so your king is able to enjoy the country's lovely landscape on moonlit nights. SICILY is rather protected from the rest of the continent, and this isolation combined with good diplomacy should see you through.

### GNP

Your economy is not very developed at present, but the conditions are in place for it to grow rapidly in the years to come. Also, your economy isn't awful, it's just that it's behind established nations like NEWCASTLE and BUDAPEST.

### Defense

Because you only border two countries, your defense worries are not as bad as those of countries that sit in the middle of the continent. You have a small army, but it is currently large enough to protect you from any one nation. Of course, you have to worry about being attacked by an alliance, so you probably need to beef up your defense and look for allies.

### Allies

You are currently on your own, but you are protected by your isolated position and the fact that you don't have any real enemies right now. In fact, the central countries, which are all involved in the BORDEAUX–MUNICH tiff, might come begging you to help them. If you play your cards right, you could come out in great shape. Because the big powers are pretty evenly matched, you and NEWCASTLE will look very attractive. Try working with NEWCASTLE to make your strength count. And make sure you protect yourself, fast.

### Sicily's Economic and Military Strength

| Year | GNP | Men under arms |
|------|-----|----------------|
| 1870 | $280 million | 200,000 |
| 1880 | | |
| 1885 | | |
| 1890 | | |
| 1895 | | |
| 1900 | | |
| 1905 | | |
| 1910 | | |
| 1915 | | |
| 1920 | | |

*Data on Other Nations' Economic and Military Strength (track it as you collect it)*

| | | |
|------|--|--|
| Newcastle | | |
| Bordeaux | | |
| Budapest | | |
| Munich | | |
| Yalta | | |

# CHAPTER 11

# Making the United Nations Work

*Students take a seat at the center of contemporary international diplomacy. Choosing the issues to be addressed, students are able to design and then fight to implement remedies to issues of central concern to the international community. Playing the roles of the 15 nations that sit on the United Nations Security Council, students are charged with identifying pressing problems faced by the nation they represent, researching and designing workable solutions to a problem, and then securing the passage of their proposal through the UN's political mine-field.*

*Designed as a year-end culminating experience, this exercise gives students a chance to show off the breadth of their knowledge, the acuity of their research and analytic skills, and their negotiating savvy. The exercise is designed so that teachers can use the nations that currently sit in the ten rotating seats on the Security Council. This structure permits students to tackle questions that are currently of pressing interest, blurring the line between scholastic learning and the evening's headlines.*

## TEACHER'S NOTE

I designed this simulation as a culminating exercise for a freshman World Geography class. It was intended to offer students a chance to show off the knowledge and the negotiating skills they had learned during the year-long course. The lesson is the least structured of the ten exercises in this book, and that loose structure makes it well suited for a number of courses. It can be used as a contemporary complement to a World History or a European History course, as part of Civics or Political Science class, or as an exercise for a Contemporary Problems class.

I have found great enthusiasm for this exercise. After participating in several structured simulations throughout the year, students welcome the loosely structured nature of this one. Students who have already learned how to negotiate, how to research necessary material, and how to engage in a simulated environment can blossom when given the chance to shape the substance of an exercise.

Students whose first love is not social studies also seize on the chance to draw on their interests in other areas when selecting policy areas to address. Various students have written up impressive proposals regarding endangered species, the green house effect, acid rain, and other environmental concerns; the need for a global capacity to deflect an incoming asteroid; plans for international space exploration; and a plan to routinize and then govern the exchange of artists and musicians between otherwise hostile nations.

Students represent the 15 nations that compose the United Nations Security Council. Their task is to tackle several of the problems plaguing the international community. The simulation gives students a chance to think about economic, political, and social problems from an international perspective. One of the particularly attractive elements of this exercise is that it is easily configured to current events and gives students an opportunity to have significant input into deciding what issues will be discussed.

## BACKGROUND ON THE UNITED NATIONS

The United Nations is the world's second attempt at an international peace-keeping body. Formed in 1945, the UN grew out of the international alliance that defeated Nazi Germany in World War II. The UN is the successor to the League of Nations, the world's failed first attempt at an international peace-keeping organization. The League of Nations was the brainchild of former U.S. President Woodrow Wilson, the former political scientist and Princeton University president. During the peace talks that concluded World War I, one of Wilson's few victories was managing to convince the negotiating powers to sign onto his League of Nations. Wilson triumphantly returned home, only to find that isolationists in the U.S. Senate controlled enough votes to block U.S. membership in Wilson's new organization. Wilson proceeded to embark on a whirlwind train tour in support of the League, during which he suffered a massive stroke that effectively incapacitated him for the last two years of his presidency. The Senate refused to ratify U.S. membership in the League, and the League existed as a largely ineffectual organization until it disintegrated in the 1930s amid escalating European tensions. In 1939, those tensions erupted into World War II.

The United Nations grew out the cooperative efforts that defeated Nazi Germany, Japan, and Italy during World War II. The name *United Nations* was devised by President Franklin D. Roosevelt as a useful nickname for the United States and its allies in the war. The phrase was first used in the "Declaration by United Nations" on January 1, 1942, in which the 26 allied nations pledged to continue their collective fight against the Axis Powers (Germany, Japan, and Italy).

The United Nations Charter was drawn up by the representatives of 50 countries at the UN Conference on International Organization between April 25 and June 26, 1945. Meeting in San Francisco, the delegates deliberated on proposals worked out by China, the Soviet Union, the United Kingdom, and the United States during 1944 meetings at Dumbarton Oaks. Representatives of the 50 countries signed the UN Charter on June 26, 1945. The United Nations officially came into existence on October 24, 1945, after the charter was ratified by China, France, the Soviet Union, the United Kingdom, the United States, and by a majority of the other signatories.

The UN consists of two main bodies, the General Assembly and the Security Council. The General Assembly, where each member nation has one vote, serves largely as a debating society and lacks significant power.

### The Security Council

The UN Charter theoretically obligates countries to settle their international disputes peacefully. Any disputes are supposed to be brought before the Security Council, which is primarily charged with maintaining international peace and security. The Security Council can be convened whenever peace is threatened. The Council has 15 members. Five of them—China, France, the Russian Federation, the United Kingdom, and the United States—are permanent members. The ten nonpermanent members of the Security Council are elected by the General Assembly for two-year terms. The nations are usually chosen to ensure representation from around the globe.

Since 1945, there have been two changes in the makeup of the permanent members who sit on the Security Council. The original Chinese seat on the Security Council was held by the U.S.-allied Chinese Nationalist government headed by Chiang Kai-shek. In 1949, the Nationalist government fled to Taiwan when the Communists seized control of mainland China. Nonetheless, under U.S. patronage, the Nationalists continued to control the Chinese seat for roughly two decades. During the Nixon administration, the United States relented in its support for Taiwan and permitted the Communist mainland government to take the Chinese Security Council seat. The other change was prompted by the dissolution of the Soviet Union in the late 1980s. The Russian Federation inherited the Security Council seat that had been previously held by the Russian-dominated Soviet Union.

Security Council decisions require nine votes, except for votes on procedural questions (they only require a majority). Significantly, each of the five permanent members was given a veto over Council decisions. Even if 14 countries vote in favor of a measure, a "no" vote from one permanent member is sufficient to block the measure. This arrangement tended to inhibit the Security Council's ability to do anything during the Cold War stand-off between the U.S.-led West and the Soviet bloc.

When a threat to international peace is brought before the Council, the Council usually begins by undertaking mediation, setting forth principles for a settlement, or pursuing some other kind of peaceful solution. If fighting breaks out, the Council tries to secure a cease-fire. Possessing no armed forces or standing army of its own, the Council relies on troops volunteered by member nations to carry out its actions. The most common Security Council activities are deploying peace-keeping troops so as to keep combatants separated, to police an area, or to reassure the local population. The Council also has the power to enforce its decisions by imposing economic sanctions and by ordering collective military action. Other Council duties include recommending a candidate for Secretary-General to the Assembly and new members for admission to the UN.

## How the UN Advances Peace

The UN's primary purpose is to preserve world peace. The UN has helped resolve disputes between nations, prevent conflicts, and put an end to fighting. The UN has varied tools with which to pursue peace. They include a Security Council decision ordering a cease-fire, a Council decision laying down guidelines for settling a dispute, a compromise worked out by a mediator, intervention by the Secretary-General, informal diplomatic arm-twisting or message-carrying, fact-finding missions, and peacekeeping forces made up of soldiers contributed by UN members.

With the end of the Cold War and the relaxation of U.S.–Soviet tensions, the UN's role in worldwide peacemaking grew dramatically. While the UN launched just 13 peace-keeping missions from World War II to 1988, it launched 21 just between 1988 and 1994.

# USING THIS SIMULATION

## Purpose of the Exercise

Substantively, the lesson is designed to have students integrate the economic, political, and social knowledge they have developed in disparate units. The exercise permits students to draw on a wide range of knowledge, and to do so while learning about the dynamics and practices of the world's most significant international body. The exercise can be used as part of a World Geography or World History class, in a Social Studies or Current Events class, or even as a broadening year-end exercise for an American or European History class.

## Skills Developed

The exercise helps to develop negotiating, public speaking, research, and analytic writing skills. Students also refine their understanding of international relations and some of the world's economic and political challenges. In contemplating solutions to an international problem that interests them, students develop their ability to analyze policy problems and solutions. Students develop collaborative and persuasive skills by working with teammates and classmates to design mutually acceptable proposals and then convincing an eclectic mix of nations to support their proposal. The essay that students need to write requires them to think through the conference and to interpret the significance of the events they witness.

Setting the exercise in the present year, and encouraging students to examine currently pressing problems, helps teach students good research habits. The need for current material discourages the use of encyclopedias (whether on-line or in print) or other sources of predigested information, propelling students toward magazines, newspapers, and on-line data sources. Not only are students pressed to use new sources, but they are forced to do their own synthesis and analysis.

## Logistics

The exercise itself generally takes about two days. However, students should be assigned their country and told about the issue-analysis assignment two to three weeks in advance of the actual exercise. Since each country can be represented by one to three students, the game can accommodate classes ranging in size from 15 to 45 students. The members of each country write an issue proposal and a short brief on the economic, political, and social needs of their country before the council meets. The exercise begins with each country passing out a one-page executive summary of its proposal, and making a two- to three-minute argument defending its analysis and its proposed solution. The Security Council, with the teacher sitting as chairperson, is then free to discuss, amend, and vote for or against any proposal. Some issues will quickly be unanimously supported, while others will prompt disagreement. Contentious issues should each be permitted about 10 to 15 minutes of debate and negotiation.

The few materials necessary for the simulation are in this chapter's Appendix. Students should be issued an Issue Analysis Guidelines Sheet, which instructs them on organizing their issue analysis and evaluating those presented by their classmates, as well as a world map.

## HOW THE SIMULATION WORKS

### Student Groups

There are 15 countries on the Security Council. Each country should be represented by one or two students. In larger classes, with more than 30 students, groups of three students should be assigned to some of the more influential nations. Depending on how much time the teacher wishes to devote to the exercise, the teacher can either have every nation prepare a proposal or have pairs of nations devise proposals.

### Object

Each group (or pair of groups) picks an international issue of concern to their nation(s). The proponents of a piece of legislation want to get it through the Security Council and want to do that while doing the greatest possible good for their nation. Farther, students are expected to produce an intelligent, thoughtful, and productive Council. Each student is charged with justifying his or her group's performance and defense of the national interest in the essay each student writes at the conclusion of the Council. In their essays, students should emphasize the fate of their proposal and how the passage, amendment, or failure of other proposals affected their country.

### Length of Exercise

The exercise runs until the class has addressed all the issue proposals. Because some issues are quickly resolved, while others can drag on, there is no way to be sure how long the exercise will run. However, the teacher should feel free to arbitrarily limit discussion on any issue in order to fit the exercise within the allotted time. (I give the exercise a maximum allotment of two 40-minute periods.)

### How the Game Is Played

Two to three weeks *before* the exercise, students are assigned their countries and told that they need to tackle an international problem of concern to their country. A single country can design an issue analysis and proposed solution, or two countries can do it as a team effort. If the teacher allows countries to partner up, it saves substantial class time. Two to three days after giving students the initial assignment—after they have had a few days to think about their country and about a problem that might interest them—students should be given about 15 to 20 minutes of class time to talk to classmates from another nation about partnering up on an issue analysis and proposed solution.

Whether one country works alone or cooperates with another country, the students are expected to write an analysis that dissects the problem, examines possible remedies, proposes a solution, and justifies that solution. Explicit directions for the students are presented in the Issue Analysis Guidelines (see Appendix), a copy of which should be passed out to each group when the initial assignments are given.

The students representing each country are also expected to prepare briefs on the status and needs of their country before the council begins. The country briefing should summarize basic political, economic, social, and military information, as well as the leading international concerns of their nation. The briefing should also inform students about the role their nation plays in the international arena and about its usual allies and sympathies.

These country briefs should be about two to three pages long. The teacher can either have each group prepare a brief or require each student to write one. These briefs are to be used for the purpose of guiding students as they seek to represent their nation's interests. The teacher may want to have students turn in their issue proposals the day before the exercise so that the two-page pieces can be photocopied and distributed around the class.

On the day the exercise begins, students should sit in a rough circle, with all students facing inward. Representatives of each country ought to sit together. The teacher calls the meeting to order, reminds students of how the Security Council operates, and then calls for the first proposal. The proponents should make their case in about four to five minutes. The Council is then free to debate, discuss, or amend the proposal. After the issue has been worked through, a vote should be taken (or the issue can be tabled for later discussion). Nine "yes" votes are needed to pass a measure. Additionally, if any of the five permanent members (United States, China, Russia, France, Great Britain) vote "no," then the measure is defeated regardless of how many "yes" votes there are.

During the debate and discussion, students are responsible for paying attention to the Council's activity. Using the Proposal Tracking Sheet (see Appendix), students are to keep track of all proposals, who proposed them, the major amendments made, and the outcome of each proposal. This information helps students to make the case that they were effective advocates for their nation when they write their analytic essay at the end of the simulation.

Depending on how large, how talkative, and how sophisticated a class is, the exercise can vary greatly in the time it will actually take. I have had a class zip through eight proposals (the minimum number a class can produce) in about 35 minutes, while engaging in little interesting or valuable discussion. Other classes have forced me to cap the exercise at two full days, because they were able to spend 20 minutes on intricate discussions of just one measure. Typically, students get through the bulk of the exercise in less than two 40-minute classes, particularly if the teacher maintains pacing and keeps the class focused.

## COMMENTS FROM EXPERIENCE

Given the exercise's loose structure, it works best after students have participated in several simulations and are used to the dynamic. This exercise works better if the students are self-policing, because it lacks concrete incentives to steer student activity. A teacher concerned about this soft focus might want to construct incentive-driven profiles (see Possible Modifications section in this chapter).

---

**SUMMARY TEACHER INSTRUCTIONS**

*Prior to the day the simulation begins*

- Objective is for students to integrate economic, political, and social knowledge while learning about the dynamics and practices of the United Nations.
- Goal is for student proponents of a proposal to get it through the Security Council having done the most good for their nations.
- At least 2 to 3 weeks before the exercise begins pass out Issue Analysis Guidelines Sheet and world map. Assign students to countries and explain that students will need to analyze and devise a solution to an international problem that concerns their country. Tell the groups they will have 2 to 3 weeks to prepare these issues analyses, which they will then present to the Council during the session. Students are also to write a 2- to 3-page country brief, either individually or in groups (teacher's option).
- Provide students with 15 to 20 minutes of class time to partner an issue with another nation for issue analysis and proposed solution.
- Students are to write an analysis and dissect the problem, examine remedies, and propose and justify a solution.
- Explain the background and responsibilities of the UN and the Security Council.

*The day the simulation begins*

- Arrange classroom seats in a circle and allow country representatives to sit together.
- Remind students how Security Council operates.
- Call for the first proposal.
- Allow the advocates of each proposal 4 to 5 minutes to present their case.
- Allow Council to debate, discuss, or amend proposal.
- Permit Council to take vote after issue is worked through (9 "yes" votes to pass a measure; if any of the 5 permanent members vote "no" the measure is defeated no matter how many "yes" votes).
- Have students keep track of proposals using the Proposal Tracking Sheet.

*After the simulation*

- Require students to write an analytic essay at the end of simulation.
- Assess simulation using issue proposal and briefing paper, classroom observations of participation, written analysis of simulation, and a quiz.

---

The teacher needs to be very aware of which students are assigned to the veto powers. Having constructive and forceful students in these roles can greatly enhance the value the entire class derives from the exercise. However, putting disengaged or contrary students in these roles creates a real possibility that the exercise will be frustrating. I don't mean to exaggerate this concern, but simply to remind teachers that they should pay attention to the makeup of the five pivotal groups.

Teachers who are concerned about the students not filling the allotted time for the lesson should have additional proposals at the ready, such as those suggested below. (Again, it is likely to be the rare class that breezes through all the proposals.) It is a good idea to have some relatively dramatic and controversial issues, ones that are likely to engender debate. The teacher may need to briefly explain why controversial measures, such as the ones mentioned in the following list, represent dramatic changes in UN policy. These are the proposals I would recommend that teachers be prepared to put before the Council:

1. A proposal to broaden the Security Council to 18 members, including the addition of three new permanent members (Japan, Germany, and a Third World nation that would need to be selected by the class).
2. A proposal to abolish the veto power held by the "Big Five" on the Security Council.

3. A proposal to create a standing United Nations army, which is under the direct command of the UN leadership, and not under the influence of the member nations.
4. A proposal to create an international 1% sales tax administered by the United Nations, for the purpose of supporting international peacekeeping and military inspection missions.

## POSSIBLE MODIFICATIONS

### More Advanced Students

For particularly advanced groups, such as a class of college freshmen, the teacher may want to require much more sophisticated country briefings and issue analyses. Students might be expected to prepare their issue analyses as term papers, lending the proceedings a substantive depth not present in the more laid-back version presented here. Students might be required to include a cost-benefit analysis, a discussion of scientific and political feasibility, an exploration of possible adverse unintended consequences, and a discussion of the effects on various nations and populations.

A second modification is that the teacher can replace the exercise's free-flowing format with one that is historically constrained. Rather than representing their nations in the present year, the entire activity can be situated in any year after 1945. The teacher may want students to struggle with international relations during the Korean War in the early 1950s, during the building of the Berlin Wall in the early 1960s, during the Vietnam War in the late 1960s and early 1970s, or during the end of the Cold War and the fall of the Soviet Union in the late 1980s and early 1990s.

Alternatively, the teacher may want to make this exercise into a more structured game, akin to those in several earlier chapters. To do so, the teacher should create specific, directive profiles for the members of the Security Council. Students representing each country are assigned concrete negotiating objectives, adding a hard-edged oppositional dimension not present in this relaxed exercise.

### Junior High and Less Advanced Students

The loosely structured nature of this exercise makes it very conducive for younger students. Because nearly all the complexities in this simulation are introduced by the students themselves, it tends to be very self-regulating. However, a teacher can further simplify this exercise by eliminating or trimming the issue proposals that students must prepare. Rather than being required to analyze and study issues from their national perspective, students can be permitted to simply propose an idea they think will make the world a better place. The discussions will be less substantive and less authentic, but I'm certainly willing to make that trade-off if it will get sixth graders talking about international trade, global warming, arms control, cooperation in space, or world hunger.

Similarly, the teacher may want to drop the requirement that students prepare country briefs, leaving students essentially free to argue as they wish about these issues. The teacher may also want to drop or shorten the analytic essay in which students plead their case, on the basis that students will lack both the knowledge and the skill to make the case for their effectiveness. If the teacher does elect to relax these rules, trading a good deal of authenticity away in order to increase student comfort, he or she may want to strip the permanent members of their vetoes. Otherwise, given that students are generally voicing personal feelings rather than trying to represent their country, the possession of the veto by some students can become a fairness issue. To avoid unnecessary headaches, and given that authenticity is already being sacrificed, it's probably easiest to drop the veto.

## ASSESSMENT

Four assessments are suggested for this exercise. Students should be informed of all assessments when they are first told that the simulation will be played, *before* the simulation begins. By requiring students to prepare for and pay attention throughout the exercise, the assessments make the exercise more productive and maximize student participation.

First, students representing each nation are required to write an issue proposal and a three-page briefing paper on the current status of their nation. The issue proposal is a two- to three-page document designed to address a contemporary international problem. The format of the issue proposal should follow the Issue Proposal Guidelines sheet (see Appendix). Each group should turn in its proposal and country briefing at the conclusion of the exercise. I evaluate the papers based on the quality and usefulness of information and the clarity of organization.

Second, I evaluate students based on my observations of their participation in the exercise. In particular, I look for students who attempt to make some concrete contribution to the class proceedings. At the end of the exercise, I also have each student fill out the Student Assessment Sheet feedback form (see Chapter 12, Final Thoughts), which asks them to assess the contributions of their teammates. Using my observations and the group evaluations, I assess students based on their contribution to their team and to the group. The feedback form takes about five minutes to fill out, so this assessment is completed by the day after the exercise.

Third, students are asked to write a two-page first-person essay that analyzes the simulation. The essay should be attached to the student's Proposal Tracking Sheet (see Appendix), which helps students to keep abreast of the various proposals and the outcome of each one. In the essay, students are asked to explain and evaluate their success at tackling pressing world concerns and at representing the interests of their particular nation.

Each student is expected to explain how effectively his or her group defended national interests. Students should emphasize the fate of their proposal and how the passage, amendment, or failure of other proposals affected their country. Students may also want to explain how they would act differently if the exercise were conducted again. Foreknowledge of this assignment helps motivate students to pay closer attention throughout the exercise, increasing student interest and attentiveness. Students are to write the paper the night after the exercise; the teacher collects it the next day.

Fourth, students are quizzed on the substance of the decisions they reached and the process by which those decisions took shape. This short quiz should be administered the day after the exercise ends, and should take no more than 15 to 20 minutes. The purpose of the quiz is to ensure that students paid attention to what transpired around them during the game, and to help ensure that students familiarize themselves with the rules guiding the Security Council. Questions should focus on the structure and history of the United Nations, the nations represented on the Security Council, the kinds of measures that were proposed, and the fate of the proposals.

The assessments are completed by the end of the day after the simulation, offering a constructive and engaging view of student participation and performance within a compact time frame.

# APPENDIX—MATERIALS

## List of Materials

- Issue Analysis Guidelines sheet (for each student)
- World map (for each student)
- Teacher's Master Proposal Tracking Sheet
- Proposal Tracking Sheet (for each student)

---

**ISSUE ANALYSIS GUIDELINES**

1. What is the problem? Will it get worse or better over time if left alone? Is it an economic, social, environmental, or political problem?

2. How does it affect your country? How will this proposal benefit your country?

3. Why is this an issue that should concern the international community?

4. What are the proposed solutions to the problem?

5. What are the strengths and weaknesses of the proposed solutions? How expensive are they? How realistic are they?

6. What are the possible undesirable side-effects the solutions may cause?

7. What are you proposing that the Security Council do? What resources will be required (in terms of money, troops, natural resources, etc.)? From where do you propose to get these resources?

8. Defend your recommendations. Why should the Security Council support your measure? Why is it in the world's best interest to solve this problem now, using your proposed solution?

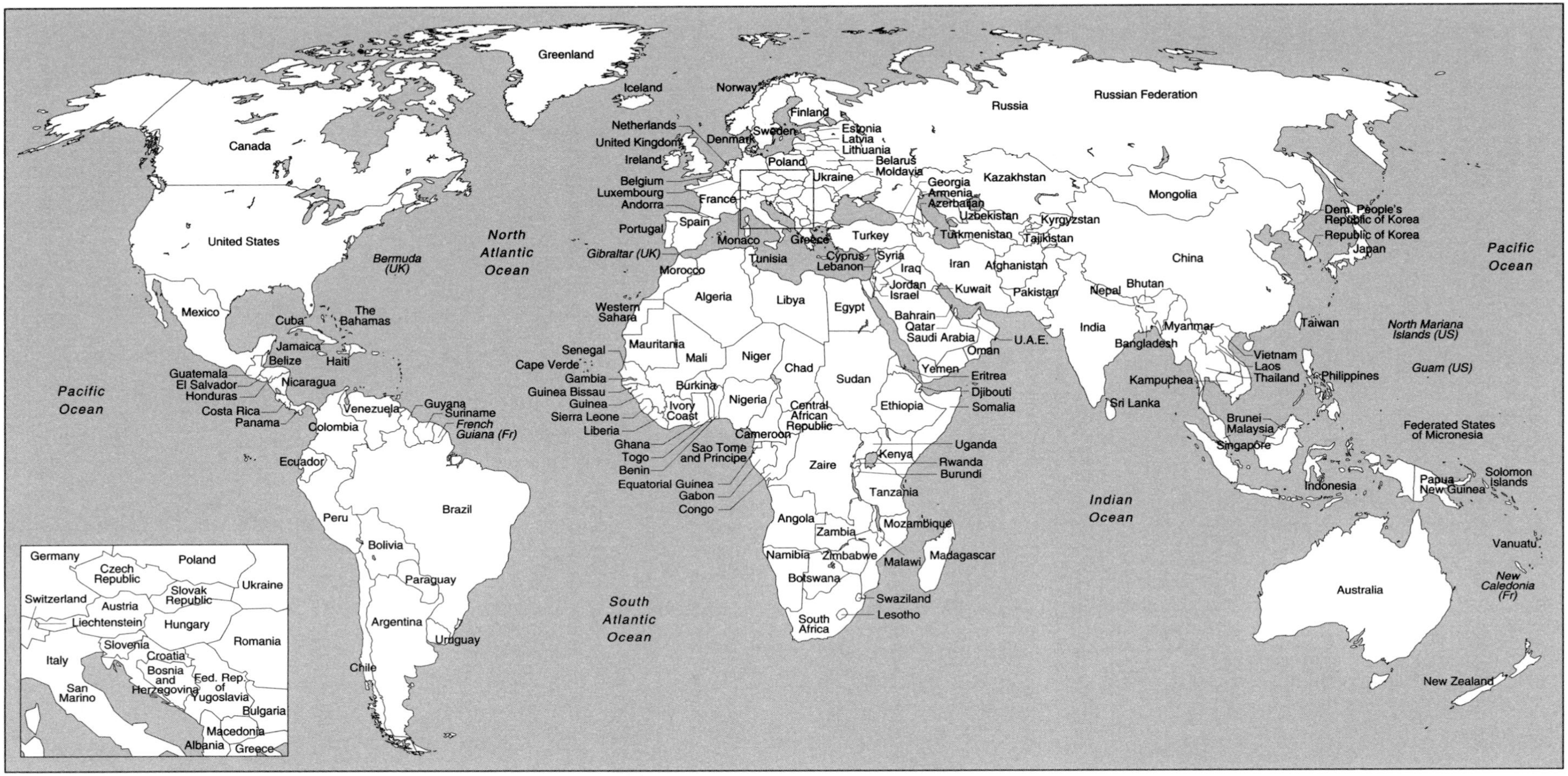

**FIGURE 11.1 Map of the World**

**Teacher's Master Proposal Tracking Sheet**

| Students | Country or countries | Proposal | Outcome |
|---|---|---|---|
| | | | |
| | | | |
| | | | |
| | | | |
| | | | |
| | | | |
| | | | |
| | | | |
| | | | |
| | | | |
| | | | |
| | | | |
| | | | |
| | | | |
| | | | |
| | | | |
| | | | |
| | | | |
| | | | |
| | | | |
| | | | |
| | | | |
| | | | |
| | | | |

**Proposal Tracking Sheet**

| Country | Proposal | Amendments | Summary analysis | Vote |
|---------|----------|------------|------------------|------|
|         |          |            |                  |      |
|         |          |            |                  |      |
|         |          |            |                  |      |
|         |          |            |                  |      |
|         |          |            |                  |      |
|         |          |            |                  |      |
|         |          |            |                  |      |
|         |          |            |                  |      |
|         |          |            |                  |      |
|         |          |            |                  |      |
|         |          |            |                  |      |
|         |          |            |                  |      |
|         |          |            |                  |      |
|         |          |            |                  |      |
|         |          |            |                  |      |
|         |          |            |                  |      |
|         |          |            |                  |      |
|         |          |            |                  |      |
|         |          |            |                  |      |
|         |          |            |                  |      |
|         |          |            |                  |      |
|         |          |            |                  |      |
|         |          |            |                  |      |

# CHAPTER 12

# *Final Thoughts*

I suggest giving simulations a try. This collection offers a number of field-tested classroom exercises that have been created and refined in the trenches. By coupling these frameworks with your ingenuity, I suspect you will find yourself increasing the number of lessons that leave your students both educated and invigorated. Although I have found these exercises to be effective and enjoyable, that does not mean you will necessarily enjoy success with any given exercise in any given class. That is why I strongly encourage you to think of these exercises as models. Try them once, taking advantage of the prepared materials to reduce the workload and the uncertainties of running a simulation for the first time. Once you have tried the exercise, evaluate how it played out. Decide whether the exercise will run more smoothly with time, whether it requires modification, or whether you would rather design your own exercises. How should you go about determining whether an exercise was successful and how it might be adjusted? I will briefly discuss these points in the final few pages.

## ASSESSING SIMULATIONS

To my mind, assessment has two purposes. One is to help evaluate student performance, the other is to help me evaluate the effectiveness of my teaching and my lesson design. The assessments included in the simulations and in this chapter have been constructed with both of those purposes in mind. Using assessments to evaluate student performance is something with which teachers are well-acquainted. There is a river of research and advice on student assessment, and every teacher already has thoughts about how student assessment should be used. So, I'll simply refer you to the recommended assessments for each simulation and leave it at that.

When the recommended assessments in the chapters suggest that you use a Student Assessment Sheet, you will find them at the end of this chapter. The Assessment Sheet for Group Exercises should be administered to each student in the class at the conclusion of a simulation that involves groups. The Assessment Sheet for Nongroup Exercises can be used for feedback on classwide exercises that do not involve groups—*Choosing a President* or *Constructing a New American Government*—if the teacher is so inclined.

### Improving Simulations

Although I find most teachers to be more or less comfortable with student assessments, I find them much more unsure how to evaluate the effectiveness of simulations and how to use evaluations to fine-tune instruction and the simulations themselves. These simulations, in different classrooms and with different teachers, can always use fine-tuning. There are two complementary goals to focus on when assessing a simulation. The first is how to make the simulation run better the next time you use it. The second is how to make the next simulation more productive and more enjoyable for this particular group of students.

No one assessment tool will prove optimal in all classrooms for all teachers. The assessments provided are only suggested tools. If you think the assessments are too extensive, not extensive enough, or need to be modified, then—at least for your classroom—you are right.

The Teacher's Exercise Assessment Sheet, included at the end of this chapter, is intended to help you evaluate the strengths and weaknesses of each simulation. I find it useful to evaluate simulations on four dimensions. One is how effectively the simulation taught the material. A second is how effectively the exercise fostered positive student interaction—whether it be sharing of research, negotiation, collaboration, or creative chicanery. A third is how successfully ancillary skills were developed; and a fourth is how much fun the exercise was.

The following are the questions I ask myself at the close of each simulation:

1. Did the simulation adequately convey the intellectual substance—both factual knowledge and theoretical principles?

2. Was the desired intellectual substance covered *and* did the exercise reinforce and help the students to apply that knowledge?

3. Did students interact in useful and productive ways?

4. Did students get a chance to develop their "people" skills?

5. Did the exercise adequately teach and reinforce the practical skills it was intended to cultivate?

6. Was the exercise as enjoyable and interesting as I hoped it would be?

Before running a simulation, it is important to clarify your expectations. The focus should be on how well a simulation did those things that it *was intended* to do—not how well it did everything under the sun. The shortcomings you observe may be due to the design of the lesson or to its execution in a given class. Those due to execution may be a product of the teacher's actions or of the dynamic of a given class. Understanding the source of any problems can help the teacher to enhance future efforts.

A given exercise will satisfy multiple objectives in varying degrees and there is no perfect way to gauge how effectively a simulation accomplished any goal. So just relax, run the exercise as well as you can, and try to understand what did not work as well as you had hoped. So long as you stay aware of your goals and think critically about where the exercises fell short, you can expect your simulations to keep getting better.

There are three key issues in simulation management that I constantly struggle with and never get quite right. The first is how authentic and complex a simulation should be. As you have no doubt noticed in this book, making a simulation more detailed also makes it much more difficult to play and to govern. Depending on the teacher, the group of students, and the course, the desired balance of detail and simplicity will fluctuate. Over time, as teachers become more familiar with simulations in general and with the particular simulations they are using, it becomes easier to gauge a good balance for a given group of students in a given course.

The second issue is the pacing of the lesson. Getting the lesson to move briskly enough to be efficient and interesting, without having it move so quickly that it is confusing or hectic, is a delicate task. For some project-oriented exercises, such as the stock market game or the travel exercise, pacing is less of a major concern. For most of the game-oriented exercises, however, getting the pace right is an ever-elusive chase. There will be times when the teacher needs to take a deep breath and slow down the exercise, because students are getting confused or because everything is so frenetic that the point of the lesson is being lost. There are other times when lethargy can set in, requiring the teacher to find ways to pick up the pace or otherwise reinvigorate the class.

The third issue is trying to make sure that the exercise plays out in a way that stays focused on the desired points and skills. A loosely conceived simulation often drifts from its intended purpose, becoming simply an amusing but ineffective use of class time. Maintaining focus can call for an occasional firm yank, depending on the nature of the class and the teacher's style. There is no one approach that will work for all teachers, but the attentive teacher will start to acquire a sense of when a little tightening is necessary to keep the class focused.

### Helping a Class Use Simulations More Effectively

Once you have run a simulation with a class, it becomes easier to make the next exercise run smoothly. Why? First, you will have a better sense of how different students react. Obviously, you will have a fair idea going in about how different students will act, but it is not unusual for students to surprise you when given the incentives and freedom of a structured simulation. In the course of these exercises, you are likely to learn that certain students have strengths that had previously remained hidden. Once a student reveals a skill, whether for leadership, persuasion, calculation, analysis, or anything else, it is much easier to find future opportunities to call on that skill. After a while, it becomes easier to build groups, assign roles, or shape activities so that they leverage students' skills and encourage students to recognize and to learn from one another's abilities.

Some groups of students simply mesh more effectively than others during an exercise. It depends on the mix of students, the way different cliques interact, and whether a given class has some unifying personalities that will help "sew" the class together. A teacher will learn how firmly the class has to be guided. Classes in which the teacher fosters student interaction, both in discussion and in coursework, generally prove more receptive to simulation-based exercises. Classes that have a more familial or cohesive feel tend to have the easiest time. It is possible to help a class mesh better by building cooperation and camaraderie in the class. In fact, effective simulations build precisely the positive social bond that helps to make future exercises more effective. Over time, the use of these kinds of exercises leaves the class more willing and better able to participate.

Some classes demonstrate more interest in simulations and more comfort with the rules. Experience helps you determine the pace at which a given group will best handle an exercise. Over time, you should be able to better anticipate how engaged a given group will be in a given exercise. This can help steer your use of simulations with that class.

Because students rarely engage in these exercises, especially as an integrated and assessed portion of the curriculum, they rarely take them seriously at first. Be patient, with the students and with yourself, and don't get discouraged if your first efforts encounter difficulty. Getting students comfortable with simulations means helping them become comfortable with interpersonal communication, cooperation, compromise, and a bevy of other necessary and productive skills. Student discomfort with these demands may lead to disappointing efforts at first, but that is all the more reason to build these crucial skills.

I suspect that you will find simulations as productive and as enjoyable as I have. Social science teachers have a unique obligation to help their students understand the world around them, and I hope you find these simulations helpful in that pursuit.

## ASSESSMENT MATERIALS

The assessment materials that follow are designed to help you evaluate the value of the exercises and the quality of student participation. I recommend having the students fill out the appropriate assessment sheet after each exercise. When the sheet is essential to evaluating student performance, the need to distribute the sheet is indicated in the Assessment portion of each chapter.

I recommend filling out the teacher's assessment sheet, for your own purposes, at the conclusion of each exercise with each class.

## TEACHER'S EXERCISE ASSESSMENT SHEET

1. What were the lesson's key goals, in terms of:

   a. Intellectual substance

   b. Practical skills

2. How effectively did the lesson accomplish these goals?

   a. Intellectual (0–10) _____ Why?

   b. Practical (0–10) _____ Why?

3. What changes would have helped the exercise accomplish these goals?

   a. Intellectual

   b. Practical

4. What changes would have helped to make the exercise more fun and/or interesting?

5. How long did the exercise take?

6. Did the simulation fit into the projected time period?

7. Was the pace of the exercise too fast, too slow, or about right?

   a. What changes would have helped with the pacing?

8. At what points, or about what elements, were the students confused?

   a. What confused them?

   b. What would help to reduce these points of confusion in the future?

9. How effective were the assessment tools for this simulation (use 0–10)?

   _____ was a _____

   _____ was a _____

   _____ was a _____

   _____ was a _____

   a. How could the assessment tools be usefully modified for future use?

10. How effective was the lead-in to the exercise and the follow-through after the exercise?

    a. What changes would have made the lead-in and follow-through more effective?

# STUDENT ASSESSMENT SHEET
# FOR GROUP EXERCISES

**1.** How effectively did your group work together?

**2.** How did the group divide the work?

    a. Did there turn out to be an even division of work?

**3.** Besides yourself, who do you think contributed the most to the group?

    a. What did they do that was particularly productive?

**4.** Which group member contributed the least to the group?

    a. What could they have done different to be more helpful?

**5.** What do you wish the group had done differently?

**6.** On a scale of 1 to 5, where 5 is *very good* and 1 is *poor*, how would you rate your group on:

    a. Preparing for the exercise _____

    b. Understanding the exercise _____

    c. Playing the exercise _____

**7.** Which group in the class really impressed you as really contributing to make the exercise work well?

    a. Why?

    b. What did they do?

**8.** Which of your classmates particularly impressed you by contributing to the exercise?

    a. Why?

    b. What did they do?

# STUDENT ASSESSMENT SHEET
# FOR NONGROUP EXERCISES

**1.** How positive was your interaction with your classmates?

**2.** Do you think that most of your classmates played their roles in the manner intended?

**3.** Which of your classmates impressed you the most during the exercise?

    a. What did they do that impressed you?

**4.** What problems arose that reduced the value of the simulation?

**5.** What changes do you think would help to make the simulation run more productively in the future?

# *INDEX*

## A

Alliances, 181
Alpert, Bracha, 5
America. *See* Whirlwind American Tour, A
Analytic skills, 38, 91–92
Analytic writing skills, 55, 142, 167, 179, 198
Appeasement, 179
Arab–Israeli conflict, 66–68
ARAMCO, 35
Articles of Confederation, 12
Assessment, 7–8, 208–210
 assessment of individual simulations, 19, 42, 59, 73, 99, 136, 147, 171, 203
 materials for, 211–213
Authenticity of simulations, 6–7

## B

Bailey, Stephen, 4
Balance of Power. *See* Delicate Balance of Power, The
Balloting, how it might look, 97
Bandwagon effect, 89
Bear market, 52
Big Board, sample, 61
Bismarck, Otto van, 176–177
Budget worksheets, 172–173
Budgeting a trip, 132
Budgeting skills, 129–139, 165–174
Bull market, 52
Businesses, financing, 51

## C

Camp David Accord, 67
Campaign Donation Transaction sheet, 102
Cartel, 33–34
 *See also* Mighty Dorito Cartel, The
*Choosing a President*, 88–128
 assessment in, 99
 background for, 89–91
 breaking delegations, 96

chalkboard chart, 93
comments on, 98
courses appropriate for, 9,88
how to play, 94–95
length of, 94
logistics for, 92–93
materials for, 100–102
modifications for, 98–99
object of, 93–94
purpose of, 91
rules of, 95–97
scoring in, 93–94
skills developed by, 10, 91–92
state delegation and interest group matrix, 101
student profiles for, 103–126
student roles in, 93
teacher instructions summary for, 98
teacher's note for, 88–89
teacher's point matrix, 100
Class atmosphere, 4
Classroom management of simulations, 6–8, 147, 209
Class size, 2–3
Cliques, 4
Cold War, 72, 175
Collaboration, 55
 competition and, 3
Collateral, 51
Competition, 3
Competitive market, 33
Compounding, 53
Constitution, U.S., 11–15, 89, 140–164
Constitutional Convention, 11–15
*Constructing a New American Government*, 11–31
 assessment in, 19–20
 background for, 12–15
 big and small state conflict in, 19
 comments on, 18–19
 courses appropriate for, 9, 11
 how to play, 16–18
 key issues in, 17–18, 21
 length of, 16
 logistics for, 15–16

*Constructing a New American Government (Cont.)*
map for, 22
materials for, 21
modifications for, 19
object of, 16
purpose of, 15
regional conflict in, 18–19
skills developed by, 10, 15
state needs sheets for, 23–31
student groups in, 16
teacher instructions summary for, 18
teacher's note on, 11–12
Country Profile sheets, 77–87
Country sheets, ODEC, 45–48
Courses, appropriate simulations for, 9
*See also specific simulations*
Creating simulations, 5
Creative writing skills, 131
Crime bill, Issues Addressed, 149
*See also* Passing a Crime Bill

## D

Debt, 166
Definition of simulations, 1
*Delicate Balance of Power, The,*
175–195
assessment in, 186
background for, 176–179
comments on, 184–185
country profile sheets for, 190–195
courses appropriate for, 9, 175
how to play, 182–184
key elements of, 181–182
length of, 180–181
logistics for, 179–180
map for, 188
materials for, 187–189
modifications for, 185–186
object of, 180
purpose of, 179
rules for, 188
skills developed by, 10, 179
student groups in, 180
teacher instructions summary for,
183
teacher's note for, 175–176
Designing simulations, 5–7
Deterrence, 179
Diplomacy, 175–195, 196–207
Dividends, 50
Dobkin, William, 5
Dorito Cartel. *See* Mighty Dorito Cartel,
The

## E

Economic concepts, 32, 33–34, 181,
183
Economic growth sheet, 187
Economic growth, teacher's master
sheet, 187
Economic skills, 49
budgeting, 129–139, 165–174
Effective use of simulations, 210
Electoral College, 89
Ententes, 181
Equity markets, 49, 50–54
historic performance of, 51–52
Exercise assessment sheets, 211–213

## F

*Federalist Papers,* 14–15
Feedback, student, 148, 208, 212–213
Filibusters, 141
Fischer, Joel, 5
Focus for simulations, 5–6, 209
*Forging a Lasting Middle East Peace,*
64–87
assessment in, 73–74
background for, 65–68
comments on, 71–72
country profile sheets for, 77–87
courses appropriate for, 9, 64
how to play, 70–71
key issues in, 70–71, 75
length of, 69–70
logistics for, 68–69
map for, 76
materials list for, 75
modifications for, 73
object of, 69
purpose of, 68
skills developed by, 10, 68
student groups in, 69
teacher instructions summary for, 72
teacher's note for, 64–65
401K plans, 51–52
Free rider syndrome, 32, 33–34
explaining, 34

## G

GNP Summary Sheet, 189
Government, 13
*See also* Constructing a New American
Government
Groundwork for simulations, 7
Guidelines, for student travel, 137

## H

Help for simulation use, 210
How simulations work. *See specific simulations*
How a Turn Might Work, 182
Hunkins, Francis, 4

## I

Improving simulations, 208–209
Incentives, 6, 8
Income, gross/net, 166
Individual Retirement Accounts (IRAs), 51–52
Inflation, 52–53
Integration
    of knowledge, 3
    of student groups, 4
Internet, finding travel information on, 130
Interpersonal skills, 6, 142
Investments, 49
    advantage of long-term, 53–54
Issue Analysis Guidelines, 204
Issues, for candidates, 101

## J

Journal, entries in travel, 133
Journal writing, for American Tour simulation, 129, 133

## K

Knowledge
    integration of, 3
    practical, 7
Koblinger, Richard, 5

## L

Lazerson, Marvin, 4
Legislative process simulation, 140–164
*Letting the Bulls Run,* 49–63
    assessment in, 59–60
    background for, 50–54
    comments on, 58–59
    courses appropriate for, 9, 49
    how to play, 56–58
    logistics for, 55
    materials for, 61–63
    modifications for, 59
    object of, 56
    purpose of, 55
    skills developed by, 10, 55
    student groups in, 55

    teacher instructions summary for, 58
    teacher's note for, 49–50
*Living on a Paycheck,* 165–174
    assessment in, 171
    background for, 166
    comments on, 169–170
    courses appropriate for, 9, 165
    length of, 167, 168
    logistics for, 167
    materials for, 172–174
    modifications for, 170
    purpose of, 167
    rules for, 168–169
    skills developed by, 10, 167
    student groups in, 167
    teacher instructions summary for, 169
    teacher's note for, 165–166
Logistics, 7
    *See also specific simulations*
Ludwig, Bernard, 5

## M

*Making the United Nations Work,* 196–207
    assessment in, 203
    background for, 197–198
    comments on, 200–202
    courses appropriate for, 9, 196
    how to play, 199–200
    length of, 199
    logistics for, 199
    map for, 205
    materials for, 204–207
    modifications for, 202
    object of, 199
    purpose of, 198
    skills developed by, 10, 198–199
    student groups in, 199
    teacher instructions summary for, 201
    teacher's note for, 196
Maps for simulations, 22, 76, 138, 188, 205
Market Logs, 63–64
Markets, competitive, 34
Markets, equity, 50–54
Materials for simulations, 21, 44, 61, 75, 100, 137, 149, 172, 187, 204, 210
Math reasoning skills, 38, 55, 91, 131, 167, 179
McLaughlin, Judith, 4
McPherson, Bruce, 4
Men Under Arms Sheet, 189

Middle East. *See* Forging a Lasting
    Middle East Peace; Mighty
    Dorito Cartel, The
*Mighty Dorito Cartel, The,* 32–48
    assessment in, 42–43
    background for, 33–38
    comments on, 41
    country sheets for, 45–48
    courses appropriate for, 9, 32
    how to play, 40–41
    key elements of, 39–40
    length of, 39
    logistics for, 38
    materials for, 44
    modifications for, 41–42
    object of, 39
    ODEC, 32, 38–40
    Price Chart for, 40, 44
    purpose of, 38
    skills developed by, 10, 38
    student groups in, 39
    teacher instructions summary for, 41
    teacher's master sheet, 44
    teacher's note for, 32–33
Modifying simulations, 8
    *See also specific simulations*
Monopoly, 33
Multipolar environment, 175
Mutual funds, 51–52

**N**

NASDAQ, 50
Negotiation skills, 15, 38, 68, 91, 142,
    179, 198
New Deal, 90–91
New Jersey Plan, at Constitutional
    Convention, 14
Nongroup Exercises, Assessment Sheet
    for, 208, 213

**O**

ODEC *See* Mighty Dorito Cartel, The
Oil crises, 35–37
Oligopoly, 33
OPEC (Organization of Petroleum
    Exporting Countries), 32,
    34–38
    decline of, 37–38
    and first oil crisis, 35–36
    history of, 35
    and second oil crisis, 36–37
Ornstein, Allan, 4

**P**

Pace, of lessons using simulations, 209
Palestinians, 68
*Passing a Crime Bill,* 140–164
    assessment in, 147–148
    background for, 140–142
    comments on, 147
    courses appropriate for, 9, 140
    how to play, 143, 145–146
    length of, 145
    logistics for, 142–143
    materials list for, 149
    modifications for, 147
    object of, 144–145
    purpose of, 142
    skills developed by, 10, 142
    student profile sheets for, 150–164
    student roles in, 143–144
    teacher instructions summary for, 146
    teacher's note for, 140
Peace. *See* Forging a Lasting Middle East
    Peace
Pendleton Act, 90
Planning, for use of simulations, 7
PLO, defined, 68
Political parties, 88–91, 141–142
Politics, 38, 88–91
Practical knowledge, about simulations,
    7
Power. *See* Delicate Balance of Power
Proposal Tracking Sheets, 206–207
President. *See* Choosing a President
Progressive movement, 90
Public speaking skills, 15, 68, 142, 198

**R**

Raffini, James, 4
Real returns, 52–53
Recordkeeping skills, 55, 131
Relevance of simulations, 1
Research skills, 15, 55, 68, 131, 167,
    198–199
Rewards, of using simulations, 6, 8
Rule of 72, 53

**S**

Savings, 165, 166
Simulations
    assessing, 208–209. *See also specific
        simulations*
    assessment of individual, 19, 42, 59,
        73, 99, 136, 147, 171, 203

assessment materials for, 211–213
authenticity and manageability in, 6–7
background on. *See specific simulations*
classroom management during, 7–8
comments from experience. *See specific simulations*
courses appropriate for, 9
creating, 5
defined, 1
designing, 5–7
dynamics in, 6
effective use of, 210
failure to use, 2
final thoughts about, 208–210
focus for, 5–6
groundwork for, 7
improving, 208–209
length of, 2–3
modifying, 8. *See also specific simulations*
planning for, 7
skills developed in, 3, 10
strengths of, 3–5
using, 7–8, 210. *See also specific simulations*
Sizer, Robert, 4–5
Skills
  developed in simulations, 3, 4, 10
  interpersonal, 6
  *See also specific simulations*
Slavery, and Constitutional Convention, 14
Special Occurrence Slips, 127–128
State delegation and interest group matrix, 101
State Needs sheets, 23–31
Stock market, 50–54
  picking stocks in, 54
  risks and, 52
Strength of simulations, 3–5
Student Assessment Sheet for Group Exercises, 208, 212
Student Assessment Sheet for Nongroup Exercises, 208, 213
Student Profile sheets, 103–118
Student Project Sheet, 172
Students, 4
  feedback from, 148, 208, 212–213
  skill levels of, 8
Summary of rules, 188
Summary of Teacher Instructions, for simulations, 18, 41, 58, 72, 98, 134, 146, 169, 183
Syndrome, free rider, 32, 33–34

**T**

Teacher's Exercise Assessment Sheet, 209, 211
Teachers
  beginning and/or student, 2
  expectations of, 209
Teacher's notes, for simulations, 11, 32, 49, 64, 88, 129, 140, 165, 175, 196
Teacher's point matrix, 100
Teamwork skills, 15, 38, 68, 179
Technology, 1
Three-fifths compromise, at Constitutional Convention, 14
Timing, of market, 53–54
Travel journal, entries, 133
Travel log, student, 139
Travel skills, learning, 129–139
Triple Alliance, 178
Triple Entente, 178
Two-thirds rule, 99

**U**

United Nations (UN). *See* Making the United Nations Work
Unit rule, 89
U.S. Congress, and a crime bill, 140–164
U.S. Constitution, 11–15, 89, 140–141
Using simulations, 7–8, 210
  *See also specific simulations*

**V**

Virginia Plan, at Constitutional Convention, 13–14

**W**

*Whirlwind American Tour, A,* 129–139
  assessment in, 136
  background for, 130
  comments on, 133–135
  courses appropriate for, 9, 129
  how to play, 132–133
  length of, 132
  logistics for, 131
  map for, 138
  materials for, 137–139
  modifications for, 135–136
  purpose of, 130–131
  skills developed by, 10, 129, 131
  student assignments in, 131
  teacher instructions summary for, 134
  teacher's note for, 129–130
World War I, and balance of power, 175–195

Writing skills, 55
    analytic, 142, 167, 179, 198
    creative, 131
    for journals, 129, 133

**Z**

Zionist movement, as part of Middle East
    simulation, 65